Sir John Harold Clapham

The causes of the War of 1792

Sir John Harold Clapham

The causes of the War of 1792

ISBN/EAN: 9783337114879

Printed in Europe, USA, Canada, Australia, Japan

Cover: Foto ©ninafisch / pixelio.de

More available books at **www.hansebooks.com**

Cambridge Historical Essays.　No. xi.

THE CAUSES OF THE WAR OF 1792

BY

J. H. CLAPHAM, M.A.
FELLOW OF KING'S COLLEGE, CAMBRIDGE

PRINCE CONSORT DISSERTATION, 1898

Cambridge
AT THE UNIVERSITY PRESS
1899

TO

THE MEMORY

OF

MY FATHER

EXTRACT FROM THE REGULATIONS FOR THE PRINCE CONSORT PRIZE.

"There shall be established in the University a prize, called the 'Prince Consort Prize,' to be awarded for dissertations involving original historical research."

"The Prize shall be open to members of the University who, at the time when their dissertations are sent in, have been admitted to a degree, and are of not more than four years' standing from admission to their first degree."

"Those dissertations which the adjudicators declare to be deserving of publication shall be published by the University, singly or in combination, in an uniform series, at the expense of the fund, under such conditions as the Syndics of the University Press shall from time to time determine."

PREFACE.

THERE is little to be said in explanation of the character and form of the present essay. It deals with a subject that has been under discussion almost continuously for a century, and lays claim only to such originality as is possible under the circumstances. The method of treatment must speak for itself. I need only say in explanation of the very slight handling of various great questions, that condensation or omission of important matter is forced upon the essay writer.

My debts to the historians are very numerous. To two I am especially indebted, to one for his writings, to the other for his lectures and advice. They are M. Albert Sorel and Lord Acton. I have to thank the adjudicators of the Prince Consort Prize for permission to rewrite and expand the original essay. Thanks are also due for the criticisms and suggestions of various friends.

The following list explains the method of reference to those books which are most often quoted in the text:—

Arneth.	*Marie Antoinette, Joseph II, und Leopold II. Ihr Briefwechsel*	= Arneth.
Bacourt.	*Correspondance entre le Comte de Mirabeau et le Comte de la Marck*	= Bacourt.
Feuillet de Conches.	*Louis XVI, Marie Antoinette, et Mme. Elisabeth*	= Feuillet de Conches.
Klinckowström.	*Le Comte de Fersen et la Cour de France*	= Fersen.
Ranke.	*Ursprung und Beginn der Revolutionskriege*	= Ranke.
Schlitter.	*Briefe der Erzherzogin Marie Christine... an Leopold II.* (Fontes Rer. Austriac. vol. 48)	= Schlitter.
Sorel.	*L'Europe et la Révolution Française*	= Sorel.
Sybel.	*Geschichte der Revolutionszeit.* 4th Ed.	= Sybel.
Vivenot.	*Quellen zur Geschichte der...Kaiserpolitik Oesterreichs*	= Vivenot.
Archives Parlementaires.	Ed. Mavidal and Laurent	= *Arch. Parl.*
Histoire Parlementaire.	Ed. Buchez and Roux	= *Hist. Parl.*

CONTENTS.

			PAGE
Chapter	I.	Introduction. France and Europe in 1789.	1
,,	II.	The Powers and the Revolution. Beginnings of Discord	15
,,	III.	The Flight to Varennes and the Policy of Leopold	44
,,	IV.	The Origin of the Austro-Prussian Alliance. The Declaration of Pilnitz and the affairs of Poland	58
,,	V.	The Constitution and the Powers . .	86
,,	VI.	The War Policy of the Legislative Assembly and the War Policy of the Court. Oct.—Dec. 1791	103
,,	VII.	Austria in direct conflict with the Assembly. Completion of the Austro-Prussian Alliance. Dec. 1791—Feb. 1792 . . .	130
,,	VIII.	The Critical Events of Feb. and March, 1792	160
,,	IX.	Dumouriez and the War	183
,,	X.	The War and the Invasion	201

		PAGE
APPENDIX.	Diplomatic Correspondence	223
I.	England and France.	224
II.	Policy of the Court of Vienna.	226
III.	Policy of the Court of Berlin.	235
IV.	Policy of the Court of Madrid	240
V.	The Powers and the Belgian Revolution	250
VI.	Miscellaneous Extracts	254
INDEX.		257

CHAPTER I.

Introduction. France and Europe in 1789.

From the very first there existed two distinct traditions as to the causes of the first conflict between Europe and revolutionary France. The conservative tradition related the deliberate and scandalous attempts of the French demagogues to overturn, by the most reprehensible means and to serve their own selfish ends, the old political system of Europe. The revolutionary tradition told of a league between the French court and the European powers, built up by the diabolic industry of the emigrants, which had for its aim the utter ruin of the Revolution and the restoration of the old order. The immense difficulty of any problem in historical causation, the exceptional complexity and obscurity of the diplomatic intrigues that preceded the war of 1792, and the special passions that the whole series of the revolutionary and Napoleonic wars gave vent to or provoked, all encouraged the growth and preservation of such one-sided and false traditions. The gradual increase of knowledge necessitated many changes in their statement. But they survived in their broad outlines and are not yet dead. Nor can they be expected to die as yet; for each has its share of truth and each has become associated with certain national or party superstitions.

The advocates of both views, and even those historians who have made the most serious attempts to be misled by neither, have generally been inclined to treat the war merely, or too exclusively, as an episode in the history of the Revolution. Such a tendency is particularly natural in narrative historians who hardly profess to handle complicated questions of cause. But at present it is ceasing to be felt. The school of French writers which has devoted itself to the study of the unity of national life, and to the undermining of the cataclysmic theories of the Revolution, is rapidly laying bare the points of contact between the diplomacy of the revolutionary leaders and that of the statesmen of the old order. As a result of their work it is becoming increasingly necessary, in the study of the great wars, to lay stress on the influence of ancient diplomatic traditions and ancient international rivalries. A first inquiry into these matters, into the forces which from afar made for war, may tend to encourage slipshod generalisation. But as the story is followed up towards the final catastrophe it becomes apparent to what an enormous extent the great new revolutionary force, and minor forces from various directions, deflected the line of action of those which had long been in operation. Indeed, as has just been said, the general tendency has been to attach too much rather than too little importance to the comparatively simple working of the forces that came into play after 1789.

In a sense, doubtless, war was inevitable. It is inconceivable that France, lying in the midst of

Europe and the centre of the state-system of the West, could have passed through a great revolution without becoming involved in war. Few things are more remarkable in the history of the years 1789—91, than the desire expressed from time to time by men of very various parties, to see the French armies take the field. Foreign statesmen too were always expecting to see France throw herself into war. The fact is important but in no way surprising. A century ago, as during the Second Empire, as in England to-day, nothing was more likely to turn men's minds away from questions of internal reform than the excitement of battle. War, it has been said, was "the classical remedy for internal troubles[1]." Europe was full of discord and unrest; occasions of strife were not far to seek; so that it is rather surprising than otherwise that the Revolution had been in progress for three years before France actually broke the peace. But just because war might conceivably have broken out at almost any time during those three years, it becomes the more interesting to trace—as far as possible—the process by which the actual accomplished war of 1792 was brought about.

Throughout the eighteenth century Europe was in an almost perpetual state of war. England was making her colonial empire; Prussia and Russia were making themselves, by means of what might not unfairly be described as systematic warfare. The periods of general peace were as short as they were few. When the States General met at Versailles in May 1789, six

[1] Sorel, *Revue des Deux Mondes*, 1884.

years had not passed since the conclusion of the last great war in the West. A great war in the East was actually in progress. Even since the peace of 1783 England and France had again been within reasonable distance of war[1].

England had not forgotten the loss of America. Although there is no evidence that her statesmen were actually seeking an opportunity for revenge, yet the whole diplomatic correspondence of the time reveals the state of uneasy jealousy in which they lived. The same is true of the French statesmen. Each side distrusted the other's good faith; each was only too ready to take offence at the other's real or supposed prosperity. But the English nation and the young English minister were certainly not anxious for war. Pitt's greatest strength lay in the conduct of domestic, and particularly economic, policy. The nation was becoming more absorbed year by year in its industrial life. Pitt had even made a serious attempt to promote harmony between the two nations—and at the same time secure substantial advantages to England—by arranging the commercial treaty of 1786 with Vergennes. The results had not been altogether as anticipated. The treaty was unpopular in many parts of France,

---

[1] In connection with the intervention of Prussia and England in Dutch affairs in 1787. On Nov. 1 of that year Wm. Eden wrote to Lord Carmarthen: "He [Montmorin, the French foreign minister] told me that in the course of our discussions this country had been much nearer going to war than from a view of the circumstances I might suppose. He said that exclusive of all objects of external interest there had been some opinions of weight that a war was the best mode of finishing the internal troubles...." The troubles referred to were the quarrels between King and Parlement.

and was not infrequently regarded as an unworthy concession to an old and lately fallen enemy[1]. But there were many Frenchmen of position who felt kindly towards England and would have welcomed a closer alliance. Opinions of this type were most common among the literary classes and the liberal aristocrats. As such men came largely to the front during the earlier stages of the Revolution, the events of 1789 tended to improve the relations between the two countries. On this side too there was a certain amount of sympathy for the French reformers. And as the Revolution at first tended to weaken France and withdraw her from active interference in European politics, the jealousy of her power declined. For the moment there seemed no reason why a moderately long spell of peace should not set in.

Up to the middle of the eighteenth century the House of Hapsburg had for generations been the constant rival and foe of the French kings. But in 1756, on the eve of the Seven Years War, the two courts had arranged a treaty[2]. This alliance was unpopular from the first, and its unpopularity increased with time. The current story of its origin was that France had entered into an unnatural and unprofitable alliance to gratify the mistress of Louis XV. The

[1] Arthur Young found it unpopular in the manufacturing districts of the N. (Abbeville and Rouen for instance), but not at Bordeaux. *Travels in France*, Ed. 1792, pp. 5, 47.

[2] The treaty of 1756 was a defensive alliance. It was followed up by a second treaty in 1757. They were largely the work of Kaunitz who had become the chief adviser of Maria Theresa in 1753. He was still the most important Austrian statesman in 1789, and held the post of chancellor.

alliance was called unnatural partly because Austria was a traditional enemy, and partly because it was directed against a former ally, in high esteem in French philosophical circles—Frederick of Prussia. The ruin of the French colonial power in the Seven Years War sufficiently explains the epithet unprofitable. As early as 1758, it was said that people in Paris were "crazy about the King of Prussia" but "detested the court of Vienna because they regarded it as the leech of the state[1]." Opposition to the Austrian alliance became a sort of political axiom to many leaders of opinion in France. Not only the 'philosophical' and literary circles adopted this view. It was expounded and justified at length in elaborate political treatises by one of the leading members of Louis XV.'s staff of secret diplomatists. The influence which the writings of this particular man—by name Favier—exercised on the foreign policy of the revolutionary period can hardly be overestimated; for he made a reasoned appeal to an old prejudice[2]. The marriage of the dauphin Louis to the daughter of Maria Theresa, in 1770, seemed a proof that the royal family meant to stand by the hated union; hence, in part at least, the unpopularity of Marie Antoinette. But when the dauphin became king as Louis XVI. his greatest foreign minister,

---

[1] Sorel, *Essais*. 'Bernis et l'alliance de 1756,' p. 149. The words are Bernis' own: he had himself arranged the treaty of 1756.

[2] Favier's two chief works were 'Conjectures...sur la situation actuelle de la France' and 'Doutes et Questions sur le Traité de 1756.' The latter appeared anonymously in 1778, and again in 1791. The former was first printed in the 'Politique de tous les Cabinets de l'Europe' by Ségur in 1801; but it was known by politicians long before its publication.

Vergennes, followed a line of policy independent of, and even in some cases opposed to, the interests of Austria.

In 1789 there was still an Austrian party among the French statesmen, and the alliance, in name at least, still existed[1]. But the hatred of Austria showed not the least sign of abating. Every sort of evidence combines to attest the vigour of that hatred[2]. It grew stronger and more bitter with each stage of the Revolution. The feeling was by no means confined to the liberal and revolutionary sections of French society. It was shared by the royal princes and by a party at the court which detested and slandered 'the Austrian,' Marie Antoinette, before the Revolution almost as viciously as did Hébert and the Paris mob on the eve of the reign of terror[3]. Even when the French royalists were beginning to be much in need of Austrian help we find the Count of Artois assuring the King of Prussia, and apparently with some sincerity, that to weaken the House of Hapsburg was his 'heart's desire[4].'

It is evident that of all possible enemies Austria

---

[1] Rumours of a great alliance between the two Imperial Courts, France, and Spain at times alarmed English diplomatists in 1789–90.

[2] Goltz (the Prussian ambassador) wrote in May, 1789, that the hatred of Austria was a marked characteristic of the new States General (Letter of May 25.) The emperor Joseph himself spoke in Nov. 1789 of "l'acharnement que la nation [française] manifeste contre l'alliance et ma personne." *Correspondance du Comte de Mercy-Argenteau avec Joseph II.*, etc. Arneth and Flammermont, II. 273. Evidence of all sorts to the same effect might easily be accumulated.

[3] Forneron, *Les Emigrés*, I. 50.

[4] Feb. 14, 1790. "Votre Majesté veut affaiblir la maison d'Autriche; c'est le vœu de mon cœur." *Hist. Zeitschrift*, 1895.

would have been the most welcome to the majority of Frenchmen in 1789. But there was not the least likelihood of Austria's adopting a hostile attitude towards France. The Hapsburgs were in need of peace and of friends. The usual internal difficulties of a huge composite state happened at this time to be particularly urgent. Hungary and Belgium had been estranged by the unwise attempts of Joseph II. to reform away their national institutions; so had the Slavonic provinces of Bohemia and Croatia. The Germans of Austria proper were indignant at the emperor's highhanded interference in ecclesiastical matters. All parts of the Austrian dominions were suffering from over heavy taxation. The neighbouring Rhenish provinces—members of the empire of which Joseph was the head—were early affected by the movement of opinion in France, and became a source of danger to Germany. Altogether it is not surprising that the Austrian statesmen were glad to hold to an old ally and anxious to avoid war. To the very end of his life—he died early in 1790—Joseph maintained that the alliance was a real benefit to France, the only cause of what small amount of deference Europe continued to show her during the mad days of '89[1].

Apart from internal matters Austria was occupied with an extensive and costly foreign war. In 1788 Joseph had joined Catherine II. of Russia in a great attack on the Ottoman Empire. The two Christian powers had dreams of a new fall of Constantinople and an eventual partition of the lands of the Porte. But

[1] Joseph to Mercy; quoted in Heigel, *Deutsche Geschichte vom Tode Friedrichs des Grossen*, etc., p. 228.

the Turks fought well, and the success of the allies in the first campaign had not been remarkable. The Russians had destroyed a Turkish fleet and stormed Oczakow; but the Austrian victories had been balanced by serious losses and failures.

Prussia had but recently passed from the hands of Frederick the Great. The licentious and unstable Frederick William II., and his minister Hertzberg, were eager to complete the scheme of expansion at the cost of Austria and Poland that had been bequeathed to them by the great maker of Prussia. As leader of the German opposition to the Hapsburgs it was the policy of Prussia to break up the Austro-French alliance. Accordingly in the early months of the Revolution an attempt was made to encourage the French hatred of Austria. Goltz, the ambassador of the court of Berlin at Paris, was in touch with many of the liberal party in the Assembly; and went so far as to assure them that their new-found liberty was in no way distasteful to the king his master[1]. Meanwhile Prussian agents were at work in the disaffected Austrian provinces, Prussian diplomatists were stirring up the Poles against Austria, and Prussian troops were ready at any moment to give assistance to Austria's foes. In Jan. 1790, the court of Berlin even concluded a treaty with the Porte. Fear of this restless enemy largely explains the renewal of the Russian alliance by Joseph, in June 1789, in spite of the comparative failure of the first Turkish campaign[2].

[1] Flammermont, *Les correspondances des agents diplomatiques étrangers en France*, p. 130.
[2] Martens, *Traités conclus par la Russie*, II. 189. Joseph was

The land-hunger and love of war that characterised the court of Berlin were in a measure restrained by the fact that Prussia was at this time not acting alone. She was closely united to England and Holland by the Triple Alliance of 1788. In 1787, when the friction between the party of the Stadtholder and the aristocratic republicans of Holland had led to civil war, Prussian troops and English influence had secured the victory for the Stadtholder. Prussia had sent her troops mainly because the wife of William IV. of Orange, who was King Frederick William's sister, had been insulted and ill-treated by the aristocratic party. England used her influence mainly because she wished to destroy an alliance recently formed between the Dutch and France; for she knew that the restored Prince of Orange would not support that alliance. Had France not been fully occupied with her own internal difficulties it is probable that a European war would have broken out. As it was, the activity of the Prussians and the sudden collapse of the Dutch opposition settled the matter almost before the French had had time to move. The Stadtholder was set up, and England at once got her reward in the shape of a treaty signed at the Hague on April 15, 1788. On the same day the same reward was bestowed on Prussia. Within a few months the three powers had completed a great defensive alliance for "preserving the public tranquillity and security, for maintaining their common interests,

following the advice of Kaunitz, who was a firm believer in the Russian alliance. Beer, *Leopold II., Franz II. und Catharina*, p. 13.

and for their mutual defence and guaranty[1]." The alliance played a most important part in European politics for three years; then it broke up under circumstances to which reference will be made in a later chapter. England used it with skill and success as an instrument for establishing peace in Europe and maintaining the balance of power. Prussia, speaking generally, concurred in this system, but she showed a constant, and to the English statesmen irritating, anxiety to meddle with the map of Europe. The greatest task which the allies set themselves was the termination of the Eastern war. England, from the first, was anxious to see all parties return to the *status quo*. But the Prussian court, and particularly Hertzberg, wished to make some profit out of the pacification. Scheme after scheme was elaborated, in which Hertzberg moved provinces like pawns, curtailing and compensating with a recklessness characteristic of the age[2]. None of these schemes pleased England. Little came of them, save in the case of Poland, and their details do not concern us here. This only is important; that in 1789 France or French territory hardly ever came under discussion in the enormous diplomatic correspondence which the work of the alliance and the dreams of Hertzberg produced. For the powers were beginning to regard France as a decadent state with whose policy and advice it was hardly necessary to reckon.

The year 1789 ended disastrously for Austria. Discontent in the Netherlands had ripened into open

---

[1] Lecky, *History of England*, v. 229. Mr Lecky's study of the Triple Alliance is particularly thorough.

[2] The chief plan is given in Sybel, i. 157.

rebellion. Prussia and England were beginning to discuss the advisability of recognising the independence of those provinces. The troubles in other parts of the empire showed no sign of abating. Joseph, a disappointed and broken man, was nearing his end, and Kaunitz was in despair. On Feb. 20, 1790, Joseph died, and his brother Leopold, hitherto known as an exceedingly liberal Grand Duke of Tuscany, succeeded to the Hungarian crown[1]. In a letter written to Maximilian, Elector of Cologne, is to be found a clear summary of the European situation as it appeared to Leopold's troubled mind shortly after his accession:— "The King of Prussia is making treaties with Poland and has promised to attack us...; he continues to sow rebellion in our provinces. England is about to suggest that we should give up Galicia, and then together they are going to declare the Low Countries independent[2]." As Prussia seems bent on war, he concludes, it will be necessary to fight her. His fears were well founded, for while he wrote the Prussian troops were awaiting

---

[1] He was a Catholic, but inclined to ecclesiastical reform; a disciple of Beccaria and the French economists—in fact an excellent type of the enlightened monarch of the 18th century. But though a reformer he had no intention of riding rough-shod over old institutions after the manner of his brother. Heigel, *Deutsche Geschichte*, p. 239.

[2] The Prussian treaty with Poland was signed on March 29, 1790. The restoration of Galicia to Poland—it was taken at the first partition—was one of Hertzberg's pet schemes. Of course Poland was to give something to Prussia in return. England never approved the scheme. She did discuss the recognition of the rebellious Belgians, and even kept up relations with them, but she was never anxious to see them independent. See Appendix v. Leopold's letter, dated March 20, is in Schlitter, p. viii.

in Silesia the signal to attack; and Hertzberg was looking forward to a war at the end of which Europe might be rearranged to suit his schemes.

Of the other powers little need be said here. Holland, one of France's nearest neighbours, was following in the wake of England. Apart from the Triple Alliance she was of little consequence. Spain was bound to France by the Family Compact of 1761, and remained her loyal if not very efficient ally. The Spanish king, Charles IV., who had only ascended the throne late in 1788, gave no evidence of energy or ability; his minister, Count Florida Blanca, took no great interest in foreign affairs; and "the separated situation of the country from the other states of Europe" struck competent observers as remarkable[1]. Spain was in a condition of great economic exhaustion, her population was declining, and her government aimed at little but the avoidance of war. It early took precautionary measures against democratic infection from France, for it had no taste for foreign novelties. But its practical isolation continued throughout 1789. In the following year it was to become for a moment a centre of interest to European diplomatists; afterwards to sink back again into comparative insignificance. The Italian courts of Naples, Sardinia, and Rome were from the very first strongly opposed to the Revolution in France. But their position and size deprived them of all real importance or interest. The same is true of such states as Portugal, Denmark, and the minor German powers.

[1] Wm. Eden [Lord Auckland] to Marquis of Carmarthen, May 19, 1788.

Outside the circle of the West lay the two great Northern rivals, Sweden and Russia. The courts of Stockholm and of St Petersburg had been in the past deeply influenced by French life and thought, that of Stockholm particularly so, but they did not stand in very close political relations with France. The great days of Sweden were over, and her king, the chivalrous and erratic Gustavus III., spent his time in coping alternately with the Russian enemy and with discontented aristocratic factions at home. In 1789 he was engaged in the former occupation, and it is not until the end of the following year that his opinions on French affairs begin to be of any special interest. As for Catherine, the Swedish and Turkish wars gave her occupation enough. And even had she not been so engaged her attention would have been concentrated on the nearer West, where lay the trunk of Poland, rather than on the affairs of the Atlantic states. Her relations with the Triple Alliance and with Austria are of the utmost importance and will be sketched in their place. But her direct dealings with France were few and unimportant; in the first year of the Revolution particularly so.

CHAPTER II.

THE POWERS AND THE REVOLUTION. BEGINNINGS OF DISCORD.

DURING the early stages of the Revolution the conception of a crusade against France hardly occurred to the leading statesmen of Europe. Few of them understood the nature of the phenomenon with which they had to deal. They naturally treated it as a mere political crisis similar to others with whose history they were familiar. Experience taught them that such crises were weakening to the state concerned; it was the business of other states to profit by that weakness[1]. This was the general principle which they proposed to apply to the case in hand. Some realised that the French doctrines were infectious, but this only made them the more eager to keep the peace, cut off all communication with the seat of disease, and so preserve their respective countries from harm. Certain English statesmen were particularly explicit in this matter;

---

[1] Speaking of the new French constitution in 1790, the emperor Leopold II. said:—" Si elle est bonne, tant mieux pour elle [the French nation], si elle est mauvaise, les autres en profiteront." Augeard, *Memoirs*, p. 240. See Sorel, I. 543.

partly because they were most of all interested in the decay of France, partly because the policy of isolation could be adopted very readily by an insular power. The following candid confession was made by an English Under Secretary of State for Foreign Affairs at the end of 1790. He is speaking of a possible attack on France by the powers, and says: "Be this as it may, it is surely our interest, and there can be no doubt of its being our plan, to preserve a strict neutrality should such an event occur. We have felt too strongly the immense advantages to be derived by this country from such a state of anarchy and weakness as France is at present plunged in, to be so mad as to interfere in any measure which may, even remotely, tend to put France into the situation, where a long and terrible experience has taught us she had the power to injure us. When she had the power I believe...she never wanted the will[1]." In the spring of the same year Lord Auckland wrote to his brother:—"The wild ideas which have taken place in France, and which will probably carry that fine country to an extreme of wretchedness and calamity, have a tendency to become contagious, and affect every established government. We have already seen their operation...That operation is progressive. It is fortunate that England regards it with disgust and horror, and she is disposed to call out garre! to every other state which will listen to her. Whether such a disposition on the part of England will produce and secure to other countries that period of quiet which they all want in

---

[1] Auckland MSS. (B. M. Additional 34, 434). J. B. Burges to Lord Auckland, Dec. 28, 1790.

order to bring back mankind to the old ideas of order and subordination remains to be seen[1]."

Turning to Austria we find that Kaunitz for many months refused to treat the Revolution as a question of first-rate importance. He held that it had reduced France to a state of complete debility. When at last he recognised the necessity of giving French affairs his serious consideration he remarked with perfect candour —in confidential letters to his fellow diplomatists— that although it was desirable to re-establish the French monarchy as a check to the power of England, yet Austria had not the least intention of allowing Louis XVI. to regain all his lost power, and with it a preponderating influence in European affairs[2]. Louis might be a useful ally; he would be a still more useful dependent.

Prussia, like Austria, was not anxious to see France entirely ruined. For she wished to make some profit out of the anti-Austrian spirit of the French nation. Yet a weak France, an assistant and not a patron, was desired as much by Frederick William and his cabinet as by Kaunitz himself. Even if all hope of assistance from France were lost it was still well that the ally of Austria, the rival of the friendly English, should remain more or less completely disorganised.

[1] Lord Auckland to Morton Eden, March 22, 1790. In June 1791 Lord Auckland wrote—"I heartily detest and abjure the whole system of the Democrates abstractedly considered; but I am not sure that the continued course of their struggles to maintain a disjointed and inefficient government would not be beneficial to our political interests..." *Dropmore Papers* (Historical Manuscripts Commission), II. 97.

[2] Kaunitz to Ludwig Cobenzl, July 1, 1791. Vivenot, I. 191.

Without further detailed examination of the expressed opinions of statesmen it may be stated once more that, for some time after the outbreak of the Revolution, the prevailing opinion in European diplomatic circles was that to prevent France from destroying her own supremacy would be shortsighted and impolitic. In 1792, when war between France and Austria was already declared, the statesmen of Vienna asserted that "the most elementary ideas of monarchical government" authorised the powers "to unite in order to help the legitimate King of France[1]." In 1789 and 1790 this solicitude for the welfare of monarchy was not strong enough to outweigh other considerations. Could the Revolution have pursued a tolerably even course and have remained merely a French movement, it would have excited little serious opposition from the European powers, so far as can be seen. Could the royal power have been curtailed without violence no statesman in Europe would have lifted a finger to save it.

Two matters play an exceptionally important part in the negotiations that preceded the war of 1792:—the absorption of Avignon by France and the spoliation of the German princes who held lands in and about Alsace. Taken by itself however, and discussed in cold blood, it is highly improbable that either occurrence would have led to anything more deadly than a long diplomatic correspondence and some sort of international convention. Yet as the action of France in these two cases was bitterly complained of by her enemies some account of that action may be given here. Avignon, and the

---

[1] Manifesto of July 5. Vivenot, I. 470.

neighbouring district of the Venaissin, had for centuries belonged to the Popes, though the French kings had more than once seized and again restored them. From the date of the first municipal revolutions of July 1789 the town and country were in a state of constant unrest. There was an actual civil war between the papal and French parties. The question of annexation was discussed by the Constituent Assembly at an early stage in its career. But it was not until Sept. 14, 1791, after the inhabitants, or at least a party of them, had formally demanded to be recognised as French citizens that the absorption was officially resolved on.

The Alsatian question is more closely and really connected with the causes of the war than is that of Avignon; for no power was specially interested in the preservation of the temporalities of the Holy See, whereas the Alsatian princes were members of the empire[1]. According to the treaty of Westphalia, by which Alsace was ceded to France, the French kings had not the right to curtail the privileges which the various Alsatian cities and landowners had possessed before the cession. These stipulations had been very imperfectly observed; so that long before 1789 the imperial towns, the clergy, and the nobles had lost much of their former independence. Alsace had practically become part of France, although much Alsatian

---

[1] There is a mass of valuable details as to Alsace in the report read to the Legislative Assembly on Feb. 1, 1792, by Professor Koch. *Arch. Parl.* xxxviii. 66 sqq. Of course the interpretations put on the clauses of the treaty of Westphalia by Frenchmen and Germans had always differed. The case is stated in the text rather from the German point of view, as given in Weiss, *Weltgeschichte*, xv. 272. Droysen, *Hist. Handatlas*, Plate 41.

land, and some land in Lorraine, still belonged to houses whose seats were in Germany proper. The revolutionary statesmen merely completed the policy of the Bourbons, who—like their Capetian predecessors —had always pruned away local privileges and liberties. By the decree of August 4, 1789, the various feudal rights, jurisdiction, the chase and the like were abolished. The suppression of the tithe affected a number of German prelates whose spiritual jurisdiction extended over parts of Alsace. It drew an indignant complaint from the Bishops of Spires and Bâle[1]. Later in the year, when the departments were being carved out, lands held by princes of the empire were treated as French soil; and when the redistribution of dioceses was effected, no regard was shown to the rights of the German bishops. The list of princes, ecclesiastical and lay, who suffered from these various measures included the Archbishops of Trèves and Cologne, the Elector Palatine, the Landgrave of Hesse-Darmstadt, and the sovereigns of Würtemberg, Zweibrücken, Baden, Salm, Löwenstein and Hohenlohe.

On May 15, 1790, the National Assembly offered compensation to the dispossessed princes; but as it suggested payment in assignats, and accompanied the offer by a declaration of the sovereignty of the French nation over Alsace, the proposal was not well received. In December of the same year Leopold complained formally on behalf of the empire. France replied —March 1791—that the matter did not concern the empire but only the individual princes. The Imperial

---

[1] Ranke, *Ursprung und Beginn der Revolutionskriege*, p. 55.

Diet then took the matter up and declared on the 6th of August, 1791, that the question did concern the whole empire and that the action of the French Assembly was unjust and therefore null. This declaration required the emperor's assent. It was not until the following December, and then only—as will appear—because he was thinking of interfering in French affairs for other reasons, that Leopold sanctioned the decree of the Diet and renewed his complaints to the French ministry. He now asserted that as by treaty the lands of German princes in Alsace were exempt from the sovereignty of the French crown France was not entitled to confiscate them however complete the compensation she might offer[1].

The action of the National Assembly, although a perfectly natural and logical consequence of the previous policy of the French kings, was undoubtedly a breach of international morality both in the case of Alsace and in that of Avignon. But it is very certain that Austria would never have gone to war solely in the interests of the princes, much less in those of the Pope; for the fact is attested by the language of her leading statesmen[2]. As to the other great powers, some had no concern whatever in the matter, all were far less interested in it than Austria.

Passing from the powers to France, from the question of Alsace to that of the emigration, we move from the sphere of the ostensible causes of the war into that of

---

[1] Letter of Dec. 3. Printed in *Arch. Parl.* xxxvi. 348.

[2] Leopold, Kaunitz, and Mercy, in their letters of 1791—2, constantly speak of the Alsatian question as a 'pretext' for war.

its true causes. The fall of the Bastille and the endless riots in the provinces that followed led to the emigration of the chiefs of that court party which had done so much to estrange the nation from the king. Of this first flight of emigrants the most important were the Count of Artois, the Prince of Condé, and the Duke of Bourbon. The 'days' of October alarmed and drove away another flock that included several ex-liberals. From that time forward emigration continued intermittently; so that when the Count of Provence left Paris, in June 1791, the number of French gentlemen who had already sought refuge abroad was immense. Hatred of the excesses that the Revolution had already occasioned drove from their minds all thought of conciliation. Men who had once passed for enlightened and liberal now became keen advocates of a violent and thorough counter-revolution. From the outset this had been the ideal of the Count of Artois. He and his confidant Calonne had set themselves the task of exciting all the courts of Europe against the Revolution. They spoke of it as a mere vicious outburst of anarchy and irreligion. Artois spent the early months of his exile at Turin with his father-in-law Victor Amadeus of Savoy. From Turin he began to scatter broadcast over Europe those hasty, impolitic, and inflammatory letters which form no small section of the diplomatic correspondence of the period. The letters were followed—in some cases preceded—by secret agents, who established themselves in the various capitals, and made it their business to gain the ear of influential people about the courts.

[1] Forneron, *Les Emigrés*, p. 249.

In January 1790 one of these agents, by name Count Roll, appeared in Berlin. Owing to the friendly offices of Prince Henry of Prussia he was well received by the king. He soon won over to his way of thinking Frederick William's favourite, General Bischoffwerder, and the Prince of Hohenlohe-Ingelfingen, an important member of the inner circle of royal advisers. Hearing of these preliminary successes Artois wrote in most fulsome fashion to the Prussian king, protesting his hatred of Austria, and making the amazing statement that all good Frenchmen 'were sighing for foreign help.' Frederick William was almost persuaded. At the beginning of April he was handed a despatch from the Prussian minister in Paris. The account which Goltz gave of the violent attacks made by the Jacobins on the Queen completed his conversion to the doctrine of counter-revolution. The emigrant agent and his allies laboured to keep the unstable king in this gracious frame of mind; but the end of the year had come before any serious results of their work began to appear[1].

These delays and the very chilling reception which his letters met with at Vienna were most galling to the Count of Artois. Though over thirty years of age he was reckless and uneducated, and his mind was full of schemes of conquest and daring which alarmed the more sober members even of his own party. Abundant proof of this is furnished by the correspondence of his friend the Count of Vaudreuil. Throughout the latter part of 1789 and the whole of 1790 Vaudreuil wrote to him constantly, and the burden of these letters is

[1] *Hist. Zeitschrift*, 1895, p. 259 sqq. Schlitter, p. xxii.

almost always the same:—nothing is to be gained by hasty and ill-considered action; the interests of the King and Queen must not be sacrificed to your love of glory; the appearance of foreign troops in France will set all the nation against those in whose cause they come [1].

A deep-rooted hatred of the Revolution, even in its mildest manifestations, and a very natural horror at the earlier acts of revolutionary violence were the feelings that had produced the first emigration. These feelings were shared by the Queen and, though perhaps less fully, by the King also. Immediately after their forced removal from Versailles to Paris, while the leaders of the emigrants were striving to win the sympathy and assistance of Europe, Louis and his Queen definitely entered upon the long course of dissimulation that was to lead to the abyss. They hated the Revolution—not without reason—but were bound to treat its leaders with deference. After the October days Mounier advised the King himself to emigrate or at least to leave Paris [2]. At the same time the Queen all but adopted a scheme, suggested by her secretary Augeard, according to which she was to flee, alone and in disguise, and make a personal appeal to her brother the Emperor [3]. From this time forward the idea of escaping from Paris and repudiating all the acts of his captivity seems to have presented itself constantly to the mind of the King.

---

[1] Vaudreuil, *Correspondance*, Vol. I.

[2] From a conversation between Mounier and Louis XVIII. quoted in Forneron, *Les Emigrés*, p. 227.

[3] Augeard, *Memoirs*, p. 197. There is no reason for rejecting this story, although the narrator is hardly so careful a writer as one could wish.

In this very month of October certain preliminary measures were adopted. A diplomatic agent of the less honourable sort, one Fontbrune, was despatched to Madrid with a letter to Charles IV. of Spain. This letter was in the form of a protest against all that the King of France might do, and all the documents he might sign, under compulsion. It was received by the Spanish King to be kept against the day of his French brother's escape, when it would serve as the base of an official repudiation of the acts of the captivity. The existence of this document and the fact that Fontbrune, who was aware of its contents, was at large in Europe caused the French court no little anxiety when, eighteen months later, it was trying to soothe the suspicious Parisians and so render possible the flight to Varennes[1].

It is evident that in this affair the French King counted on the friendship and hoped for the assistance of the Spanish Bourbons. And he was well advised so to do. The further the Revolution progressed the more real became the sympathetic concern with which the crowned heads of Europe heard of the misfortunes of His Most Christian Majesty. That this concern was in some cases slightly hypocritical and in others not sufficiently strong to induce a sacrifice of interest is

---

[1] Fersen, writing to Breteuil, April 2, 1791, explained the whole matter at the Queen's request and remarked on the necessity "de ménager M. de Fontbrune." Fersen, *Correspondance*, etc. I. 96. Further references, I. 290. Compare Des Cars, *Memoirs*, p. 198; and the details as to Fontbrune's career in Schlitter, p. xi. I suspect that he is the same person as a certain "Chevalier de Fonsbrune" who in Sept. 1787, visited England "to inform himself respecting the state of our armaments and other circumstances," *i.e.* as a spy. Wm. Eden to Lord Carmarthen, Sept. 28, 1787.

true. But the very assumption that it existed was enough to encourage French royalists to rely on the final interference of the powers. And the general belief that such sympathy would lead to interference explains, and goes far towards justifying, the suspicious attitude of the revolutionary leaders towards the court and towards Europe.

For interference in the affairs of a country in a state of revolution was a normal proceeding in the international politics of the time. The interfering power usually appealed to some honoured principle. Behind this principle it hid, perhaps the personal attachment of its monarch to the leader of one of the conflicting parties, perhaps its own general interests. Had it not been for the fierce struggle of parties in Poland, encouraged by the powers themselves, the interference that led to the partition of 1772 could not easily have been effected. In 1787 England and Prussia had interfered to set up the authority of the Stadtholder in Holland. In the two following years Prussia had encouraged and sought to profit by the troubles in the Hapsburg dominions. Had it not been for England she would almost certainly have utilised the revolution in the Low Countries to split those provinces from Austria. At the same time a party in France had sought to do precisely the same thing in its own interests.

From the first then an intervention of some or all the powers was confidently expected in France. The more each individual Frenchman was convinced of the greatness of his country and the importance of its Revolution—and most Frenchmen were firmly convinced of both—the more likely did it seem to him that Europe would not long leave France to herself. His newspapers and pamphlets coupled together praise of liberty and stories of the plottings of tyrants against it. His suspicions were aroused; his pride was touched. "It is certain," wrote an anonymous patriot in Sept. 1789, "that a scheme has been formed in the foreign courts against the enterprises of the French nation... The plan is to open a diet in the town of Frankfort. The eleven Christian monarchs of Europe will send deputies to it and in this assembly they will dare to accuse the French people of the crime of revolt"; eventually they will reestablish the old monarchy[1]. Such opinions were common enough. Serious statesmen shared them. In Jan. 1790 no less a person than Montmorin, the minister of foreign affairs, told the agent of the United States that "if the French did not soon make war it would soon be made upon them[2]." In streets and cafés and patriotic clubs the designs of Europe against French liberty had been denounced long before they had begun to take shape in the minds of foreign statesmen.

Very naturally the vast majority of the French nation, including men of almost all parties, was resolved not to tolerate any such interference. Suspicion begot resolution; resolution much brooded on begot further suspicion. The result was an 'electric' frame of mind

---

[1] Quoted in a news-letter from Brussels to the English Foreign Office, Sept. 8, 1789.

[2] Morris, *Diaries etc.*, I. 275. At that time Montmorin was inclined towards war but nervous lest the French finances should break down.

in the nation at large; an unfortunate but perfectly explicable, perhaps praiseworthy, state of things. The great idea that lay at the base of all the suspicion has never been better stated than by Talleyrand, when, in 1792, he had occasion to justify the attitude of Frenchmen towards foreign powers. He knew perfectly well, so he asserted, the faults of the new constitution; he desired to see it amended. But he, and his whole nation, were resolved not to undertake any amendment save when and how they themselves might think fit:— "car bien certainement personne n'a le droit de nous dire: 'Nous prétendons que vous soyez mieux que vous n'êtes'." Talleyrand prophesied that against the firm resolve of the French nation to manage its own affairs in its own way all the schemes of Europe would be shattered[1]:—as eventually they were, after the suspicious dread of interference had contributed not a little to bring an interference about.

Among the courts of the very first rank the one which manifested the most genuine sympathy for the fate of the French royal family was, as would be expected, that of Vienna. It has been seen that from a very early date the King of Prussia had taken up an attitude of hostility towards the Revolution; but he confined himself at first to suggestions and promises

---

[1] Pallain, *La mission de Talleyrand à Londres en* 1792, p. 103. Talleyrand to Delessart, Feb. 17, 1792. A forcible British rendering of the same thought was given by Burns some twelve years later when England in her turn was threatened with invasion:—

"The kettle o' the Kirk and State
  Perhaps a clout may fail in't;
But deil a foreign tinker loon
  Shall ever ca' a nail in't."

that produced no direct result. Leopold also showed no great anxiety to act with vigour during the first year of his reign. He was involved in difficulties of all sorts and checked by the cynical policy of his chancellor. Yet certain advice which he gave to the French court so early as the autumn of 1790 is very closely connected with the outbreak of war eighteen months later. In September 1790 Leopold went to Frankfort to receive the imperial crown[1]. There he met Augeard who reported his attempt to persuade the Queen to escape from Paris. The Emperor thoroughly approved of the plan, but declined to take any direct part in carrying it out, lest his action should become known and so lead to some murderous assault on his sister and her husband. He had already been warned by the French court not to support the violent plans of the emigrants. He knew that the Queen was not anxious as yet for an open breach with the Revolution. The proposal of a flight from Paris exactly coincided with his own point of view[2]. In the course of his conversation with Augeard it transpired that the latter was well acquainted with feudal land law and cognate matters. On hearing this Leopold—so we are assured—said:—" Listen. If the

---

[1] He was elected on Sept. 30, and crowned on Oct. 9.

[2] Fontbrune had been at Vienna in May 1790; he was commissioned by the King and Queen to check the schemes of the princes because of the danger which they involved for those who were still in Paris. Fontbrune was succeeded by another agent with a similar commission. For details and for evidence of Leopold's advocacy of the flight at this time see Schlitter, p. xi. sqq. Marie Antoinette wrote on Aug. 17: " Je crois qu'il faut patienter encore," and on Oct. 3: " Le temps et la patience sont les vrais remèdes à nos maux." Arneth, pp. 136—7.

Queen cannot escape the King must find a minister faithful enough to make the Assembly declare war on me. In that case I should not be bound to assign any reasons for taking up arms. Failing that, the Imperial Diet must be induced to force me to declare war about the Alsatian affair."

The Emperor did not intend to go to war, save as a very last measure, but he took this favourable opportunity of arranging pretexts for interference. To this end he bade Augeard stir up the German princes, giving him a letter of introduction to the most influential and able of those concerned—the Bishops of Spires. "I spent all November 1790 and January 1791," says Augeard, "in going to the different German courts, to the princes who held lands in Alsace and Lorraine, to prevent their agreeing to receive any money compensation from the National Assembly." So early as March 1791, we are told, the 'conclusum' of the Diet, declaring the action of France unjust and null, was drawn up. But Leopold did not wish it to be formally adopted until the King and Queen were safely out of Paris. It is significant that it was so adopted in August—when Leopold was first attempting to bring about a concert of the powers for the settlement of French affairs—and was sanctioned in December—when the concert scheme, which had been suspended, was being again taken down[1].

---

[1] These last facts confirm Augeard's narrative (*Memoirs*, pp. 239—59). Perhaps he has over-coloured his picture somewhat; but the whole story agrees too well with Leopold's character and with the subsequent course of events to be a fabrication. This contradicts Sybel's assertion (I. 197) that "neither Frederick William nor Leopold wanted the princes to complain in the Reichstag."

In obedience to his sister's wish the Emperor coupled with these proposals and arrangements for giving her help, should she be in a position to avail herself of it, the most steady opposition to the schemes of Artois, which involved a complete counter-revolution. He refused the pompous offers of the emigrant Mirabeau Tonneau, who professed to have an army of a thousand "great hearted gentlemen" at his back, and declared himself ready to shed "the last drop of his blood for the restoration of the rights of his sovereign[1]." But when the Emperor went so far as to assure Augeard that he would be no party to the restoration of despotic power in France, we may suppose that he was influenced by more motives than the desire to please his sister by discouraging the emigrants:—his own liberal sympathies, for instance, and the wish to see France fairly weak and consequently pliable.

In Prussia, as has already been stated, the sympathies of the sovereign himself were early enlisted on the side of the court and the counter-revolution. Of the ministers and courtiers only a small party at first adopted the King's point of view. But they did not dislike the Revolution less than he, and this dislike could be interpreted by Frenchmen as a confession of belief in the emigrant faith. The same is true, though in a less degree, of England. There the dislike of the Revolution was perhaps less general than in Prussia but it was very real. The ministers—as a body and after the first few months—hated it while they recognised its utility to Great Britain. George III. sympathised

---

[1] Mirabeau to Leopold, Oct. 13, 1790. Schlitter, p. xv.

most sincerely with his former enemy the King of France; for the 'brotherhood' among crowned heads was after all more than a mere name[1]. And in the case of England the French public was provided with a means of gauging public opinion that was not at first forthcoming in the case of Prussia. The hearty welcome given by the majority of the governing class to Burke's 'Reflections,' which appeared in the autumn of 1790, proved finally that respect for precedent and love of monarchy, worship of the divinity which for the leaders of the National Assembly no longer attached to the 'head of the executive power', still prevailed in England. There can be little doubt that Burke hastened both the struggle between the monarchy and the nation in France and that between the French nation and Europe[2].

The Bourbons of Spain were perhaps more honestly solicitous for the fate of Louis and his Queen and more bitterly opposed to the Revolution than any reigning house in Europe. Already in July 1789 Count Florida-Blanca had expressed to foreign ministers his dislike of the Revolution and had hinted that Spain might assist the French King to quell the insurrection of the third estate and the populace. It was rumoured at Madrid that in June a message had been sent to Paris stating that the alliance between the different branches of the

---

[1] A number of his letters, written at the various crises in the Revolution, are in Vol. II. of the *Dropmore Papers*.

[2] The reference is to his published works, the *Reflections*, and *Letter to a member of the National Assembly* (Feb. 1791). In private he wrote frequently to emigrant royalists and others to urge a European crusade against the Revolution.

House of Bourbon "did not allow that any alteration should take place in the form of government of the kingdoms belonging to that family." In view of the protest against the Revolution that came from Paris to Madrid in the autumn this rumour may well have been authentic. The Spanish government, as one would expect, did all in its power to prevent the circulation of French news south of the Pyrenees. From the autumn of 1789 troops were held in readiness to be used as a cordon along the northern frontier. It seems probable that had not Spain fallen foul of England in the following spring, and consequently been anxious to retain the friendship of France, she might have taken serious action of some sort against the Revolution, in spite of her dislike of war, her exhausted treasury, and her ineffective administration[1]. Even throughout the Franco-Spanish negotiations of 1790 the dislike of the court of Madrid for the French democratic party made itself apparent. "They are a wretched set," said Florida Blanca in August, "it is impossible to treat with them. If I had my way, I would put a cordon along the frontier, as if for a plague[2]." It is not surprising that nothing came of the French proposal to turn the Family Compact into a National Compact, nor that from the latter part of 1790 onwards Spain made no secret of her complete disapproval of the Revolution.

The little court of Sardinia was naturally anxious to avoid giving needless offence to the dominant party in France. Yet the fact that up to the end of 1790

---

[1] See the extracts of despatches from Madrid in Appendix IV.

[2] Grandmaison, *L'Ambassade Française en Espagne pendant la révolution*, p. 28.

Turin was the headquarters of the Count of Artois must have seemed significant to many French reformers. The real state of the case was not however revealed by that fact. Victor Amadeus soon became weary of the wild schemes of his brother-in-law. The Count of Artois in his turn grew impatient at the cautious policy and disgusted with the formal etiquette and the parsimony of the Sardinian court. He left Turin in Jan. 1791. Yet Victor Amadeus was and remained really attached to the interests of the King and Queen and fully prepared to co-operate, so far as his means would allow, in the plans for their salvation which Leopold of Austria from time to time suggested[1].

The northern powers hated the Revolution almost as much as Spain itself. Catherine of Russia cared little enough for the fate of Louis or of France, but she was concerned for the cause of royalty in general. Her letters contain attacks in the most violent language on the Revolution[2]. Gustavus III. of Sweden, who knew something of revolutions and of how to plan a *coup d'état*, blamed the irresolution of the French King and marvelled at his neglect of the most obvious means of checking popular movements—cavalry and cannon. Immediately after the first emigration Gustavus wrote to offer an asylum to Artois and Condé. He was not in the least disturbed when Staël, the Swedish ambassador at Paris, told him with some anxiety that this letter was being read and freely

---

[1] Victor Amadeus to Leopold, 8 Nov. 1790, 13 July, 1791. Schlitter, pp. xix. and lviii. See too correspondence of Mr Trevor with the English Foreign Office, *e.g.* Trevor to Carmarthen, Jan. 1, 1790.

[2] Larivière, *Catherine II. et la révolution française.*

criticised in clubs and cafés. The events of October further incensed him against the Revolution. Before the year was out his confidant Taube was at Aix-la-Chapelle engaged in secret and 'counter-revolutionary' negotiations. Early in 1791 Gustavus refused to recognise the new French tricolour flag; and when, in June of the same year, the question of an embassy from France to Sweden was raised, he informed Staël that he regarded all agents of the National Assembly as so many conspirators paid to light the fire of civil war in the various states of Europe[1].

As more or less distorted accounts of the attitude of the various European courts spread abroad in France, first in diplomatic and political circles, then—by means of pamphlets and newspapers and stump orations—throughout the whole nation, active hostility towards the old political system of Europe was aroused and began to prevail. And as these accounts generally contained explicit reference to the situation and interests of the French King and Queen, the unpopularity of the great state prisoners in the Tuileries tended to increase at the same time.

It is easy to arrive at the general conclusion that this active hostility towards the old Europe was of the very essence of the Revolution, and to imagine that the revolutionary leaders were eager from the outset to forcibly overthrow the institutions of neighbouring lands. But such a conclusion is hardly sound. It is true that in November 1792 the convention decreed that "it would accord brotherhood and help to all

---

[1] Geffroy, *Gustave III. et la cour de France*, pp. 102—5, and p. 134.

nations who might desire liberty"; and it proceeded to revolutionize conquered countries without much regard to their desires. It is true also that foretastes of this policy are to be found in the speeches and writings of various extreme democrats in the summer of 1791. But the decrees of 1792 belong to a stage of the Revolution with which we are not now concerned, and the threats of 1791 are mostly subsequent to the flight to Varennes:—the event which seemed to many Frenchmen to prove that the court and the powers were in league against freedom. Indeed during the first two years of the Revolution opposition to the old order of Europe was, as a rule, of a very moderate and philosophical sort. The principles of '89 were undoubtedly democratic and those who held them aimed at the establishment of governments on a popular basis. But the mass even of advanced liberals in 1789, '90 and 91' did not aim at a violent reconstruction of European society. They set about their task with much more deliberation and regard to the past than has often been supposed. Propagandists they were; but the doctrine of armed propaganda formed no part of their political creed.

That this was so even the testimony of their political enemies proves. For instance:—there was circulated among European statesmen in 1791 an account of a secret society, called The Society of the Propaganda, which was said to exist at Paris. Some said that it dated from before the Revolution, others that it did not exist before 1789. La Rochefoucault, Condorcet, and Sieyès were its reputed founders. Its aim was to control opinion and it employed the usual apparatus of vows, ceremonies, and what not. The members were pledged to support the influence of the people in all governments, to oppose arbitrary power, and to work in the cause of complete religious toleration. But it was one of their principles that attempts at sudden and complete change were not desirable, for "it was better to wait another fifty years than to fall by too great precipitation." Emissaries, it is said, were sent by this society into all neighbouring countries; and these emissaries met with considerable success in Savoy, Holland, and the Austrian Netherlands. But at first their methods conformed in the main to the rules laid down by the society. The day of revolution forced on from outside was not yet[1].

The Austrian Netherlands were not only the nearest but also the most favourable field for the display of the proselytising zeal of the French reformers; for they were already full of unrest in the spring of 1789, and before the year was over the Hapsburg government had for the time collapsed. The predominant party among the Belgians was clerical and aristocratic; it directed its attacks rather against the enlightened despotism of Joseph II., with its tendency to abolish local privileges and interfere in Church affairs, than against arbitrary power in general. Yet a strong democratic party existed. It shared the views of the

---

[1] This account comes from a memoir given to Lord Auckland by the Pensionary of the United Provinces in May 1791. *Dropmore Papers*, II. 69. The society is also mentioned in the despatches of Goltz from Paris, Sybel, I. 322. The two accounts do not agree absolutely. For the present purpose it is immaterial to know precisely how much truth there was in them.

French liberals and received their sympathy and support. Here was a revolution ready made. There was no question of delay in such a case. Naturally enough every liberal in France hoped that the Belgian democratic party would prevail and encouraged that party as he had occasion. From moral support and personal encouragement to public, even armed, interference is not a long journey. The fact that French statesmen from time to time seriously discussed the desirability of taking that journey, a fact of which Europe was perfectly well aware, increased greatly the chances of a collision between France and her neighbours. But schemes of interference in Belgium were only to a certain limited extent a development of the principle of democratic propaganda.

The spirit of propaganda was new and characteristic of the Revolution. Together with it older forces were working:—the desire to strengthen and extend the French empire and the passion for military glory. The former produced the incidents in Avignon and Alsace. The latter was to distort strangely the ultimate course of the Revolution. Both were in a sense bequests from the dead absolute monarchy. They tended to produce a certain love of war for its own sake, which can almost be separated from that desire for war as a means of distracting public attention from internal affairs which so constantly made itself felt in the earlier years of the Revolution. Those politicians who wanted war for either reason naturally turned their attention towards the hereditary enemy England or the still more unpopular Austria. For a time, in the summer of 1790, it seemed not unlikely that the lot would fall on

England. The colonial rivalry between England and Spain had come to a head once more. In Jan. 1790 news had reached Europe of the violent interference by Spanish ships of war with the English trading establishment in Nootka Sound on the coast of Vancouver Island. England proceeded to demand satisfaction from Spain without any preliminary discussion of the question of right. Pitt had Holland and Prussia at his back, so that Spain naturally looked to France for support. The details of the various debates in the French Assembly and of the negotiations which preceded the final discomfiture of Spain in October are too complicated for present discussion. It is important however to notice the attitude of the various nations and parties concerned. The English ministry fancied more than once in the course of the negotiations that Spain might be mad enough to risk war, but one searches in vain in the despatches for any traces of fear of the French. Evidently the belief in the decadence of France was very real. Spain seems to have been influenced mainly by the stubborn unreasoning pride that lost her the last shreds of empire but yesterday. Yet there is every reason to suppose that in the early summer the Spanish court was influenced by another motive. A strong aristocratic party in France wanted only a pretext for attacking England; for it saw safety for the monarchy in war. This fact was known at Madrid. Could Spain have felt certain that the conduct of a war would rest with the aristocratic party she might have forced on a breach with England out of sympathy for the French King. But the National Assembly stood in the way. Some of its members were aristocrats and wanted war for its own sake. Others, of a more liberal type, followed Lafayette who had dreams of humbling England once more. But the majority was not particularly warlike. Certain members of this majority felt kindly towards constitutional England. All were disposed to criticise a policy that the aristocrats favoured, and disliked the idea of the nation being involved in war in consequence of a dynastic agreement such as the Family Compact. In the Assembly, in the diplomatic committee, and in his secret notes for the court, Mirabeau did his utmost to press the arguments against war. His report on the question decided the Assembly (August 25) to vote for the change of the Family Compact into a National Compact. With this proposal the court of Madrid had not the least sympathy. It proved finally that the aristocratic party in France was helpless. That being so there was nothing whatever to be gained by further connection with a country that Florida Blanca and his master regarded as the plague spot of Europe. England was given all that she had demanded. France was no longer regarded as an ally; and the Nootka Sound incident with all its possibilities was past[1].

A colonial dispute was the appropriate prelude to a war of the traditional type with England. The corresponding prelude in the case of Austria was some disturbance or interference in the Low Countries. Those provinces lay at hand, rich and tempting,

[1] Yet in May 1791, Montmorin, the minister of foreign affairs, told Morris that "he would, if in office, bring on a sea war next year." Gouverneur Morris, *Diaries*, I. 416. For Spain see the extracts in Appendix IV.

separated from France by no natural barrier[1]. War after war against Austria had been opened by a northward march of the French over the flat country about the Belgian frontier. Belgium was hard to defend, and more closely connected by nature with Paris than with Vienna. The anti-Austrian party in France had in consequence always maintained that its conquest was natural and suitable, almost inevitable.

Thus it was towards Belgium that the warlike politicians as well as the more peaceful propagandists first turned their attention. Towards that point the lines of action of the old and new forces converged. There was thus every opportunity for the employment of force in the cause of liberty, and, ultimately, of the name of liberty in the cause of mere national ambition. Lafayette, who was both a propagandist and a warlike politician, was from the first eager to exploit the Belgian rising in the interests of liberty, and of France. He would have preferred 'a revolution more favourable to democratic principles' than that which he saw before him, but he resolved to make trial of it nevertheless. Late in 1789 he sent an agent, Sémonville, to observe the state of affairs in Brussels and enter into relations with the democrats there. Sémonville talked rather freely of the armed support which the French intended to give to the democrats in case the powers of the Triple Alliance should interfere in Belgium. But when those powers began to make arrangements for inter-

[1] In 1790 there remained no serious artificial barrier. When Joseph II. overthrew the mixed dominion in the Netherlands, and turned the Dutch garrisons out of the barrier fortresses (1781) several of those fortresses had been dismantled.

ference, in Jan. 1790, it became evident that he had promised more than he could perform[1]. France did nothing despite Lafayette; and Sémonville went home. In the summer of 1790 a fresh agent, no less a person than Dumouriez, paid a flying visit to Belgium. He brought back such an unfavourable account of the state of parties, and the character of party leaders among the Belgians, and of the financial and military affairs of the revolutionary government that Lafayette abandoned for the time all hope of utilising the Belgian revolution[2].

The desire of France to interfere in the Netherlands did not escape the notice of Austria. The desire was indeed a normal factor in the political calculations of the time. But gradually it became known at Vienna that the meditated interference might take the form of assistance to the democrats. In May 1790 the Austrian ambassador at Berlin announced that certain French liberals were engaged in sounding the Prussian court as to its willingness to tolerate such interference[3]. The letter contained almost the first hint of the possibility of a propagandist war that reached the Austrian court. Kaunitz however was slow to take the alarm. He reckoned rightly on the opposition

---

[1] Lafayette, *Memoirs*, III. 13. See in Appendix V. the letters from Colonel Gardiner, an English agent at Brussels, to the Duke of Leeds of Feb. 2, 12, 1790. On Jan. 9, the powers of the Triple Alliance signed a convention in which they agreed to settle together the affairs of Brabant and Flanders.

[2] Dumouriez, *Memoirs*, III. 84. Gardiner to Leeds, July 26, August 2.

[3] Beer, *Leopold II. Franz II., und Catharina*, p. 26. Reuss to Kaunitz.

between the aristocratic revolution of Belgium and the democratic revolution of France. Further, he was of opinion (and here he showed less sagacity) that the French government, present or to come, would never dare to think of appropriating the Low Countries[1]. Before the end of the year the Austrian armies had reduced the rebellious Flemings without any mishap. This confirmed Kaunitz in his contempt for revolutionists and in his hopeful view of the probable attitude of France towards Belgium. He seems to have adhered to that view until late in 1791, although so accurate an observer as the Count of Mercy had no confidence in the apparent acquiescence of the Belgians in their defeat, and although the Emperor's sister, the wife of the Imperial Viceroy in the Netherlands, continued to send alarming accounts of the spread of French principles throughout the country[2].

[1] Vivenot, I. 38. Letter of Oct. 31, 1790.
[2] Mercy to Kaunitz, Feb. 1791. Zeissberg, *Zwei Jahre Belgischer Geschichte*. Reports of the Academy of Sciences: Vienna 1891. Marie Christine to Leopold, June 9, 1791. Schlitter, p. 114.

CHAPTER III.

THE FLIGHT TO VARENNES AND THE POLICY OF LEOPOLD.

THE series of events that led more directly to the war of 1792 began in June of the previous year with the flight to Varennes. The flight is at once the most dramatic and historically, perhaps, the most significant and decisive event in the first four years of the Revolution. Projects of escape had often occupied the attention of the court and its well-wishers, both in France and abroad; but apparently it was not until the ecclesiastical laws of July and December 1790 had touched his conscience, that the kindly and irresolute Louis finally decided to fly from Paris at the first opportunity, and guide the Revolution in his own way from some suitable post in the provinces. Various schemes were considered. Finally that of a flight to the N.E. frontier was adopted. In January 1791 Mercy was aware that an escape might be expected in the near future. Early in the following month the Queen herself sent him word that Montmédy, hard by the frontier of Luxemburg, was the goal. On the 1st of April Fersen, who had for some time been engaged in arranging the details for the great adventure, stated definitely that within two months his royal mistress and the King would steal away from Paris by night. But delays arose and it was not until the night of June 20—1 that the eloping monarch and his family gave their guardians the slip and set out on the road to Montmédy[1].

The details of the story do not concern us here. But it is important to know what was the precise plan of the King and Queen, and what the attitude of the Emperor, the only one of the European sovereigns who took any direct part in the negotiations that preceded the flight. Certainly the King had no intention of attempting to restore the old order intact. He wished rather to establish a reformed monarchy somewhat of the type that Mirabeau, right up to the time of his death in April 1791, had not ceased to advocate in his secret letters to the court. Mirabeau, like every other real royalist, had insisted that the absolute freedom of of the King's person was the indispensable preliminary to any such monarchical restoration. The unlucky declaration which Louis drew up before leaving Paris throws abundant light on his intentions with regard to this matter. In that document he first reproached the

---

[1] Marie Antoinette to Mercy, Feb. 13, 1791. Feuillet de Conches, I. 444. Fersen to Taube, April 1. Fersen, I. 90. The first volume of Feuillet de Conches' work contains a number of spurious documents. The letter quoted is one of those which have not as yet been proved to be authentic; but there is no reason to suspect it. The dates given in the text are in part intended to prove that it was not after the riot of April 18—as some historians have asserted—that the scheme was finally adopted. As a matter of fact the famous berline was ordered in Dec. 1790.

representatives of the nation for the ingratitude which they had shown in return for his many acts of self-sacrifice; he next protested against the deeds of his captivity; recapitulated all the violent episodes of the Revolution; severely criticised the new constitution and finally appealed to all Frenchmen to rally round one who was at the same time their King and their truest friend[1]. It is a return to the old theory of enlightened despotism, to the doctrine expressed in the 'seul je ferai le bien de mes peuples,' with which Louis had tried to calm the first outbursts of revolutionary feeling in 1789. The royal plan included the appearance on the frontier of Austrian troops, whose menaces—which were not to be followed by invasion—should frighten the nation into seeking safety by supporting the King and accepting his proposals[2]. That is to say the King was to reap the benefit of the policy of salvation by war—a policy based on the assumption that in time of war, actual or impending, the force of the executive authority will increase—whilst, owing to his secret understanding with the enemy, he was to spare his people the misery of an actual invasion.

The policy of Leopold in the summer of 1791 is not easy to follow and has given rise to a considerable amount of controversy. One can at times almost imagine that he was subject to the rare complaint known as alternating personalities. There is the brother, keenly interested in the laments and entreaties of Marie Antoinette, and there is the prince, obedient

---

[1] Feuillet de Conches, II. 95. The declaration is dated June 20.

[2] For the general policy, see Sybel, I. 248, and Lenz, *Historische Zeitschrift*, 1894.

to the cool and often perverse reasonings of Kaunitz[1]. His position with regard to France was exceedingly difficult. It was rendered the more difficult by the comparative indifference of the other powers, and by the reckless conduct of the emigrants. He had for some time meditated a settlement of the French troubles by means of a concert of the powers. The idea was not his only; it had been suggested to the Queen by Mirabeau in June 1790, but had been abandoned in the following October because Mirabeau then saw no prospect of a stable alliance between Austria and Prussia[2]. It would seem that in December, Artois had broached the subject to the Emperor. After consulting Kaunitz, Leopold laid down certain conditions upon the fulfilment of which the formation of a concert should depend: the King of France was to secure his liberty, to denounce the Revolution, and make a formal appeal in the first instance to the court of Madrid; after this the powers might begin to move[3]. This confirms once more the view that Leopold regarded the escape from Paris as 'le préalable à tout[4].' It shows too, what is apparent from other sources, that he saw no very immediate prospect of united action on

---

[1] Beer (*Hist. Zeit.* 1872) maintains that the differences of opinion between emperor and chancellor, of whom now one now the other carried his point, sufficiently explain the very complicated and seemingly inconsistent policy of the reign. See too App. Holland, 27. Certainly it is upon these lines that the problem should be approached.

[2] Marie Antoinette to Mercy, June 12. Arneth, p. 129. Mirabeau to La Marck, Oct. 27. Bacourt, II. 272.

[3] Memoir drawn up by Kaunitz, Dec. 20, 1790, and sanctioned by Leopold. Schlitter, p. xviii.

[4] Mercy's words to the Queen, March 7, 1791. Arneth, p. 147.

the part of Europe. He was at the time uncertain as to the attitude of Prussia. He thought too that, until the Russo-Turkish war was over and the obstinate indifference of England overcome, there was small hope of a successful concert[1].

The spring and summer of 1791 were spent by the Emperor in Italy. The history of his policy in these few months is exceptionally important and as exceptionally difficult. Some have held that he really was above all things interested in French affairs and eager to release his sister from her hateful captivity. Others maintain that his desire to help the Queen was more affected than real. Yet others explain that his anxiety to conceal his own policy and that of his sister until a successful escape from Paris should have removed all danger from publicity, accounts satisfactorily for his apparent inconsistencies. It would be rash to assert that Leopold was perfectly candid or entirely disinterested; yet a close examination of his conduct tends to confirm this last more favourable explanation and estimate. It tends also to confirm, in a sort the old accusations of conspiracy against the French Revolution[2].

According to the old-fashioned revolutionary tradition, Leopold entered into an unholy alliance with the Count of Artois on May 17 at Mantua. But the actual occurrences of the Mantua meeting hardly bear

---

[1] For Prussia and Russia, see Ch. IV. The French court had thought of bribing England to join the concert with colonial concessions. Fersen, I. 94.

[2] Compare the views of Herrmann, *Forschungen zur Deut. Gesch.* V 257. Lenz, *Hist. Zeit.* 1894. Schlitter, p. XL.

out this legend. Those occurrences, as we now know, were briefly thus: Artois laid before the Emperor an elaborate memoir in which he advocated an immediate march of troops, the publication of a threatening manifesto, a dash by the emigrants across the French frontier near Valenciennes, and an appeal for assistance to Spain, Sardinia, and Switzerland, with other hasty and ill-timed measures. Leopold commented on this document in his usual cautious style; he flatly rejected or skilfully parried the more violent proposals, and declined to commit himself in any way until the King should have escaped from Paris, and until satisfactory arrangements for the establishment of a concert of the powers should have been made. Seeing that he was aware of the plans of the French court and had been often warned against giving ear to the suggestions of Artois, his caution cannot be described as either unnecessary or treacherous[1].

But Artois and his agents did not transmit to Paris the replies that the Emperor gave them. The court had sent a certain Count Durfort to Italy to gather news of Leopold's movements and intentions. Durfort fell into the hands of the emigrants and consented to work with them. Towards the end of May he brought to the Tuileries an undated and unsigned document, written in his own hand, that purported to be based on the Emperor's expressed opinions. This document contained promises of invasion and rescue, and, in short, a résumé of the policy which the emigrants had.

[1] The proposals of Artois and Leopold's comments in Lenz, *Hist. Zeit.*, 1894. Leopold's letter to Kaunitz enclosing the proposals and comments in Beer, *Joseph II., Leopold II. und Kaunitz*, p. 404.

always favoured, and the court always discouraged. Among other things, the King and Queen were bidden not to fly from Paris but to await there the rescuing army[1]. Now Artois and his clique, who were responsible for this forgery, knew that no army would come. What then was their aim? May it not have been to keep the King in Paris until the rising violence of the Revolution should force him to abandon the comparatively liberal policy towards which he inclined and which the Emperor would have supported in case of a successful escape? By this means the Artois faction may have hoped to demonstrate the futility of moderate counsels and the need for a complete and radical counter-revolution. There is one other possibility which is not pleasant to think of. The Emperor refrained from violent proposals or measures lest they should bring about some murderous assault on royalty at Paris. It can hardly be that those who invented for him a violent policy wished to bring about that which he was above all things anxious to prevent.

But the Mantua forgery hardly deceived the Queen. She wrote to her brother on the first of June asking for further explanations, and expressing doubts as to the document which had just come to hand. The following day her confidant, Fersen, expressed similar doubts in a letter to a friend; he mentioned that the royal family was about to fly in spite of the direct command to the contrary. On the fifth Marie Antoinette repeated her reasons for suspicion to Mercy. She

---

[1] The story by which Durfort accounted for the existence of so irregular a document was exceedingly flimsy.

received in reply a clear confirmation of the justice of these suspicions: "The result [of the Mantua conference] as it has been reported at Paris is most suspicious; we cannot rely on it until the Emperor shall have explained himself on this point directly[1]." There can be no doubt that the Queen never believed that this Mantua policy was really that of her brother; but her alarm at the bare possibility of its being so proves that his action in making all dependent on a successful escape met with her entire approval, however much his slow and circuitous procedure may have galled her impetuous spirit.

Leopold and Mercy regarded the flight as dangerous but necessary. Kaunitz went further. He thought it well-nigh impossible. "I shall not believe in the escape of the royal family until I see it," he wrote on June 9[2]. Not only was it impossible, but to encourage it was impolitic. Suppose, it was argued in a memoir that he forwarded to Leopold about this time, suppose that all goes well, which is highly improbable, and that

---

[1] The Queen to Leopold, June 1, Arneth, p. 167. She mistrusts Durfort's memoir: "comme il n'est signé de personne." Fersen to Taube, June 2, Fersen, I. 134. Queen to Mercy, June 5, Arneth, p. 171. Mercy to the Queen, June 9, Arneth, p. 175. As Mercy was in Belgium, we may safely assume that this letter is a reply to Marie Antoinette's of the 5th.

[2] For Leopold and Mercy see Arneth, p. 156, and Schlitter, pp. xxxii. and xlii. For Kaunitz, Schlitter, p. xliii. Compare his letter to Mercy of June 23 : "Ich bin...überzeugt, dass Niemand auf sich nehmen könne, dem König und der Königin diese Flucht anzurathen; dass vielmehr alle möglichen dringenden Bewegursachen vorhanden sind, sie davon abzuhalten." Vivenot, I. 538. Evidently he had spoken of a flight to be followed by a concert—above p. 47—mainly to gratify the Emperor.

the King escapes. The Assembly will order him to return, and, if he refuses to obey, will depose him. England will not lift a finger to restore the absolute monarchy, nor would it be in Austria's interest to support any attempt of that sort. If, on the other hand, the King agrees to accept the constitution as drawn up by the Assembly in order to keep his throne we shall have no right to interfere. It could hardly be incumbent upon us to declare that his consent was not given freely unless the evidence of the fact were overwhelming[1]. This most important memoir shows very clearly how divided the counsels of Austria were, and how remote were all prospects of a European concert at the moment of the flight.

Safe in Italy from the chilling personal influence of his impracticable chancellor Leopold began to disregard difficulties and to throw himself heartily into the work of helping his sister. He wrote to her on June 12 to say that, should the flight prove successful, Mercy would be prepared to assist her; that money, troops, all that he had, would be at her disposal[2]. In the first days of July the rumour that the royal party had made its escape without mishap went the round of the capitals of the West. It found Leopold at Padua. He was in a state of the utmost delight. The Count of Vaudreuil, an ardent royalist, who but a few days before had been complaining of the Emperor's 'intolerable vacillation,' now reported that his conduct was 'perfect,' and told

---

[1] The memoir was drafted by Spielmann. Schlitter, p. xliii.

[2] Arneth, p. 177. He promised also to hold Artois in check and to do nothing hastily. Possibly this letter did not reach Paris before the royal family left.

with enthusiasm how he came in person at four o'clock in the morning to rouse the Duke of Polignac, who, in his night-shirt, received the good news from the imperial lips. Vaudreuil was unbounded in his admiration of the excellent skill with which the King and the Emperor had outwitted their foes and kept all secret up to the last moment[1]. Leopold was determined to act promptly and with decision. On July 5 he wrote to his ambassador at Madrid ordering him to make some arrangement with the Spanish court forthwith, since he meant to support the King and Queen of France in every possible way[2]. The same day he despatched to the sceptical Kaunitz a most important letter, which deserves to be quoted at length. "My decision is taken. Seeing that the King of France is free, has won back his authority, and has revoked all that was done in his name and that he was forced to sanction, I intend—as his relative, friend, and ally—to support him and assist him with all my force: be it by providing him with the necessary funds, of which at the moment he may be in want; or by issuing a most threatening declaration to the National Assembly; or by moving my Belgian troops to the French frontier, and even letting them enter the country, should circumstances demand it; or finally by summoning, as head of the empire, the German princes, the King of Prussia and the Swiss to stand by the King of France[3]."

[1] Vaudreuil, *Correspondance*, II. 1, 8, June 26 and July 3.
[2] Feuillet de Conches, II. 152. Compare his letters of the same date to Marie Christine and Mercy, Feuillet de Conches, III. 373.
[3] Schlitter, p. xlix. The German original is in the Vienna archives.

Leopold was now willing, and even eager, to do all that ardent royalists could wish; almost in fact what he had refused to do at Mantua when the escape from Paris was not admitted as the necessary preliminary to action. In the light of this letter, even after allowance has been made for the natural excitement of the moment, it may fairly be concluded that his previous policy had been on the whole sincere and consistent. As fairly it may be said that he was privy to a 'conspiracy' against the Revolution. He and Louis were at one as to the policy of repudiation. Together, and if possible with the assistance of the other powers, they intended to terrorise the National Assembly and force it to accept reforms and a constitution of the royal making. In short the revolutionary doctrine of the sovereignty of the people was to give place to the doctrine of enlightened despotism as held and practised by Frederick the Great and Leopold himself. Neither monarch meditated a complete counter-revolution; yet it is very possible that the influence of the extreme royalist party might have proved as pernicious to the restored Louis XVI. as it proved, nearly a generation later, to the restored Louis XVIII. But Louis XVI. was not restored. The berline was stopped at Varennes; and on the very day that Leopold wrote so confidently to Kaunitz certain news of the disaster arrived in Padua.

The turning point which Kaunitz and Spielmann had foreseen was come. The French nation, having brought back its King, would either depose him or force him to give an apparently willing consent to the constitution. At first there was talk of deposition, and certain sections of the Parisian populace, under able and determined leadership, advocated that course persistently and with much demonstration. Yet even in Paris it is doubtful whether there was much real republicanism at this time. Discontent with the King and indignation at his duplicity there certainly was; but the mass of the people was still so monarchical in sentiment, and most of the popular leaders were still so firmly convinced of the inexpediency of abolishing royalty, that Louis was in no great danger of losing his crown when once the first ebullition of feeling caused by his flight had died away. But nothing did more to undermine both the sentiment and the conviction with regard to royalty than the three months of practical republicanism (June—September, 1791), at the end of which, by an act of grace as it were on the part of the nation, Louis was allowed to return to his throne on conditions. Henceforward Frenchmen knew that, should war between France and Europe actually break out, they would be able to manage their affairs without a King, if the King whom the constitution had preserved to them were to show a dangerous sympathy with the nation's foes.

Leopold did not at first recognise the full importance of the Varennes mishap, nor did he at once give up the schemes for interference in French affairs that he had so recently expounded. Immediately on hearing of the arrest of the royal family he drew up a circular note, copies of which were forwarded to the Empress of Russia, the Kings of England, Prussia, Spain, Sicily, and Sardinia, and the Elector of Mainz. In this document he argued that, as the recent lamentable event definitely established the illegal character of the whole Revolution, and compromised directly "the honour of all sovereigns and the safety of all governments," concerted action on the part of the powers to "vindicate the liberty and honour of the Most Christian King and his family and to limit the dangerous extremes of the French Revolution" was most urgently required[1]. As a preliminary measure it was suggested that the ambassadors of the powers at Paris should hand in a strongly worded declaration. A draft of this suggested 'identical note' was sent with the circular. It stated that as the freedom of the King of France was now obviously a mere fiction the powers could no longer delay to do what honour, blood, and the interests of order demanded. The King must be set at liberty without delay. Due respect must be accorded to him. For the allies would unite to avenge signally any further attacks on his honour or his person; they would decline to recognise any French law or constitution that had not received his free assent, and they would use all possible means to put an end to the scandal of an usurpation in case it should arise. Leopold proposed that still more vigorous measures should be adopted if the French democrats were not cowed by this impressive and unanimous expression of opinion.

On July 17 a second circular, of a rather different character, was drawn up by Kaunitz at Vienna. The difference in character is partly explained, and at the same time light is thrown on the general policy of Austria, by the fact that a draft of this Vienna circular

---

[1] Vivenot, I. 185, July 6, 1791. The document is usually known as the Padua circular.

had been sent to the Emperor on June 30—before the result of the flight was known[1]. The completed document begins, like its predecessor, with an enumeration of the reasons that render interference desirable. Among these the danger of contagion holds a prominent place[2]. The aim of the interference is to stop further violence and to bring about a modification of the new constitution in accordance with the freely expressed wishes of the King. This cautious and moderate language is significant. As means suitable for the coercion of the democrats Kaunitz suggests, in addition to the declaration, the suspension of commercial relations between France and the allied powers, the recall of ambassadors, and the assembling of a European congress at Aix-la-Chapelle or Spa. The whole is not very precise nor very vigorous. It gives the impression that the case for which he was pleading did not lie near the heart of the old chancellor. Yet the two circulars taken together constituted a formal and pressing appeal to the leading governments of Europe to interfere in the internal affairs of France. It remains to be seen what was the state of European politics at the time and what grounds, if any, Leopold and Kaunitz had for supposing that their suggestions were likely to be well received.

[1] Schlitter, p. li. The circular in Vivenot, i. 208.
[2] In a second letter, to the various Austrian embassies, Kaunitz refers to the questions of Alsace and Avignon, and insists on the necessity of forcing France to put a stop to warlike preparations and the revolutionary propaganda, and to respect treaties. Vivenot, i. 213.

CHAPTER IV.

THE ORIGIN OF THE AUSTRO-PRUSSIAN ALLIANCE. THE DECLARATION OF PILNITZ, AND THE AFFAIRS OF POLAND.

At the time of his accession, early in 1790, Leopold had with good reason anticipated a war with Prussia. But just before the flight to Varennes he had been assured by an influential person from Berlin that "as soon as the King of France should have escaped, the troops of the King of Prussia would be at his disposal to help him[1]." The diplomatic revolution which these words implied is of especial significance in the present connection. Begun in 1790, but not completed until early in 1792, it is related most intimately at every stage to the series of causes that led to the outbreak of war in the latter year, indeed it might itself be described as one of those causes.

In spite of the desperate condition of the Hapsburg dominions in the early spring of 1790, Kaunitz seems not to have entertained any thought of coming to terms with Prussia, the power which had done so much to humble and despoil his former mistress Maria Theresa and to thwart the policy of her successor. He clung to

[1] Vivenot, I. 170. *Journal über die Unterhandlung mit Bischoff-werder.* Cp. Schlitter, p. xlix.

the Austro-Russian alliance and still hoped to retain the profitable connection with France that he had himself brought into existence thirty-four years earlier. But Leopold was naturally of a conciliatory and pacific disposition. He was eager to secure the imperial crown and to devote all his energy to internal affairs. Consequently he was altogether averse to war with Prussia. "It gives me much displeasure to be forced into war," he wrote in March 1790[1], when a collision between the two powers seemed inevitable. A few days later he made a preliminary attempt to smooth matters over by sending a friendly letter to the Prussian King[2]. At this time Leopold had no intention of abandoning the Russian alliance entirely, although he was not anxious to continue the useless and costly campaign against Turkey. But Kaunitz held that any understanding with Prussia, or the whole Triple Alliance, would involve the desertion of Catherine, to whose policy the allies were known to be averse. Therefore he opposed his new master's inclinations. This opposition, together with the momentary eagerness of Frederick William to imitate his predecessors by winning military glory in war against Austria, helped to render Leopold's first friendly advances unfruitful.

But the contest was delayed. Prussia was hardly inclined to engage almost single handed with the two imperial courts; and her ally England, though anxious to save the Porte from destruction by Russia and to terminate the war in the East, preferred if possible to

---

[1] Schlitter, p. viii.
[2] March 25. Beer, *Leopold II., Joseph II. und Catharina*, p. 16.

do so without fighting, and certainly had no mind to join in any spoliation of Austria merely that some fanciful territorial juggle of Hertzberg's might be successfully executed. In the spring of 1790 the particular redistribution towards which Hertzberg and his master inclined was this: Austria was to give back Galicia to Poland, receiving in return some Turkish lands; Poland was to cede to Prussia the valuable districts in the neighbourhood of Dantzig on the lower Vistula; the Belgian provinces were to be declared independent Russia was to retain part of her conquests from Turkey the town of Oczakow for instance[1]. England wished to see peace concluded between Russia, Austria, and the Porte on the basis of the strict *status quo*. She did not wish to recognise the independence of the Low Countries—largely out of fear lest they should fall under the domination of France—though she was prepared to do so on emergency. She regarded the Galicia scheme and the alliance that Prussia had arranged with the Porte as altogether objectionable[2]. On hearing of the friendly disposition of Leopold she threw all her weight into the scale of peace, and her foreign minister spoke in the warmest terms of the character of the new ruler

---

[1] Sybel, I. 180. Lecky, v. 244 sqq.

[2] "There appears indeed to be so little justice in insisting upon such an arrangement [that about Galicia]...and it is so evidently contrary to our defensive system, that,...it would be impossible for this country to give any expectation of supporting Prussia in a contest begun on such grounds." Leeds to Ewart (at Berlin), March 19. "The Prussian ministers appear totally blind...in short to have neither eyes nor ears except for their own projects relative to Galicia and the independence of the Netherlands." Auckland to Leeds April 16. See too Appendix V.

at Vienna[1]. She urged Prussia to take no hasty action in the matter of Belgium, but to support her in arranging some satisfactory mediation between the Hapsburgs and their revolted subjects, and in terminating the war in the East. Pitt had the Nootka Sound affair on his hands, a fact which rendered him the more eager to pacify Europe; and certainly the Prussian schemes did not tend to pacification.

Austria meanwhile armed for war and moved troops into Moravia and Bohemia. In April Leopold had gratified England by accepting her offer of mediation in the Low Countries[2]. In June he made a last effort on the side of Prussia, sending to Frederick William a letter which might almost be described as an ultimatum[3]. From that time forward his willingness to make peace with Turkey and England's desire to avoid war began to break down the various obstacles in the way towards a pacific arrangement with Prussia. The King of Prussia empowered Hertzberg to open negotiations at Reichenbach in Silesia with Baron Spielmann and the Prince of Reuss, who represented Austria. Ewart and the Baron de Reede, who attended as representatives of the maritime powers, were largely responsible for the final adjustment. Hertzberg was, as ever, anxious to bring about some redistribution of territory and his master hardly knew what he himself wanted. But after a time England succeeded in bringing both statesmen, more or less reluctantly, to adopt her point of view. Frederick William abruptly decided to insist on one main point only: Austria was to declare her

[1] In the letter of March 19.
[2] Leopold to George III., April 3.   [3] Dated June 17.

intention of signing forthwith an armistice with the Porte, to be followed by a congress for the final settlement of the Turkish question and the conclusion of a treaty of peace on the basis of the *status quo*. To the surprise of many politicians, and to the disgust of the Prussian war party, Leopold promptly accepted this rather hard proposal; and on August 4 Reuss presented the declaration with his master's signature attached. Austria also announced her intention of accepting the mediation of the Triple Alliance in the settlement of Belgian affairs and of guaranteeing the preservation of the ancient Belgic customs and privileges.

It seemed, for the moment, as if the allies, and more especially Prussia, had gained a signal diplomatic triumph. Such was the popular opinion; but Hertzberg, whose real dislike of the new policy had caused a breach between him and the King, saw that Austria might easily turn the whole to her own advantage; whilst Prussia had wasted the millions spent on military preparations and alienated the Poles—who were eager for the restoration of Galicia—the Belgians, and the anti-Austrian party in Hungary. On September 19 the promised armistice was signed at Giurgevo; but Austria was not careful to proceed further, and it was not until late in December that the peace congress was opened at Sistova[1].

Almost immediately after the negotiations of Reichenbach Leopold was elected and crowned Emperor.

---

[1] This short account is based on the narratives of Sybel, Lecky and Heigel (*Deutsche Geschichte*), and on the despatches of Ewart and Keith. See too Neumann, *Traités...conclus par l'Autriche*, I. 414 and 431.

Possibly his desire to secure the Prussian vote had influenced his conduct throughout. His mind was already occupied with French affairs, but he agreed with Kaunitz in holding that the pacification of the Netherlands and the treaty with the Porte demanded, for the moment, all the attention of Austria. At Reichenbach not the remotest reference was made to France; but Frederick William, as we have seen, had already begun to turn his eyes towards Paris, and to listen to the advice and exhortations of Bischoffwerder and of Roll, the agent of the Count of Artois. At the very moment when Leopold, at Frankfort, was advising Augeard to stir up the German princes against the Revolution, the Prussian court—or that section of it which sympathised with the emigrants—drew up a tentative scheme for interference in French affairs. The Prussian court was fond of hypothetical politics; its proposals by no means necessarily implied intentions; but this proposal is not the less interesting on that account. On September 13, Hohenlohe told the Prince of Reuss that his court was anxious to join with that of Vienna in some plan for helping Louis XVI. It is interesting to observe that Prussia had no intention of giving her assistance without return. Indeed she had already fixed on her reward. Whilst offering French Hainault to Austria she proposed to take as her own compensation the Duchies of Jülich and Berg, whose owner—the Elector Palatine—was to secure an equivalent from the lands to be conquered from France in Alsace[1].

[1] Reuss, Sept. 14. Beer, *Leopold II., Franz II. und Catharina*, p. 36. Yet Sybel wrote (v. 529), "Beunruhigte durch die Hülfenrufe

But as yet it was no time for joint action. Throughout the summer Leopold had been busily working at the settlement of his dominions. He availed himself of the jealousy between Slav and Magyar to check the disquieting manœuvres of the Hungarian Diet at Ofen. Immediately after the imperial coronation he proceeded to Pressburg to receive the Hungarian crown. There he adopted the national costume; regulated the relations between the peasantry and the landowners; facilitated the rise of commoners to office; rearranged the military contributions; and secured to the nobles the majority of their feudal rights. These various concessions won him the almost enthusiastic loyalty of all sections of the Hungarian nation. Meanwhile he had done what he could to lighten and readjust financial burdens throughout his dominions, had partially abolished his brother's unpopular ecclesiastical innovations—thereby gratifying the Germans of Austria proper—and had secured the support of Bohemia by the establishment of a professorship of the Czech language in the University of Prague[1]. There remained only the Low Countries. There Leopold decided to employ force seeing that there only had there been open rebellion. His commander, Marshal Bender, met with little opposition from the Belgian rebels. As Bender advanced Count Mercy, the Austrian ambassador at Paris who had come to the Hague to

Ludwigs XVI., aber erst auf die Kriegserklärung der Gironde widerwillig unter die Waffen getreten, hatten die Mächte damals nur den Gedanken gehabt, den aufgenöthigten Streit zur eignen Vergrösserung zu benutzen."

[1] Heigel, p. 342 sqq. Keith's despatches, *passim*.

negotiate with the representatives of the Triple Alliance, began to show that Leopold's policy was not all concession. Military operations began in September. In the first days of December the imperial troops entered Brussels. On the tenth Mercy, abandoning ostensibly the rather uncompromising attitude which he had recently adopted, signed a convention at the Hague in company with Lord Auckland, Count von Keller, and Van der Spiegel. Austria agreed to restore the ancient Belgian privileges, to grant an amnesty to the rebels, and in various ways to reverse the policy of Joseph :—by abandoning the conscription, the claim to levy taxes without the consent of the estates, and certain edicts interfering with Catholic seminaries and universities[1]. But this convention was never ratified. The mediating powers complained that Leopold restored not the ancient Belgian system as it had existed under Charles VI. but a modified form of it which resembled in certain points the unpopular constitution of Joseph. Leopold apparently felt himself strong enough to do without the guarantee which they offered and so disregarded the complaint[2].

[1] Neumann, I. 435. Auckland's Despatches, *passim*. A proof of the suspicious attitude of the National Assembly had been given in August, when it refused to allow Austrian troops to cross French territory on their way to the Netherlands. This act was "looked upon as the certain forerunner of the total abrogation of the Treaty of Alliance" between the two powers. Mercy's withdrawal from Paris was, it would seem, in part due to this act of unfriendliness. Keith to Leeds, 18 Aug. 1790. From this time forward Mercy remained at Brussels and conducted the correspondence between Marie Antoinette and Leopold.

[2] Sybel, I. 341.

Naturally the whole conduct of the undertaking against Belgium caused much irritation at Berlin. The Prussian court had to a certain extent committed itself to the cause of the Belgian rebels. Yet Austria had crushed them by force and now disregarded all pleas on their behalf. There was also a special cause of complaint. After the fall of Brussels Austrian troops marched to the assistance of the Prince Bishop of Liège against the democrats in his own diocese. Liège was part of the empire and so had claims on Leopold's assistance. But Prussia was not minded to acquiesce in any revival of real imperial power in the hands of the Hapsburgs. Yet she could not interfere. On Jan. 10, some two hundred 'patriots' of Liège retired on to French territory; the next day the Kaiser's troops entered the city, and in February the Bishop, who had been forced to emigrate, was reinstated[1].

Evidently Austria had gained at least as much as Prussia by the convention of Reichenbach. England was not dissatisfied on the whole. The peace had at least been kept, and there was a prospect of some sort of Eastern settlement in the near future. But Austria profited by the advantageous position in which she found herself at the end of 1790 to delay that settlement, in the interests of Russia, and in the hope of obtaining more favourable terms for herself. The policy was that of Kaunitz. To what extent Leopold acquiesced in it at this time is not clear; he seems to have followed no precise or consistent course. Kaunitz

---

[1] Heigel, 370 sqq. In October Mirabeau had declared the Austro-Prussian understanding doomed. To La Marck. Bacourt, II. 272.

saw that, could the negotiations in the newly opened congress at Sistova be delayed until Catherine's armies should have met with success great enough to render the fact of a peace between Austria and the Porte immaterial to the empress, he would gratify her without actually breaking his master's promise at Reichenbach. Not that he fully approved of that promise; he had no love for the new policy of friendship with Prussia, and did what he could to discourage its further progress; but he must have realised that, for the time at least, it was useful, and he had some respect for the accomplished fact.

England and Prussia were now anxious to strengthen the slight bonds that held Austria to their policy. Both had adopted, and proposed to enforce, the *status quo* as the basis of a general pacification. Austria had accepted this position in principle. Russia had not. The allies had offered their mediation on these terms and had been refused; for Russia meant to retain at least Oczakow, the chief of her conquests. Consequently the allies were engaged in an attempt to split Austria definitely from Russia. They thought that Leopold might even be induced to adopt some form of treaty with them, to become party to a Quadruple defensive Alliance. One of the tasks of Lord Elgin, who was sent on a special mission to the Austrian court at the end of 1790, was to promote some arrangement of this sort. The court of Berlin secretly despatched Bischoffwerder on a similar errand in Jan. 1791. So far as can be seen schemes for joint action in French affairs had dropped into the background; but there is no doubt that Bischoffwerder himself was strongly in favour of the policy of interference[1]. The favourite was well received at the imperial court in spite of the fact that Kaunitz handed in to the Emperor a whole series of memoirs intended to demonstrate the folly of an Austro-Prussian alliance[2]. At Berlin, as at Vienna, there was a strong party in the ministry that disliked the whole negotiation. Hertzberg was at the head of this party. His objection was based, as one would expect, on a general disapproval of the doctrine of the *status quo*. But circumstances aided the plans of the monarchs and defeated those of the ministers. England and Prussia were preparing, as all the world thought, to force the *status quo* on Catherine when suddenly, early in April, Pitt drew back. He had found that England had no desire to waste money in saving a place called Oczakow, about which no one knew or cared much, from the grasp of Russia; that of all the powers Prussia alone would stand by him in case of war; and that some of his most trusted advisers disapproved of his policy[3]. This unexpected conduct on the part of its ally offended the Prussian court deeply. The Triple Alliance practically went to pieces. Prussia was left in a position of most uncomfortable isolation, and began to regard an understanding with Austria as more than ever necessary[4].

---

[1] The various arguments that induced the Prussian court to seek for a friendly understanding with Austria are given in Ranke, *Ursprung...der Revolutionskriege*, p. 14, and Sybel, I. 279. The hope of splitting Leopold from Catherine was certainly the most influential of these arguments.

[2] Beer, *Leopold II., Franz II. und Catharina*, p. 44.

[3] Browning, *Essays*, p. 115; and the exhaustive discussion in Lecky, v. ch. XIX.

[4] At the time, as Mr Lecky says, "the determination of the

England continued to pursue her attempt to detach Leopold from Russia. In the early summer Lord Elgin followed the Austrian court to Italy. Leopold was at that time busy with the projected flight of the French royal family and occupied in interviewing the emigrant princes and the king's agents. It is not surprising that Elgin should have come to the conclusion that "the restoration of affairs in France" was "the chief spring" of the emperor's political system; nor that his letters constantly speak of Leopold's absorption in French questions and indifference to other branches of foreign policy[1]. These facts struck Elgin the more because his own government was firmly resolved not to entangle itself in any scheme of interference. Leopold dallied with the English scheme for a great defensive alliance, from which only the Bourbons and Russia were to be excluded, and made certain suggestions which show that the idea of a concert of the powers for the settlement of the French question was fully developed before the flight to Varennes. In the first week of May, for instance, "he went so far as to suggest the expediency of guarantying not only the possessions, but also the constitutions of the different states of Europe[2]."

English government was received at Berlin with regret, but more graciously than might perhaps have been expected." But the whole subsequent relation of England and Prussia fully bears out what Ewart wrote on Aug. 21, 1791: "...I know now that though the King and Colonel Bischoffwerder professed to be satisfied with the explanation I gave them [after the Oczakow incident], they immediately lost confidence in the resources both of the Alliance, and of this country..."

[1] Herrmann, *Forschungen*, v. The letter quoted is of May 26.
[2] Elgin to Grenville, May 9.

Frederick William now sent a formal invitation to Leopold to enter into an alliance. The task of presenting it was entrusted to Bischoffwerder, who made his appearance at Milan on the 9th of June. Ostensibly he and Elgin were working for the same end, and at first their relations were cordial and confidential. But Prussia no longer fully trusted England, and in consequence the harmony between the two ministers was not complete. Further, Bischoffwerder and his sovereign sympathised with Leopold's French policy; whilst Elgin and his government did not. Consequently the Prussian was more successful than the Englishman. Leopold was anxious to make some arrangement which would finally settle affairs in the East—where the congress at Sistova still dragged on —and leave his hands free in case the flight from Paris should necessitate vigorous action in the West. Kaunitz wished no alliance to be made to which Catherine was not a party. To gratify the chancellor Leopold, whilst carrying on negotiations with both Bischoffwerder and Elgin, wrote to assure Catherine that he was procrastinating at Sistova entirely with a view to her benefit. This was on June 18[1]. A few days later, before the news of Varennes reached Padua, Leopold announced to Kaunitz with some satisfaction the state of the Prussian negotiation. He had promised Bischoffwerder to bring matters at Sistova to a conclusion and had given the necessary orders to the Austrian diplomatists. A preliminary defensive alliance was to be signed at Vienna on his return from Italy.

---

[1] Beer, *Leopold II., Franz II. und Catharina*, p. 146.

To this alliance Russia, England, and Saxony were to be permitted to accede. Finally, a meeting between himself and the King of Prussia was to take place at Pilnitz in Saxony, with the consent of course of the Elector[1]. Elgin was not acquainted with all these contemplated arrangements, although he knew that some sort of separate convention was being discussed between the Emperor and the Prussian favourite. Thus matters stood at the moment when the Austrian government issued its July circulars calling upon Europe to unite in opposition to the Revolution.

Kaunitz was at length acting in full accordance with Leopold's wishes and pushing forward the Prussian alliance[2]. So when Bischoffwerder came to Vienna, early in July, he found the chancellor ready to treat with him. At Berlin the ministers Schulenburg and Alvensleben suspected this suspiciously new friendliness towards Prussia and warned Bischoffwerder against it[3]. But their warnings either were disregarded, or came too late. Eager to play an important part and flattered by the attentions of Kaunitz, Bischoffwerder signed the promised agreement, without much consideration, on July 25. The contracting parties were to arrange a final treaty as soon as peace should have been signed between Russia and the Porte. By the July convention it was

---

[1] For Bischoffwerder's negotiation see Sybel, i. 281. Elgin's correspondence from June 10 to July 28. The letter here referred to is dated June 26. Beer, *Joseph II., Leopold II. und Kaunitz*, p. 410.

[2] To Leopold, June 26. Beer, *Joseph II., Leopold II. und Kaunitz*, p. 419. Kaunitz' sincerity in this matter may well be doubted.

[3] Letters of July 16, 25 and 29. Herrmann, *Forschungen*, v. 270—4.

agreed that the bases of this final treaty were to be:—
a mutual guarantee of territories; the confirmation of
all previous treaties; an agreement to conclude no new
treaties without mutual consent; and united action to
bring about a concert for the settlement of French
affairs. Further the integrity and free constitution of
Poland were to be guaranteed by the high contracting
parties and Russia. A secret clause dealt with the two
principalities of Anspach and Baireuth, the reversion to
which Prussia was anxious to secure[1].

Bischoffwerder's action in signing this convention
caused much discontent among the members of the
anti-Austrian party at Berlin. The favourite was
accused, and it would seem with reason, of exceeding
and even transgressing his powers[2]. His critics were
somewhat pacified however when it became apparent
that Leopold intended to fulfil his promise of terminating the congress at Sistova. The treaty between
Austria and the Porte, based upon the *status quo* as
agreed upon at Reichenbach, was actually signed on
the fourth of August and ratified at Vienna on the
thirteenth—to the infinite relief of Sir Robert Keith,
the English plenipotentiary, and his colleagues[3]. On
the eleventh Catherine's agents signed preliminaries of
peace with Turkey at Galatz. The empress fully
approved of their action; for the delay in the negotia-

---

[1] Neumann, *Traités*, I. 452.

[2] Herrmann, *Russische Geschichte;* Ergänzungsband, p. 40.

[3] Neumann, I. 454. A separate convention between Austria and the Porte specified "the small and voluntary concessions that the Turks were disposed to grant" (Keith to Grenville, Aug. 2); so that the *status quo* was not observed quite strictly.

tions at Sistova and the partial collapse of the Triple Alliance had enabled her to secure Oczakow and Bessarabia beyond dispute. A fortnight later the Emperor and the King of Prussia met at Pilnitz.

Before the meeting took place replies to the Padua circular had arrived from several quarters. England, as was to be expected, would commit herself to nothing. She had never given the powers to suppose that there was much chance of her so doing. But until the Sistova matter was concluded she did not absolutely refuse to join the concert lest the Emperor should take offence. Once his signature was attached to the treaty there was no further occasion to temporize. "The conclusion of the Sistova business," wrote Lord Grenville just before the Pilnitz meeting, "has removed every difficulty which there was in the way of our speaking out, and avowing our determination of the most scrupulous neutrality in the French business—and I now hold this language to all the foreign ministers, in order that it may be clearly understood that we are no parties to any step the King of Prussia may take on this subject[1]." Sardinia, Naples, and Spain welcomed the proposed concert and promised to act in full accordance with the Emperor's wishes, though no one of these courts was particularly anxious for war[2]. Catherine of Russia

---

[1] To Lord Auckland, Aug. 23 [Auckland MSS. 34,239]. The official letter of July 23, Vivenot, I. 227, is not a rejection of the concert scheme; nor is it an acceptance.

[2] Letters of July 13, 14 and 15. Schlitter, p. lviii. Of Spain Lord St Helens wrote to Lord Grenville on Aug. 15, "...the fact is... independent of Count Florida Blanca's natural predilection for a temporizing system, this court cannot now in prudence pursue any

continued to lavish hard words on the Revolution, and to encourage all its most uncompromising enemies; but although she had recently made a treaty with the chief of those enemies, Gustavus of Sweden, it was not evident that she seriously intended to join the concert. She assured the Emperor that she approved of his scheme. She showed her sympathy for the cause by insulting Genêt, the French ambassador at St Petersburg, and by forwarding a considerable sum of money to the princes. Further she would not go. "The Empress will not interfere directly in French affairs," was the report of the Swedish ambassador in July; "she says the season is too far advanced, that she is too far off..., that she must await the replies of the other powers." This was probably before Leopold's circular reached St Petersburg. Late in August, however, Catherine writes in the same strain, and adds:—"for the coming spring the question is different; I shall try to bethink myself of some means for lending a hand, if circumstances allow it[1]." It may very fairly be assumed that 'circumstances' might have been translated by 'the state of the Polish question.'

Gustavus was honestly devoted to the cause of monarchy and disinclined for all moderate measures. He was prepared to set up one of the emigrant princes

other." Mr Trevor from Turin (Aug. 17) spoke of "the embarrassing situation" of Sardinia, and "the extreme degree of political debility into which it has insensibly fallen."

[1] Catherine to Leopold, Aug. 2. Beer, *Leopold II., Franz II. und Catharina*, p. 149. To Genêt; Sorel, II. 244. To Provence and Artois (Aug. 19), and to Nassau Siegen. Feuillet de Conches, II. 238, 242. Stedingk to Gustavus III. Geffroy, *Gustave III.*, &c., p. 177.

on the French throne should Louis himself prove too willing to compromise the dignity of the crown. But as the Queen had sent him a golden sword, with the legend 'for the defence of the oppressed,' his chivalrous devotion to her cause tended to get the better of his half-contempt for Louis. About the middle of June he came to Aix-la-Chapelle, and soon entered into close relations with the Count of Provence, who had escaped safely from Paris on the night of the flight to Varennes. Gustavus helped to elaborate the various untimely schemes which the party of the emigration constantly laid before Leopold and Catherine. A few typical suggestions from these schemes will serve to indicate their character:—the powers were to declare that the regency of France had devolved by right on the Count of Provence, owing to the captivity of the King; they were to send an ultimatum to the French ministry, which was to be answered within twenty-four hours, and to be followed by a vast combined invasion should the answer be unsatisfactory; and the like [1].

In the middle of August the Count of Artois, accompanied by Calonne and Esterhazy, arrived unexpectedly at Vienna and succeeded in extracting from Leopold permission to accompany him to Pilnitz. A few days later the Emperor received from his unwelcome guest a long series of questions, an answer to which he was requested to give without delay:—Would he sanction the regency scheme? Would he give the

---

[1] Geffroy, pp. 173 sqq. Compare the schemes in Vivenot, I. 229, and Feuillet de Conches, II. 185. It should be mentioned that on July 7, Louis had drawn up full powers for Provence and Artois to treat with the courts of Europe in his name. Fersen, I. 145.

emigrants leave to keep up an army on imperial soil? Did he approve of the plan of issuing a violent manifesto? His reply was evasive; he would give a formal answer after his interview with the King of Prussia[1]. It is probable that Leopold intended to secure from Frederick William at Pilnitz confirmation of the promises given by Bischoffwerder at Vienna in the previous month. He was not anxious to commit himself publicly to any interference in French affairs. According to the account of Spielmann, who accompanied him and knew his mind, nothing definite would have been done had it not been for the presence and importunity of Artois and the emigrants; but this can only apply to the public declaration[2]. The influence of the King of Prussia, who was not of a cautious disposition and did not distrust the princes, was thrown, it would seem, into the emigrant scale. A few weeks earlier it had been reported from Berlin that "his eagerness to take an active part in French affairs was increasing" and that "he had given such positive assurances to the French agents that they relied on vigorous measures being taken that season[3]."

The net result of the interview was the notorious declaration of Pilnitz, drawn up and signed on August 27. In it the Emperor and the King declared that, having heard the wishes of the French princes, they regarded the situation of the King of France "as an object of interest to all the sovereigns of Europe."

[1] Questions in Vivenot, i. 231; answer in Schlitter, p. lxiv.
[2] Spielmann to Kaunitz, Aug. 31. Vivenot, i. 236.
[3] Ewart to Grenville, Aug. 9. The agents referred to are emigrant agents, particularly Baron Roll.

They expressed the hope that the powers would recognise this fact, and would unite to establish in France a monarchical system, which would give full scope to the rightful authority of the King, and yet not conflict with the interests of the nation. If the powers should do so ["alors et dans ce cas"] the contracting parties would proceed to take active measures. Meanwhile they would keep their forces ready for action. Various secret articles were appended to the declaration. By the first Austria and Prussia agreed to request and, if a request should fail, to demand of France the strict observance of treaties, doubtless with reference to the Alsatian question. The second sanctioned the establishment of an hereditary monarchy in Poland, subject to the approval of Russia[1]. By the third the right to exchange 'present or future acquisitions' was recognised; possibly with a view to conquests in France, the thought of which was never far from the minds of the German diplomatists[2]. In the sixth Austria agreed to support the claims of Prussia to Thorn and Danzig, provided that Prussia in turn should support 'the desired modifications in the convention concluded at the Hague with reference to the affairs of Belgium': this Prussia eventually did, thereby moving still further away from her late ally England[3].

It is not certain that Leopold intended this famous document to be published in France. He must have regretted subsequently that even so cautious a declaration of hostility to the Revolution saw the light in

[1] Below, p. 84.
[2] For instance, Ewart to Grenville, Aug. 4; Lecky, v. 555.
[3] Declaration and secret articles in Neumann, I. 468.

Paris immediately after the acceptance of the new constitution by Louis, at the end of the second week in September. Not that the declaration itself excited much alarm, or very much irritation; its indefinite character was so obvious that, after its publication, prices on the Bourse actually rose. But the princes appended to it a most preposterous and indiscreet manifesto which did much to nullify the cautious procedure of the Emperor. To the issue of this Leopold very certainly never agreed[1]. This manifesto took the form of an address to the King. His brothers assured him that he had 'the consolation of seeing the powers conspire' to put an end to his misfortunes; and that he might count on 'the assistance of all Europe' in his struggle against a rebellious faction and its 'extravagant innovation.' They begged him to withhold his assent from the new constitution; they promised that if a hair of his head were touched the armies of Europe should gather to crush the criminals. If he were constrained to accept the new system, they swore not to recognise his acceptance, since it could not possibly be sincere. They protested against this new system in the name of France, of religion, and of the fundamental principles of the monarchy. Finally they reminded him that he had *no right* to consent to any diminution

---

[1] The emigrants told his sister that he had agreed to the publication of the original document. Marie Christine to Leopold, Sept. 18. Zeissberg, *Zwei Jahre Belgischer Geschichte*, p. 253. The information about the Bourse comes from Staël, *Correspondance*, p. 236, 18—22 Sept. The declaration, without the secret articles of course, and the manifesto are printed together in the *Moniteur* of Sept. 23. Louis accepted the constitution on the 13.

of the honour due to the crown, and assured him that they would continue to execute his true will, in spite of anything that he might be forced to say or do with a view to hindering their action. The manifesto was a frank invitation to every Frenchman to distrust the King. To the King himself it was evidence that no amount of caution and self-sacrifice in his relations with the popular leaders could save him from the imputation of double dealing.

Leopold's action at Pilnitz has been made the object of many and bitter criticisms. No one now maintains that it amounted to a formal conspiracy to overthrow the entire Revolution. The tendency of critics is indeed rather towards the directly contrary view. The last and ablest, M. Sorel, implies that he played throughout exclusively for his own hand and had no honest interest in French affairs: the declaration was 'all hypothetical,' since at the moment of signing it Leopold knew that England would not join the concert, and so committed himself to nothing; it was signed with all the "secret understandings and reservations that in the mind of those who signed it rendered it insignificant[1]." Leopold's position was so singularly difficult that a just appreciation of his policy is not easily reached. Varennes had failed; the Padua circular had as yet produced little effect, though it had hardly had full time to act; it was beginning to be apparent that the French court did not wish its friends to adopt a threatening language. Leopold, who was not warlike, was probably well pleased to be relieved of

---

[1] Sorel, II. 257—8.

the obligation to support his sister with force. He was particularly anxious not to give too much sanction to the belief that the emigrant princes were his advisers and near friends; for he disliked and distrusted them thoroughly. Exactly how far he was influenced by a desire to help his sister, and how far by the reasonings of Kaunitz, cannot be determined. Fersen, who saw him at Vienna in September, certainly received the impression that he was culpably dilatory, and that, though personally well-disposed towards the cause of the Queen, he was not strong enough to resist his less generous advisers; but Fersen was not at the moment disposed to make allowances for honest hesitation, much less for any obedience to self-interest[1]. And when we come to examine the policy of Marie Antoinette, it will be seen that, from the royalist as distinct from the emigrant point of view, Leopold was not seriously to blame. The last letter which he had received from the Queen before the declaration was signed, contained these words: "Je persiste toujours à désirer que les puissances traitent avec une force en arrière d'elles, mais je crois qu'il serait extrêmement dangereux d'avoir l'air de vouloir entrer[2]." Certainly a more definite declaration than that actually issued would very easily have given to those who signed it "l'air de vouloir entrer."

While following, on the whole, the course indicated

---

[1] Fersen, I. 20, 28.

[2] To Mercy, Aug. 9, 1791. Arneth, p. 196. Mercy was in the habit of forwarding the Queen's letters, or the substance of them, to the Emperor. We may therefore suppose that this opinion was known to Leopold before Aug. 27.

from Paris, Leopold was at the same time greatly under the influence of his ministers. It happened that, so far as action was concerned, the advice of Kaunitz did not differ widely from that of Marie Antoinette; so that the dual control was not so disastrous as it might have been. Early in July Kaunitz had explained to Cobenzl that the Emperor's love for his sister, the fear of revolutionary infection in Italy and the Netherlands, and the necessity of preventing all attempts to restore the French monarchy to its former position of supremacy, rendered at least a passive concert desirable. The third reason reveals the secret of the Chancellor's policy :—France was to be kept weak, but she was not to be allowed to fall into complete anarchy lest she should become dangerous to her neighbours. He calculated, and rightly, that England would not object to this system; but he was somewhat apprehensive of Prussia, whose policy it had always been to keep up a secret understanding with the French court, and whose King at this particular time inclined to 'emigrant' views of the concert and its aims. The inmost wishes of Kaunitz were that the two imperial courts of the East should preponderate in Europe; that the Anglo-Prussian alliance, already moribund, should be despatched; and that France should be utilised to hold England in check. These considerations, combined with the wise conviction that France, with her splendid fortresses and the new enthusiasm of her people, could not easily be conquered, induced him to advocate measures not unlike those suggested from Paris. The powers were to secure for the French King the respect that was his due and

c. 6

'such a measure of authority and influence as should save France from anarchy'—no more. Kaunitz was not aware that this scheme for reducing France to the level of a sort of western Poland had long been known to Fersen, was suspected by Marie Antoinette, and was openly proclaimed by the French radicals[1].

The affairs of Poland itself were now occupying very much of the attention of Russia, Prussia and Austria. Those affairs can only be treated in the most superficial manner here; but no account of the origin or course of the revolutionary wars would be even moderately complete that failed to bring out the importance of the Polish question. Had that question been settled before 1792, Prussia and Austria might have sent all their forces against France, whereas in fact they sent but a part. Russia, whose ruler was disposed to attack the Revolution unless other and more profitable enterprises came in the way, might have aided them. "Add that having no Poland to divide to cover the expenses of the campaign, the allies are anxious to get paid back from the spoils of France. Instead of 1792 you have 1814[2]."

Ever since the first partition Russia and Prussia had cast hungry eyes on the remainder of Poland. Prussia was especially anxious to increase her possessions along the Vistula and secure complete control of the district around its mouth. She wanted first of all Thorn and Danzig. The Prussian diplomatists piped

---

[1] This whole account is from two long letters to Cobenzl of July 8 and 23. Vivenot, I. 187, 203. Compare Lenz, *Preussische Jahrbücher*, Oct.—Dec. 1894, p. 294.

[2] Sorel, *Essais d'histoire et de critique*, p. 184.

many different airs at this time; but, whatever the air, the drone growled on continuously, 'Thorn and Danzig, Danzig and Thorn.' Austria was less anxious to increase her own territory at Poland's expense than to checkmate Prussia at all costs. She wished to keep Poland weak and submissive but yet strong enough to resist the advance of her western neighbour[1]. Prussia, on the other hand, held, in the words of Hertzberg, that she had no more dangerous enemy than a well-ordered Polish kingdom, under a king who could and would use his strength[2].

The anxiety of Russia to expand westward as well as southward was undisguised and notorious. One of the reasons which induced Kaunitz to cling so long and stubbornly to the Russian alliance, in spite of the comparative indifference of Leopold, was the fear lest Catherine, irritated by the desertion of Austria in the Turkish war, should give heed to some fresh scheme of partition suggested from Berlin. He had connived at the delays at Sistova in order to gratify Russia. He was desirous to strengthen Poland somewhat, if possible, that she might be able to resist the coming storm. It has been maintained that Kaunitz and the Emperor, in pursuance of this policy, had long planned a change in the Polish constitution; that the great reform of May 1791, which crowned the political revival of Poland, was largely of Austrian workmanship. It would seem however that the constitution of '91 was really an indigenous growth, that owed little or nothing

[1] See two letters of Kaunitz, Nov. 12, 1791 and March 17, 1792; Vivenot, I. 271, and Herrmann, *Forschungen*, IV. 429.

[2] Heigel, p. 380.

to the fostering care of Austria[1]. The domestic reforms promulgated in that year do not concern us. It is sufficient to note that they were all directed to the increasing of social and political unity. The two provisions of the constitution that are of first-rate importance from the international point of view are the establishment of an hereditary Polish monarchy in the Electoral House of Saxony, and the abolition of the *liberum veto* formerly enjoyed by the nobles[2].

This revival of Poland, most welcome to the Austrian statesmen, was essentially distasteful to Poland's ally, Prussia, and to the Empress Catherine. For a time Prussia hesitated to show her hand openly. In diplomatic circles at Berlin the whole affair was treated as the result of an Austrian intrigue; yet it was followed by the mission of Bischoffwerder to Milan, the agreement of July 25, and the declaration of Pilnitz. Both these documents contained—as has already been mentioned—general clauses in favour of the new Polish constitution; and the latter, as was natural considering that it was drawn up in presence of the Elector of Saxony himself, approved of the new hereditary monarchy in very precise terms. Frederick William seemed to have adopted the policy of Kaunitz and broken with Prussian tradition. He was an unstable person, so that it is hard to say whether he was or was not consciously playing double. Catherine of Russia, who was anything but unstable, saw at once

---

[1] The question was the subject of an elaborate controversy between Sybel and Herrmann.

[2] On the death of the reigning king, Stanislas II., the throne was to pass to Frederick Augustus III. of Saxony and his heirs.

that she must concentrate her attention on Poland more carefully than ever. Before she could do so with complete safety, it was necessary to come to terms with Turkey, and conclude a final treaty with Sweden. A provisional treaty with the latter power had been signed in August 1790, and in August 1791 the preliminaries of Galatz opened a way to peace with the Porte. But it was not until more solid results had been attained, and until Prussia and Austria had become more deeply involved in French affairs, that Catherine's policy was fully revealed. That policy was in existence however in August 1791. Its existence helps to explain the real indifference of the Empress, an indifference which the vigour of her language did not altogether conceal, towards the proposals made by Leopold in July. The Polish question, with its complex negotiations and unpleasant passages, remained at least as important as the French question for the German powers and Russia, until the last of Poland disappeared in the year that saw the Directory established in France. It was no cause of the war of 1792; rather it was a hindrance to its outbreak. But it helped to give the war its peculiar character, and, in the end, contributed not a little to the success of the French and the ruin of their King.

CHAPTER V.

THE CONSTITUTION AND THE POWERS.

DURING the three months that intervened between the return from Varennes and the final establishment of the new French constitution there was a distinct reaction in favour of monarchy among the leaders of the Constituent Assembly. The overthrow of the party that clamoured for the deposition of the King, in the 'massacre of the Champ de Mars' (July 17), did much to encourage republicanism in the long run, but for the moment it rendered the moderates, the Feuillants, supreme. Among the most important of the Feuillant leaders were Barnave, Adrien du Port, and the brothers Lameth—members of the liberal noblesse, then Jacobins of the left, converted and sobered by their rise to power since the death of Mirabeau[1]. Barnave had been in touch with the Queen since he had been sent to escort the royal fugitives back from Varennes. He

---

[1] There were three Lameths:—Alexandre and Charles, who both sat in the Constituent Assembly, and Théodore, who sat in the Legislative. Alexandre is the best known of the three. He, Barnave, and Duport formed the so-called triumvirate.

and his friends hoped to make use of this connection, and of the revived spirit of loyalty, to establish securely a constitutional monarchy. They were anxious to form a coalition of all the moderate parties, and accordingly made advances to Lafayette, the man of action among the moderates, who was in many ways the most influential politician in France at the time. But their union with him was neither close nor permanent. The Queen loathed Lafayette. As commander of the armed force of Paris he acted as her jailor at the Tuileries, and the past had given her cause to fear him. Consequently she did nothing to help on the negotiation. Moreover the party of Barnave was unable to agree with him on the most important question of the day—the extent and nature of the revision to which the constitution was to be subjected. Equally unsuccessful was an attempt made by the 'triumvirate' to secure the assistance of the more old-fashioned royalists of the right in the work of revision. They sounded Malouet, the most open-minded of the party; but the right had small mind for any constitution at all, so that Malouet was unable to command its support[1]. In the end the constitution underwent very little revision, and it bore traces to the last of the passions that had influenced the making of its various, and not too consistent, sections.

The flight to Varennes had awakened all the suspicions of the Assembly and the nation, as was to be expected. Now more than ever the certainty of an interference and the need for military preparations were proclaimed. Was it not evident that the King

---

[1] Glagau, *Die Legislative*, pp. 3 sqq.

had intended to throw himself into the arms of the foreign, the Austrian, tyrant? Might not the suspension of the monarchy, and the consequent cessation of regular diplomatic intercourse between France and the powers, facilitate the schemes of that tyrant? So argued the popular politicians; and not altogether without reason. Even moderate men realised that France must be on her guard; and as rumours of the Padua circular and the scheme for a concert reached Paris, they too joined in the agitation in favour of vigorous measures. In the latter part of June, and throughout July and August, the organisation of the army and the national guard occupied much of the time of the Assembly. The latter was formally 'put in a state of activity'; attempts were made to put the former on a war footing. Reports on the state of the frontier fortresses and the general condition of the national defences were regularly laid before the now sovereign legislators[1].

Yet peace was the great aim of the Feuillants[2]. Peace was necessary for the successful working of the new institutions and for the firm establishment of their patrons in power. Accordingly the Feuillants conceived the notion of approaching Leopold—of whom they stood somewhat in awe—by way of the Queen. They wished to wean him from the emigrants, to whom he was supposed to be unduly partial, and to secure his sympathetic tolerance of the new order in France.

---

[1] See *Arch. Parl.*, xxvii., xxviii.

[2] The nickname is applied, here and subsequently, to the constitutional royalists of the Barnave type and particularly to the leaders of the Barnave clique. The 'Fayettists' are in a class apart.

The first step was to convince him that a period of stable equilibrium was at hand. They prevailed upon Marie Antoinette to forward to Leopold, at the end of July, an inspired memoir which contained a very sanguine account of the state of public feeling. The authors insinuated that, by means of patience and an honest attempt to make the new constitution work, the royal family might in time win back some of its lost influence[1]. The second step was to put the Count of Artois in a false position, by rendering him liable to the reproach of having rejected fair proposals and disregarded his brother's advice. Accordingly another inspired letter, signed this time by the King, was entrusted to the agent who left Paris on the last day of July in charge of the memoir for Leopold[2]. Louis was made to commend the Count for his discreet conduct in the past. Let him prove his continued loyalty by returning at once, and so anticipating the summons which the Assembly might be expected to issue shortly; for the Assembly had heard that he was taking a prominent place among the discontented abroad. Above all things let him avoid violent measures, and so facilitate that return of confidence and quiet in France from which alone good results were now to be expected; seeing that the King, face to face with the alternative of acceptance of the constitu-

---

[1] Marie Antoinette to Leopold, July 30. Arneth, 188.

[2] The motive assigned to the Feuillants in the text is that attributed to them by La Marck (to Mercy, Aug. 23, Bacourt, III. 184): it can hardly be supposed that they really hoped to win Artois to their policy. The letter to Artois is in Bacourt, III. 163, July 31. The bearer was a certain Chevalier de Coigni.

tion or deposition, was resolved to accept and to trust the future for some amelioration of his fallen estate. The third step of the Feuillants consisted in an attempt to induce Mercy—the trusted adviser of both Marie Antoinette and Leopold—to visit Paris and confer with them. To this end they sent a certain Abbé Louis to Brussels, in the first week of August, bearing letters of recommendation from the Queen herself.

The influence of the Queen was now more than ever predominant in the Tuileries, and from this time forward her correspondence becomes increasingly important. Her relation to the Feuillants was thoroughly false. They flattered themselves that she was in sympathy with them, but nothing was further from the truth. No sooner had the memoir, with her signature attached, been sent by way of Brussels to the Emperor than she wrote excitedly to Mercy disowning it:—in her present position she was obliged " to do and write all that was demanded of her[1]." She spoke with contempt of the Abbé Louis and his mission:—"He says that he is accredited by me to confer with you. It is absolutely necessary that you should affect to listen to him, but you must not allow yourself to be influenced by his ideas[2]." In a third letter she explained her notions as to the course which the powers ought to pursue; and finally, some fortnight before the official acceptance of the constitution, she wrote a now famous letter which reveals plainly the desperate strait in which the court found itself. We

[1] July 31. Arneth, p. 193.
[2] Aug. 1. Arneth, p. 194.

are forced, she writes, to accept the constitution. What else could we do since the powers have not lifted a finger to save us? To refuse is out of the question. Yet it is no longer possible to contemplate existence under the preposterous new regime: "Il ne s'agit pour nous que de les endormir et de leur donner confiance en nous pour les mieux déjouer après." The powers must act; the Emperor must place himself at their head; and (for she feared and hated others than her Feuillant advisers) the emigrants must be kept in the background[1].

As to the King he seems to have remained as ever, passive, kindly, and plastic. On July 7 he had empowered the Princes to treat in his name, but on one condition:—that should the powers decide to check the Revolution in any way negotiations were to precede force. On the 31st of the same month he signed the memoir in which Artois was exhorted to return to France. On one point his mind was clear:—he intended to sanction the constitution. He could hardly have done otherwise; and almost all his most trusted advisers, from the Queen downwards, approved his resolution. The chief exception was Mercy. Towards the end of August a letter from Mercy, with an enclosure from Edmund Burke, reached Paris. The burden of both was the same—"if the King accepts their constitution you are lost for ever[2]." The King however rejected this strong but most dangerous policy in favour of that

[1] To Mercy, Aug. 16—26. Arneth, p. 205. The third letter referred to is that quoted on p. 80.
[2] Mercy to the Queen, Aug. 20. Feuillet de Conches, II. 243. The words are Mercy's.

of acceptance and temporary conciliation. The scheme by which he was chiefly guided is to be found in a memoir drawn up, at La Marck's request, by Pellenc, the former literary collaborator of Mirabeau. Pellenc argued that a second revolution was inevitable, and that its result would be either the modification of the constitution in the interests of the King or the establishment of a republic. So the King must honestly carry out his promises and thereby win popularity. Then, should the state of anarchy continue, it would become evident that the fault lay not in him but in the laws. By this means the monarchy and not the republicans would benefit by the Revolution of the near future. If the King failed to win popularity, the throne would fall, and France would eventually pass into the hands of a dictator[1].

Between this policy of temporary concession and that of an immediate appeal to the powers the court wavered during September and October. Such hesitation increased its difficulties and those of its agents and friends abroad. Apparently for a few weeks Louis honestly tried to carry out the advice of Pellenc; upon it he based his speech on the day when the constitution was inaugurated. Nothing would have pleased him better than the interference of the powers; but he wanted France itself to demand foreign help. In the last week of September he expressed a hope that the new Legislative Assembly might give so much offence that the majority of the nation would be driven to appeal to the good offices of Europe[2]. As for the Queen

[1] La Marck to Mercy, Sept. 6. Bacourt, III. 191.
[2] Louis to the Princes, Sept. 25. This is a secret letter which

she cared little for majorities and kept her eyes steadily fixed on Vienna.

The acceptance of the constitution—Sept. 13—aroused little enthusiasm. No party really regarded it as a final solution to the problems of the Revolution, and the Assembly which made it had been waxing unpopular in its old age. Men were looking forward with hope, though for very different reasons, to the new Legislative Assembly, the elections for which had long been in progress, for they were of that complex character which the earlier revolutionary leaders had prescribed. The extreme party hoped for some further limitation of the royal power, which they dreaded to see employed in the interests of a counter-revolution. The King and his Feuillant advisers looked forward to a season of reaction, or to such folly on the part of the new deputies as would discredit the system of which they were the representatives. Altogether the constitution that was to have opened a new era in human history, the constitution whose sacred provisions were not to be changed for a generation, produced a feeling of unrest among politicians and men of affairs; a feeling which was revealed by a fall in the public funds[1]. Among the populace however the word constitution created some enthusiasm, and the old French loyalty flared up once more to gladden the King and Queen. They appeared in public again; they were cheered at the opera. Indeed they did so much to court popularity and prove

expresses the King's real opinion and not that of Barnave. An official letter, which was sent to the Princes about the same time, contains Barnave's suggestions. Feuillet de Conches, II. 328, 364.

[1] Gower, *Despatches*, p. 123, Sept. 16, 1791.

their love of the new order, that those who were in their dreary secret began to criticise the indiscretion which would render more difficult the coming change of front[1]. Meanwhile the act of acceptance was communicated to all the powers.

The Emperor had always declared that any French constitution must receive the full and free consent of the King before it could be regarded as valid by Europe. Kaunitz and Spielmann, criticising this declaration, had asked the pertinent question:—If the King consents without obvious coercion how can Europe prove that it is justified in interfering with the affairs of France[2]? Yet, up to September, Leopold continued to insist on this point in all his public utterances. It is very clearly expressed in his reply to the Queen's inspired memoir of July 30. This reply was written about a week before the meeting at Pilnitz[3]. On leaving Pilnitz Leopold went south to Prague to assume the Bohemian crown. Thither he was followed by certain leaders of the emigrants, whose suggestions increased in recklessness after their recent success. But he gave no heed to them now. The recognised exponent of the Queen's views, Fersen, had a somewhat warmer reception; but the cautious tone that Leopold adopted in speaking of the effects of Louis' latest step on the policy of Austria disgusted Count Axel, who finally left the imperial presence sad at heart and "enchanted to get away[4]."

[1] Staël, *Correspondance*, p. 236, Sept. 18 and 22.
[2] Above, p. 52.
[3] Aug. 17. Arneth, p. 199.
[4] Fersen, I. 28—30, Sept. 13—28.

Privately the Emperor was convinced that his brother-in-law had signed the constitution unwillingly; yet it was impossible—as he wrote to his sister Marie Christine—"to reply that they did not believe what he said[1]." For the time Louis was acting, and seemed anxious to be treated, as a constitutional King; he was begging the emigrants to return, begging the naval and military officers who had not emigrated to stand to their posts and aid him in his work of conciliation and restoration[2]. Even the Queen, who continued to write to Mercy in favour of an armed European congress, was most anxious to prevent any overt act of hostility, and was still trusting to gradual and more or less pacific measures. "I hope," she said to Bertrand de Molleville on Oct. 1st, "that if we use patience, firmness, and a connected policy all is not yet lost[3]." So without abandoning all notions of interference Leopold decided to give the King's system a trial. "We desire," he wrote in his reply to the announcement of the new constitution—the passage when read in the Legislative Assembly excited angry murmurs—"We desire that the course which the King has seen fit to take may have the success which he expects...and at the same time that the causes...which have aroused gloomy forebodings may cease for the future, and that the necessity for taking serious precautions against their return may be

---

[1] Schlitter, p. lxxix. Other quotations in the same strain could easily be found.

[2] Various letters written in October to the Count of Provence, the officers, and emigrant gentry in *Hist. Parl.*, XII. 158—228.

[3] Bertrand de Molleville, *Memoirs*, I. 103. Bertrand had just been appointed minister of marine.

prevented[1]." It may be supposed that Leopold suspended his schemes of interference the more readily because he had himself learnt the value of conciliatory measures in the restoration of a disorganised state, and because the French constitution was of all things the one most welcome to Kaunitz.

The delight of the Chancellor on hearing that Louis had accepted was unmistakable. He wrote to Spielmann, on September 28, giving vent to his joy in an expressive compound of French and German. "Le roi a mieux aimé être roi sur le pied de la constitution que de ne plus l'être du tout ; das ist, däucht mir, ungefähr das Resultat von allem, was man dieserwegen sagen könnte, und nach meinem Sinne sollten wir et Compagnie Gott danken, dass ce bon homme de Roi nous ait tiré par sa détermination du mauvais pas, dans lequel nous nous trouvions embarqués[2]." Kaunitz seemed to see in the future France weak, divided, and submissive; and nothing gave him greater pleasure. He believed, not altogether wrongly, that the threatening attitude of the powers had been the chief cause of the release and restoration of Louis XVI. after Varennes[3]. As this release was all that he had ever desired, he saw no further use for an active concert or an armed con-

---

[1] *Arch. Parl.*, xxxv. 92. The letter, drawn up by Spielmann (Schlitter, p. lxxxv.), is dated Oct. 23. It was read on Nov. 16.

[2] Vivenot, I. 259.

[3] On Ap. 21, 1792, referring to 1791, he wrote of the powers, "...l'appréhension de leur réunion prochaine opéra l'effet que le roi de France fut relâché..." Vivenot, II. 2. The view is confirmed by Staël, writing in Feb. 1792 :—"L'unique cause pour laquelle on ne détrôna pas Louis XVI. était la crainte d'une guerre avec l'empereur." *Correspondance*, p. 254.

gress[1]. He overestimated the strength of the moderate party in France and had not yet learnt the temper of the new Assembly. Yet, although so late as Nov. 12 he continued to lay stress on the hopeful state of public opinion in France, on that very day, in a circular addressed to the various Austrian embassies, he mentioned the possibility of a return to the policy of concerted action. Evidently he did not consider himself as yet out of the wood[2]. He was beginning to feel for the first time really uneasy in view of the reported increase of the party of aggression in France.

The hesitation of Austria at this time was even greater than that of Prussia, although the court of Berlin with its erratic monarch and divided counsels moved slowly enough. The Prussian ministers were in the main opposed to any sort of interference. But "the most able of them had no weight but through the favourite, the sect of the Illuminés, or the tribe of mistresses past and present[3]"; so as the favourite was mainly responsible for the Austrian connection, and was well inclined towards the agents of the Princes at Berlin, Frederick William continued his relations with Vienna and his declarations of sympathy for Louis XVI. He repeatedly expressed his intention of imitating with the most scrupulous care every measure of his imperial ally, and he even kept some troops ready for action[4]. But questions of compensation and profit seem to have

[1] Kaunitz to the Elector of Mainz, Nov. 11. Vivenot, I. 266.
[2] Vivenot, I. 270—1. Circular note and letter to L. Cobenzl.
[3] Sir Morton Eden to Grenville, Dec. 31, 1791. *Dropmore Papers*, II. 245.
[4] Fersen, I. 160.

occupied most of his attention. The notion that a war with France might put Austria in possession of Alsace and Lorraine haunted his mind, and he was anxious to make provision against such an occurrence by securing promises that would safeguard the interests of Prussia[1]. Then came the acceptance of the constitution. "I understand that his Prussian Majesty has been much disappointed and mortified...," wrote Ewart on Sept. 30, "but he is still made to believe that the majority of the nation is against it and that a civil war will ensue. Excepting this object he seems very indifferent about all foreign concerns[2]." Frederick William showed his mortification by blustering a little to the royal agent Moustier. Then he replied to the formal notification of acceptance by a few conventional protestations of affection for the Most Christian King, without referring either with praise or blame to the new order in France[3]. And having done so he waited for civil war or the call from Vienna.

England continued to preserve an attitude of most scrupulous neutrality and from her isolated position to watch the troubled face of Europe. The events of September hardly affected the policy of 'exact and perfect neutrality' which she had already adopted. In that month however she formally and definitely declined to associate herself with the Austro-Prussian alliance[4].

---

[1] Vivenot, I. 218. "The court of Berlin," wrote Lord Auckland from the Hague (Aug. 8), "is allured by a speculation of dismemberment." *Grenville Papers*, II. 158.

[2] To Grenville.

[3] Sorel, II. 280; and the letter in *Arch. Parl.*, XXXIV. 553.

[4] Grenville to Keith, Sept. 19.

But she did not immediately recognise the constitution. Her official reply, like that of Prussia, contained nothing decisive. This suspicious reserve doubtless contributed to confirm the French popular party in the superstition that Pitt, in spite of his affectation of neutrality, was secretly hounding on the enemies of France. He was doing nothing of the kind; if he had thoughts of revenge at all they were shown rather in his indifference to the schemes of the allies than in any support given to those schemes.

Spain did what she could for the cause of royalty. She could not attack France single-handed or exert much influence in the counsels of Europe, but she managed, in spite of her empty exchequer, to contribute to the support of the emigrants; and she even went so far as to brave the displeasure of the French nation and of the cautious originator of the concert by declining to recognise the constitution, on the ground that it had not received the free assent of the King[1]. In so doing Count Florida Blanca imagined that he was carrying out the wishes of Louis XVI., for had not the French King's protest against all the acts of his captivity lain in the archives at Madrid since the autumn of 1789? He fancied too that the other powers would adopt the same policy, and was not a little alarmed when he learnt that they had half recognised the new French system[2]. His alarm resulted in various hesitating or retrograde steps taken towards the end of the year; for he was horribly afraid of a French war. The minor

---

[1] *Arch. Parl.*, xxxiv. 553. The Spanish reply was read on Oct. 31.
[2] St Helens to Grenville, Oct. 17. See Appendix IV.

powers, such as Sardinia, Tuscany, Switzerland, Poland, and a number of the Princes of the Empire, replied to the official letters that announced the acceptance of the constitution in the friendly but indefinite tone adopted by England and Prussia[1].

The two great northern powers, Russia and Sweden, shared the views of the Spanish Bourbons and held to them persistently. Catherine was not prepared to fight for Louis XVI. but she had no intention of approving the Revolution; accordingly she declined to recognise the new order. Gustavus followed her example. Moreover he seemed inclined to act; so much so that for a time ardent royalists fancied that he would lead the European crusade against the Revolution[2]. Gustavus was disgusted with the weakness of Louis XVI., disgusted too with his attempts to check the activity of his brothers and friends; for the Swedish King saw French affairs through emigrant glasses. He despised the Emperor and shared Fersen's opinion as to his duplicity. He dismissed with a few scornful words the darling scheme of Marie Antoinette, an armed congress of the powers:—How, he asked, could a congress discuss the constitution of an independent state? There was not, and never had been, any means of salvation other than war[3]. His minister, Taube, was anxious to see a league constructed independently of the Emperor. For

---

[1] *Arch. Parl.*, xxxiv. 553 and xxxv. 93.

[2] Provence and Artois to Catherine, July 31: Feuillet de Conches, II. 156. The Swedish fleet is already prepared to invade France, so it is asserted; all that is needed is a supplementary force of eight thousand Russians and a little money.

[3] To Fersen, Nov. 11. Fersen, I. 222.

he knew that England would not move, and believed that Leopold was using the inaction of the Court of St James' as a screen to hide his own cowardly withdrawal[1].

The treaty of peace signed between Sweden and Russia on October 19 at Drottingholm seemed to many the first move in the crusade of the northern powers. Taube believed that Catherine really intended to take up the cause of monarchy. Even the Swedish ambassador at St Petersburg, Stedingk, who in July had announced that the Empress would not interfere directly in French affairs, seems now to have been convinced of her genuine anxiety to help the good cause[2]. But, beyond a little money and much advice, Catherine never to the day of her death gave the least assistance to the emigrants. Even Gustavus talked rather than acted. His exchequer was not full nor were his dominions altogether in good order. Whilst at Aix in the summer he had spoken freely of an invasion of France by sea. In August he went home to prepare for the expedition; so thought the emigrants. But when, in the following month, the Chevalier d'Escars, who had been sent to represent the Princes, arrived at Stockholm, he found that the Swedish fleet was utterly unprepared and that there was not the least possibility of an autumn campaign. D'Escars in his despondency busied himself in drawing up a long, pathetic, and rhetorical memoir, such as his party affected. He tried to move Gustavus by assuring him

---

[1] Taube to Gustavus, Nov. 15. Fersen, I. 226.

[2] Above, p. 74 and Fersen, I. 200, 217: Taube to Fersen and Stedingk to Fersen.

that already countless watchers lined the Norman coasts, scanning the horizon, with eager but weary eyes, for the sails of the Swedish fleets[1]. But words could not man those fleets. The winter began to close in on the North and all thought of assistance from that quarter had to be postponed until the spring of the coming year.

[1] Geffroy, *Gustave III.*, p. 191—7. Des Cars (in 1791, the name was usually written as above, D'Escars), *Memoirs*, pp. 227, sqq.

CHAPTER VI.

THE WAR POLICY OF THE LEGISLATIVE ASSEMBLY AND THE WAR POLICY OF THE COURT. OCT.—DEC. 1791.

THE first Legislative Assembly of the reconstituted French monarchy met in Paris on Oct. 1, 1791. As a result of the unfortunate self-denying ordinance that the makers of the constitution had imposed upon themselves, the working of the new machine was left to men who had had no hand in the construction. The Legislative contained able men enough. Many of these had already served the state, either under the old order, or as members of the various local assemblies and administrative bodies created since 1789. Yet they were necessarily deficient in the wider political experience. The majority was moderate, devoted in the abstract to the new constitution, and well inclined towards the King. For as the first stage in the complex system of election was completed before the flight to Varennes, the new legislators had been chosen from a body of men that contained few decided republicans[1]. But

[1] M. Aulard in *Hist. Gen.*, VIII. 119—20.

though the decided republicans might be few, those who distrusted the King and court were many; and this distrust was shared by almost all the leading orators of the Assembly. Their enemies reported that nothing but the absolute destruction of the monarchy would content them; for they had taken as their adviser and prophet one of the most distinguished members of the late Assembly, the Abbé Sieyès, a man who was said to be devoting all his great ability and considerable powers of intrigue to the task of pulling down the King[1]. However that may be, there can be no question as to the wide-spread distrust of the court. The Jacobins Club was now the meeting ground for all those who were turning against every form of monarchy. The club had lost much of its popularity among politicians of weight in July; but already in October its position had improved, and it counted among its members a number of the most distinguished of the new deputies[2].

As a body, the Legislative Assembly was if not exactly pugnacious yet jealous of the honour of France, fully conscious that Europe regarded her new institutions with suspicion, and rather eager to prove that she was still "that strength which in old days moved earth and heaven." There were men in almost all sections

---

[1] La Marck to Mercy, Oct. 30. Bacourt, III. 258. The part of this report that applies to Sieyès is almost certainly true. How far those whom he influenced had at this time moved towards republicanism cannot be determined.

[2] A comparison of the lists of membership of the Feuillant Club for July and October shows how short lived the popularity of that anti-Jacobin organisation was. What the Feuillants lost the Jacobins gained. Challamel, *Les clubs contre-révolutionnaires*.

of the Assembly who believed, for various reasons, that a state of war would help on the settlement of internal disorder. The Parisian press studiously stimulated the warlike passions of people and deputies alike. Hébert did the work for the mob in the filthy pages of his *Père Duchesne*. The royalist editor of *L'ami du Roi* had long been looking forward to the armed intervention of the powers. In September his prophesyings became more and more confident, as a result of the Pilnitz declaration and the commentary of the exiled Princes. Pamphlets of an inflammatory sort littered the bookstalls[1]. In the press, by means of his *Patriote Français*, at the Jacobins, and in the Assembly Brissot did his utmost to excite enmity towards the court and a belief in the necessity of war. His policy was adopted, more or less fully, by that loose association of groups in the Assembly which is often spoken of as 'the Gironde.' This term, having been extended so as to include men who, though advocates of war, were neither enemies of the King nor disciples of Brissot, is apt to lead to confusion. But Vergniaud, Gensonné, Isnard and other leading members of the true Gironde were convinced 'Brissotins,' as the phrase then was. By their brilliant oratory and infectious suspicions they helped to win from the unstable mass of open-minded men, which formed the centre of the Assembly, the violent decrees that have so often been regarded as the true and sufficient cause of the war of 1792. Brissot's policy

---

[1] Convenient series of quotations from the journals at this time are given in *Hist. Parl.*, XII. A number of the war pamphlets of this period are collected in volumes 316 and 317 of the F. R. series in the British Museum.

varied little, if at all, during the course of the months from Oct. 1791 to April 1792. He described it in December thus[1]:—"During the last six mouths [i.e. since Varennes], and even throughout the whole of the revolution, I have meditated on the opinion that I am about to maintain...I am convinced that a nation which has conquered its liberty after ten centuries of slavery has need of war. It needs war to consolidate its liberty, to purge it from the evils of despotism; it needs war in order that men who might corrupt it may be expelled from its bosom." He went on to speak of the favour shown by Europe to the French rebel emigrants and concluded with a famous and significant sentence:— "A Louis XIV. could declare war on Spain because his ambassador had been insulted...and we who are free, should we for a moment hesitate?"

Undoubtedly Brissot and his allies did more than any other one political party or group of statesmen to bring on the war of '92. But those professed enemies of the Revolution, who try to throw upon them alone the whole responsibility of the evils to which that war led, are often guilty of making statements that are neither historically accurate nor morally just. In reading critics of the Sybel school one gathers that, in the autumn of 1791 and the spring of 1792, Europe had no intention of attacking France, would indeed have been well content to leave her to make what she could of her new institutions. But 'the Gironde' was set on a second revolution that it might have the King down and seize on supreme power. Therefore it worked

---

[1] In a speech at the Jacobins, *Hist. Parl.*, XII. 409.

towards war as a means to revolution and attacked Austria wantonly[1]. Now it is not strictly true that any definite Girondin party, whose sole aim was the overthrow of the King, ever existed. And it is most improbable that war would have been declared at all had not the anti-royalist groups received assistance from those, including the King himself, who saw in the outbreak of war a possible means of salvation for the throne. That Brissot and certain of his circle were animated by a vicious and partly unjustifiable hatred of the court is true[2]; but they themselves, and still more those who voted with them, were influenced also by the very well-founded suspicion that the King and Queen in their hearts disliked the actual fundamentals of the Revolution and were seeking an opportunity to repudiate it. Again, it may be that in connection with the diplomatic correspondence that passed between Paris and Vienna in the winter of 1791—2 the French ministers committed more errors, and the French Assembly showed more insolence, than Kaunitz and his fellows. It may be so, though the matter is open to discussion. Yet the whole attitude of Austria towards France from June

---

[1] See, for example, Sybel, I. 325. "Das neue Frankreich...hätte in voller Verträglichkeit neben dem...Reiche bestehen können, so gut wie heute das republikanische Amerika neben den europäischen Monarchen besteht, wenn nicht die brausende Leidenschaft der Gironde in dem Bruch mit Deutschland das wirksamste Mittel für ihre zweite Revolution gefunden hätte."

[2] Brissot avows naïvely that envy was with him a ruling passion. As a boy, he says, "Je ne voyais pas pourquoi il [le roi] était sur le trône ; tandis que j'étais né fils d'un traiteur. Je prévoyais avec quelque complaisance que je pourrai le voir tomber du trône et que je pourrais y assister." Brissot, *Mem.*, I. 2.

1791 onwards was overbearing in the extreme and such as no self-respecting nation could fail to resent. Further the view under discussion overlooks all causes of the war which are not directly connected with the Revolution, deep-rooted national antipathies and ancient political traditions. In short it isolates, in a somewhat partisan and unscientific fashion, one of the more obvious forces that made for war and neglects the rest. Thereby those who hold it are confirmed in the comfortable belief that the revolutionary leaders, whom they like to handle *en bloc*, were a mere gang of unscrupulous political fanatics. This view has been criticised by anticipation in the earlier chapters of the present essay. Not a little of what remains to be said will be intended to supplement and substantiate the general criticisms just put forward.

There was one party in France at the moment when the Legislative met that was thoroughly averse to war; it might almost be said frightened of war. That was, as has already appeared, the group of Feuillant leaders that had of late gained the upper hand in the government. But the 'Triumvirate' had never had a strong following, although there were deputies in plenty who sympathised with their domestic policy, and a few who would have been really reluctant to go to war. The lower class democrats and the leaders of Paris detested the clique that had kept Louis on the throne and brought about the 'massacre' of July 17. Brissot, whose influence among the more educated adherents of the Revolution was very great, made systematic attacks on them as opponents of the war policy and advisers of the Queen. Nor did the court love them. It disliked both the triumvirate and the existing ministry[1]; although for the moment it concealed its dislike. For Louis and his Queen were trying, in a half-hearted sort of way, their policy of conciliation; yet without having abandoned the hope of finding means to bring about the intervention of the powers. Altogether the chance that the Feuillants would be able to keep the peace can hardly have seemed great.

The state of the provinces that bordered the French frontier to the North and East must have occasioned uneasy thoughts to those who dreaded war. For two years the emigration had continued. Month by month the crowds of ci-devant seigneurs had drifted into the towns of Belgium and the Rhenish Provinces. No one in France had been allowed to forget that they meant to come back one day with an army at their heels. Their really insignificant military preparations had been studiously magnified by the pamphleteers and hired alarmists of their party. Their very moderate success in extracting promises of assistance from the monarchs of Europe had been treated in the same way. Their arrogant confidence in the certainty of the coming day of reckoning made them the laughing-stock of well-informed politicians throughout Europe[2], but it could not fail to arouse some alarm and much irritation in

---

[1] Ministers in Oct. 1791:—Tarbé (Finance), Montmorin (Foreign Affairs), Delessart (Interior), Duportail (War), Bertrand de Molleville (Marine), Duport du Tertre (Justice). In Nov. Delessart succeeded Montmorin and Cahier de Gerville took the place vacated by Delessart. The ministry was constitutional and averse to war, as a whole. Montmorin—who had been in office since 1787, save for three days in July 1789—was the minister most trusted by the court.

[2] One illustration will be found in Appendix VI.

France. All along the French frontiers were dotted the various emigrant posts. Early in 1791 the Count of Artois had established himself at Coblence, on the territory of the Elector of Trèves. In July his brother joined him. There was formed a little emigrant Versailles, with all the old scandals, the intrigues, the parties, the mistresses; a court at which the wildest schemes of Calonne received a ready hearing, at which the news of the King's arrest at Varennes was received with joy, and such military preparations were made as the slender means of the Princes would allow[1]. In the neighbourhood of Worms the Prince of Condé had assembled a ragged and fanatical troop of gentlemen which he struggled desperately to turn into an efficient army[2]. Further South, not far from Strasburg, was Mirabeau-Tonneau with a force which even his enemies did not reckon at more than six hundred men[3]. The Netherlands were flooded with exiled royalists, as indiscreet and violent as those of Coblence. At Brussels, their headquarters, they revived the elegant social life of the ancien régime and organised a score of extravagant devices for demonstrating their loyalty and their hatred of the Revolution. They were a perpetual annoyance to the governors of the Belgic provinces, Albert of Saxe-Teschen and his wife Marie Christine. The latter shared her brother's objection to the Princes and their following and realised that they were a source of danger to the half re-established Austrian government.

[1] See a very bitter account of Coblence in Augeard, *Mem.*, p. 281; the joy at the King's arrest (which the Mantua plot explains), p. 274.
[2] Forneron, *Les Emigrés*, pp. 250 sqq.
[3] Koch's report to the Assembly, Nov. 22, *Arch. Parl.*, xxxv. 290.

Week by week, throughout the summer and autumn, she warned Leopold of this danger. "Would to God," she once wrote of the Count of Artois, "that he and his council and his schemes were a million leagues away from you and from us here." Her repeated representations were not without effect. On Oct. 22 Leopold gave orders for the dispersal of all the groups of armed Frenchmen on Belgian soil and for the prevention of every sort of military preparations[1].

The Emperor did well to walk warily; for Belgium, always open to the attacks of France, was discontented and half-inclined to welcome French aggression. In the autumn of 1790 Kaunitz had held that the religious and aristocratic character of the Belgian revolution separated it sharply from that of France, so that the French government would never dream of trying to annex the Low Countries. The first part at least of this opinion was fully justified by the facts. After the armed rebellion had been crushed in Dec. 1790, the concessions made by Leopold had not sufficed to pacify the country. All through 1791 a struggle went on between the government and the Estates of Brabant[2]. In July of that year Marie Christine wrote that "there were districts which might be regarded as remaining in a state of open revolt. Such, among others, was the town of Antwerp[3]." A month later she reported the alarming news that the Belgians, "even those most

---

[1] See the correspondence, June to October, in Schlitter, pp. 110—200. Among other things the emigrants demanded assistance in recruiting and leave to utilise the imperial barracks. Zeissberg, pp. 252 sqq.

[2] Zeissberg, pp. 160 sqq.   [3] Schlitter, pp. 130—1.

attached to their ancient fanaticism, were beginning to regard the French as their liberators[1]." Belgian exiles from both the anti-Austrian parties were gathered on the French side of the frontier. Already in August certain of the Vonckists, or democratic party, had presented a petition to the Assembly at Paris, in the hope of winning sympathy and assistance[2]. On Sept. 16 La Marck wrote from Paris to Mercy warning him that, in view of the recent theft of Avignon and the Venaissin by the French, it would be in no way surprising should the new Assembly order an attack on Belgium and Liège[3]. The fear of such an attack and the knowledge that resistance, with a disaffected population, would be difficult, increased Leopold's anxious desire to avoid all provocative measures at the time when Louis was trying the policy of conciliation. The result was the decree of Oct. 22. The Emperor seems to have hoped that the Legislative Assembly would, in its turn, withhold all patronage from the Belgian emigrants. It did in fact forbid warlike gatherings two months later[4]. Yet, throughout the winter, Walckiers, a prominent Vonckist, and Lebrun-Tondu, who had made himself the mouthpiece of the exiled democrats of Liège, remained in Paris as members of the 'comité réuni des Belges et des Liègeois.' Their aim was the emancipation of the Low Countries by means of a fresh revolution; and in this work they were encouraged by

[1] Schlitter, p. 142.
[2] Zeissberg, p. 206.
[3] Bacourt, III. 230. Reference to the decree of annexation of Sept. 12.
[4] Dec. 21st, 1791.

some of the more ardent French politicians and propagandists, notably Dumouriez, Brissot, and Condorcet[1]. This fact was not unknown to the government of Brussels. In December Marie-Christine reported that the Belgian revolutionary clubs had entered into close relations with those of France. 'The French,' she added, 'who dread your influence in a counter-revolution..., are doing all they can to raise the Low Countries once more, with intent to use them as a barrier and protection against the advance of your troops[2].' This shrewd guess at the secret motives of the war party in Paris does credit to the political insight of the Archduchess.

From the first, questions of diplomacy and war occupied the attention of the Legislative Assembly. There was no longer a constitution to make. Something had to be discussed; and almost every discussion of current topics could be given a warlike turn. In the first fortnight of October however little was done. The time was spent in electing committees and other purely technical work. Even this brief delay annoyed the war party. Brissot had succeeded in introducing into a written speech on the subject of committees references to Pilnitz and the impudence of the allied Kings. He was unable to get a hearing in the Salle

---

[1] Zeissberg, pp. 208 sqq. For some curious information concerning Lebrun's career see W. A. Miles, *Correspondence*, I. 145. He had been a printer and journalist at Liège, and was involved in the Revolution there. He became minister of foreign affairs after the tenth of August; was guillotined in Dec. 1793.

[2] Schlitter, p. 216. Marie-Christine to Leopold, Dec. 24.

de Manège and so unburdened his soul to the Jacobins[1]. But an opportunity of addressing the greater body soon arose. The Assembly, as soon as its preliminary business was concluded, proceeded to a great debate on the emigration. The King, dreading the probable results of such a debate, had issued official letters to the nation and the emigrants on the 14th and 16th of October. He besought those who were his true friends to remain in France or to return thither without delay. He begged his brothers at least to abandon their martial attitude even if they would not consent to return. Privately he had already told them that he still hoped for the intervention of the powers[2]. His public utterances produced no effect. The emigrants did not return. The hostility of the representatives of the people was not disarmed.

On the first day of the debate, Oct. 20, Brissot spoke at great length, as his custom was. Rumour said that the Powers intended to hold an armed congress at Aix for the purpose of discussing the French constitution. This Brissot took as his text. 'Is it true,' he indignantly asked, 'that this insolent scheme...is to be carried out in spite of the King's declaration that he accepts the constitution?' (It was not true; but at this very time the Queen was doing her utmost to make it so[3].) Such insolence was not to be tolerated. The

---

[1] Discours...destiné à être prononcé à l'Assemblée nationale le 12 octobre 1791, prononcé aux Jacobins le 14...par J. B. Brissot. *Arch. Parl.*, xxxiv. 225.

[2] Above, p. 92. The official letters in F. de Conches, iv. 201, and *Hist. Parl.*, xii. 160.

[3] See her letters to Mercy about this time. Arneth, pp. 214 sqq.

neighbours of France must be taught to render sincere homage to her constitution and, as a natural consequence, to withdraw all patronage and assistance from those who were in arms against it. Should the monarchs refuse to do so, or should they attempt an armed mediation, there was but one course of action open to the French nation:—'it is not merely necessary to think of defence, the attack must be anticipated; you yourselves must attack[1].' Undoubtedly Brissot was thinking of Belgium.

A few days later Vergniaud, in a speech that has become famous, defended and justified to his own satisfaction the policy of taking violent measures against the emigrants[2]. On Oct. 31, it was decreed that if Louis Joseph Stanislas Xavier (the Count of Provence) did not return to France forthwith he should forfeit his constitutional right to the regency in case of the King's death. The same day Montmorin, the minister of foreign affairs, who was anxious to calm the rising fury of the Assembly, declared that at the moment there were no signs of any enterprise in which the great powers would take part[3]. He made this declaration after reading a not too satisfactory report on the negotiations with the Alsatian princes and the attitude of the various European states towards the new consti-

---

[1] *Arch. Parl.*, xxxiv. 298 sqq.

[2] Oct. 25. Morse Stephens, *Orators of the French Revolution*, I. 250.

[3] *Arch. Parl.*, xxxiv. 556 sqq. Montmorin was highly unpopular with the war party and quite out of touch with the Assembly. He resigned his post shortly after the reading of this report. For the circumstances of his resignation see Masson, *Le département des affaires étrangères pendant la révolution*, p. 117.

tution. So in spite of his efforts, and those of other Royalists and Feuillants of various shades, the Assembly held on its course. It divided its attention between the emigrants and the non-juring clergy. On Nov. 9 it was decreed that if on Jan. 1, 1792, the emigrants should still remain assembled on the frontiers, they would be declared guilty of conspiracy and liable to the punishment of death, and their goods would be confiscated for the benefit of the nation. A variety of supplementary provisions dealt with the most flagrant offenders, royal princes and public functionaries who had deserted their posts. Finally the diplomatic committee was instructed to suggest measures which the King might employ against such foreign powers as harboured the French rebels[1].

Louis, at the suggestion of the Lameths who hated the Assembly[2], resolved to exercise his veto on this savage decree. As a sop to the nation, and as a reminder to the Count of Provence that both court and parliament objected to his violent conduct, that of Oct. 31 was allowed to run its course. The King wrote to his brothers once more, on Nov. 11, inviting, ordering them to return and reminding them of the conditions upon which they enjoyed their constitutional privileges. The next day the veto and the sanction were announced in the Assembly. They were received amid a great silence[3]. A further attempt to appease

[1] *Arch. Parl.*, xxxiv. 724.
[2] Glagau, *Die Legislative*, p. 50.
[3] *Arch. Parl.*, xxxv. 27. The King's letter in Feuillet de Conches, iv. 241. The reply of the Princes (Nov. 16) reminded the King again, insolently enough, that he held his kingdom on trust:—" vous avez

the disappointed legislators was made, a few days later, by the minister Delessart. He announced the dispersal of the emigrants in the Low Countries and mentioned that the King had written to request the Rhenish Electors to follow the Emperor's example in this matter[1].

The report of the diplomatic committee on the emigrant question was read on Nov. 22 by the celebrated publicist Professor Koch of Strasburg[2]. He began by detailing the evidence for certain acts of violence committed on the eastern frontier by the bands of Mirabeau-Tonneau. He complained that the support given to the emigrants by the Electors of Mainz and Trèves and the ex-bishop of Strasburg was a defiance not only of international but of Germanic law; for the latter forbade such minor states to raise fresh troops without the permission of the Empire. Koch was a man of moderate views, and he suggested merely that strong complaints should be made to the princes concerned, to the Imperial Diet, and to the Emperor. He expressed the hope that this would be sufficient; for were not the powers of Europe turning away from the violent schemes for a counter-revolution? But his report was succeeded by another in which evidence was given of an attempt made by the emigrants to bribe General Wimpfen and so gain an entry

un compte à rendre à vos successeurs, et à leur remettre l'Empire dans le même état que vous l'avez reçu des rois nos ancêtres." *Arch. Parl.*, xxxvi. 740.

[1] Nov. 16. *Arch. Parl.*, xxxv. 97.

[2] *Arch. Parl.*, xxxv. 290. The members of the committee were Koch, Ruhl, Gensonné, Brissot, Lemontey, Briche, Baert, Ramond, Mailhe, Schirmer, Treilh-Pardaillan, and Jaucourt.

into Neuf-Brisach. This news roused the fears and passions of the Assembly. Three days later Merlin of Thionville moved that the emigrant princes, with their agents and adherents, should be formally impeached. No vote was taken on the point, but the motion itself was proof enough of the failure of Koch's report[1]. On the 27th Ruhl rose to explain that enlistment for the emigrant army was actually going on 'at a place called Bobenheim, less than a league from the town of Worms.' He suggested that the Electors should be threatened with war if they did not at once disperse and expel the French rebels, that the frontier fortresses should be repaired, and that an address should be circulated throughout the nation in which the treachery of the emigrants was to be explained and the policy of the Assembly justified. Ruhl was followed by Daverhoult, who proposed that a deputation should wait on the King and lay before him three suggestions:—that he should demand the entire dispersion of the emigrant bands within three weeks; that none but 'patriots' should be employed in the diplomatic service; and that the negotiations with the Alsatian princes should be terminated with all speed[2].

The debate of Nov. 29[3] was preceded by the reading of a royal message that announced the appointment of Delessart to the ministry of foreign affairs, in place of Montmorin, and of Cahier de Gerville to that of the interior, vacated by Delessart. The change increased the influence of the Feuillants in the ministry, for Montmorin was rather an old-fashioned royalist than a

---

[1] *Arch. Parl.*, xxxv. 359.   [2] *Arch. Parl.*, xxxv. 397 sqq.
[3] *Arch. Parl.*, xxxv. 433 sqq.

Feuillant. Koch was the first speaker on the 29th. He accepted the substance of Daverhoult's motion but urged that it was not reasonable to expect that the demands of France could be complied with in so short a space as three weeks. After a passage of arms between Ruhl and Delessart, the matter in dispute being the 'patriotism' of the diplomatic service, Isnard rose and supported the motion of Daverhoult in a powerful and violent speech. 'Let us tell the ministers,' he exclaimed, 'that hitherto the nation has not been altogether well pleased with them...and that by the word responsibility we mean death....' Let us tell the King 'that the nation is his sovereign and that he is subject to the law.' To Europe we will say that we love peace but that 'if the cabinets of foreign courts try to stir up a war of kings against France we will stir up for them a war of peoples against kings.' This typical Brissotin harangue was received with great enthusiasm; and, after a draft of the proposed address had been read, Daverhoult's motion—in the words of the report—was adopted 'almost unanimously...amid the sound of acclamation from the tribunes and applause from the Assembly.' Without further delay the deputation waited on the King. His reply was announced the same evening. He promised to give the matter his most serious consideration; and he assured the representatives of the nation that 'he had neglected nothing that might help to secure general tranquility, to maintain the constitution, and make it respected abroad[1].'

[1] *Arch. Parl.*, xxxv. 453. The address to the King, which was circulated throughout France, fixes no definite period within which

On this very day—Nov. 29—it was decreed that all priests who had not yet taken the oath of allegiance to the New Constitution should do so within a week. The penalty for those who refused was expulsion from their benefices. The decree is of the greatest importance in connection with the subsequent policy of the King.

For with the beginning of December that policy began to take its final form. It is only with considerable difficulty that a tolerably satisfactory account of the various forces acting upon the poor inert King can be made out. This much, however, is clear:—the law against the non-jurors, which touched him very nearly, made him more than usually docile in the hands of the Queen. He was anxious to put a veto on that law without too great a sacrifice of popularity. He had of late made serious efforts to adapt himself to the views of his Feuillant advisers. For he had hoped, in his dull way, that if he acted in a constitutional fashion the nation itself might somehow come to see the need for a change, perhaps even the need for a foreign intervention. He still wanted to keep up his popularity, but now at last he seems to have abandoned the idea that in time his power would be restored to him spontaneously by the majority of the nation, when it had wearied of the follies of its elected legislators. He therefore adopted a plan that was intended to increase

---

the demands of the French were to be complied with. One most interesting passage declares that Louis XIV. would never have allowed the Protestants, exiled after the revocation of the Edict of Nantes, to act as the emigrants were then acting. Cp. Sorel, III. 184.

his popularity and retain it until the moment of the great change of front.

The plan was not his own. He had it from Marie Antoinette; and she had it, in part at least, from Fersen. In October the faithful correspondent had seen with alarm that the French court seemed to have adopted the policy of conciliation. He wrote to the Queen to know whether this really was so or not. At the end of his letter he asked three definite questions:— had they finally decided to come to terms with the Revolution? did they still want help or were all negotiations to be dropped? had they a plan of any sort, and if so, what was it[1]? Two days later (Oct. 12) he suggested that a European congress might be summoned, at the Pope's request, to discuss the affairs of Avignon, without provoking increased hostility against the court in France. On the 25th he again wrote to advocate a congress. He spoke very strongly of Leopold's indifference and procrastination. Nothing would go well until he was roused from this inactive condition; and to this end it was advisable that the Queen should 'exaggerate her fears with regard to the Princes and tell him that a congress would calm them[2].' Marie Antoinette's letter of reply is dated Oct. 31. She speaks bitterly of the Princes and their advisers and once more protests that she still holds firmly to the congress scheme[3].

---

[1] Fersen, I. 194, Oct. 10. That Fersen could suppose that the policy of conciliation might be really intended to replace for a time that of war fully explains a similar supposition on the part of Leopold.

[2] Fersen, I. 195, 202.

[3] Fersen, I. 206.

The emigrants and their mainstay, Gustavus of Sweden, thought but meanly of a counter-revolution by congress. Nor, so far as can be seen, was that plan ever cordially entertained either by Leopold or Mercy[1]. But the Queen was determined to hold to it; for it came from Fersen. On Nov. 25 she expressed to Mercy, even more decisively than usual, her ardent desire to see a congress assembled at the earliest possible opportunity[2]. The parliamentary events of the 29th favoured her schemes. It may be that Louis was still half averse from war. But he had always hoped that some occasion for an interference by the powers might arise. The attack made by the Assembly on the clergy rendered that interference more necessary than ever in his eyes. The troubles with the Rhenish Electors might furnish a suitable pretext. He resolved therefore to appeal definitely to his fellow monarchs.

The letter of appeal to the King of Prussia was despatched on the 3rd of December. Louis explained how that in spite of his patience and his acceptance of the constitution discontented factions were ruining the state. He was writing therefore to the Emperor, the Empress of Russia, and the Kings of Spain, Sweden, and Prussia to suggest the expedience of organizing an armed congress[3]. In the letter to the King of

---

[1] There exists a memoir sent by Leopold to the Queen, dated Oct. 1791 [the day not given], in which he speaks of the scheme as premature, regard being had to the unsatisfactory state of the concert. Feuillet de Conches, II. 421. Compare Mercy's letters in Arneth, pp. 214—6.

[2] Arneth, p. 226.

[3] Feuillet de Conches, IV. 269. This letter has had an uncommon fate. Printed in the *Mém. d'un Homme d'État* with the false date

Sweden it was explained that the French princes were not privy to the new system and that the accredited agent of the Tuileries was the Baron de Breteuil[1]. These letters were a direct result of Fersen's advice. Before they had left Paris, in all probability, the Queen received another long memoir from Fersen on the state of Europe. The Emperor, he wrote, was weak, easily led by his ministers, and so not to be trusted. The King of Prussia was little better. The northern powers and Spain were most likely to act with vigour; upon them, accordingly, the weight of the European league must mainly rest[2]. On Dec. 4 he wrote again in the same strain. This time he went so far as to censure the Queen for her omission to urge active measures. This inaction served as a pretext for that of the court of Vienna. Let her act decidedly in conjunction with the loyal powers and so she might force her brother's hand. Such a message from Fersen was all that was needed to fill the Queen's cup of bitterness. She replied to it in grief and amazement. What was said of her letters to the Emperor could not be true; she had written nothing to justify the charge brought against her; someone must be forging her hand. In the latter part of the letter she mentioned the probability of war being declared against the Electors. 'The imbeciles do not see that to do this is to help us;

1790 it has been made the basis of various mistaken theories as to the King's policy. See Sybel, I. 249; criticisms on Louis Blanc, v. 172.

[1] Feuillet de Conches, IV. 271, Dec. 10. Breteuil had first been authorised by Louis to treat in his name in Nov. 1790. Feuillet de Conches, I. 370.

[2] Dated Nov. 26. Fersen. I. 233 sqq.

for it is very sure, if we begin war, that all the other powers will join in....[1]'

When the Queen next wrote to Mercy she carried out Fersen's advice to the letter, exaggerated her fears, and left her brother no possible excuse for further delay. She made light of the danger for her life and that of her husband, knowing that fear of some murderous attack on them was one of the causes of Leopold's hesitation. 'It is no longer the time,' she wrote, 'to fear for our persons; the course that we have adopted here, the course that is of pretending to move in the direction that they wish, renders us safe; and the greatest danger of all would be to remain always as we are.' She concluded with a passionate appeal:—'This is the moment to help us; if they miss it all is over; and the Emperor will have left to him nothing but the shame and reproach...of having allowed his sister, his nephew, and his ally to be dragged into dishonour, when he might have saved them[2].' This letter left Paris on Dec. 16. Two days earlier Louis had explained the royal policy in all its intricacy to Breteuil[3]. He pointed out that he had been forced to demand the dispersal of the emigrants, for he wished to maintain the character of a constitutional monarch. Had he not done so he would have been unable to veto the law of Nov. 9. Further, his system had always been that

---

[1] Fersen, I. 266 and 271. The Queen's letter is of Dec. 9.

[2] Arneth, p. 231.

[3] Feuillet de Conches, IV. 296. Louis XVI. to Breteuil, Dec. 14. The fact that both Breteuil and the Princes had authority from the King to treat with the powers caused considerable annoyance in Europe. It shows how varying and uncertain the King's policy was.

of keeping the Princes in the background. And the attack on the Electors would probably furnish a pretext for the interference of the powers:—'instead of a civil war, it will become a political war, and our chances will be much better.' It would be a great pity if the Electors were to yield to his threats and disperse the emigrants before the powers had had an opportunity of speaking. Should the powers take the matter up, have the emigrants dispersed, but at the same time protect the Electors from French aggression, very good results might be expected. If such armed demonstrations did not produce sufficient effect on the internal state of France the powers, as a last resort, would have to attack her. She would succumb in half a campaign. Then it would be the King's business so to act that the nation in its misfortune might throw itself into his arms.

An interesting commentary on this letter is supplied by the study of Louis' public actions during the first weeks of December. The Feuillants were striving, ever more and more ineffectually, to secure for themselves popularity and for the nation peace. One useful means to this end was the appointment of popular ministers who would yet acquiesce in the plans of the triumvirate. It so happened that for some time the friends of Lafayette, and in particular Me. de Staël and Talleyrand, had been anxious to secure some post for the Count of Narbonne. Narbonne seems to have struck the Feuillants as a likely man for their task. Apparently another circumstance prejudiced the King in his favour. After the decree of Nov. 29 against the priests the leaders of the party with which Narbonne was in touch, together with the Feuillant leaders, organized a petition requesting the King to employ his veto[1]. The same day (Dec. 5) the minister of war, Duportail, a man who was far from popular, was dismissed and his place was forthwith given to Narbonne[2].

The new minister was a man of a good presence, genial, accomplished, and clear-headed. He was neither particularly profound nor particularly earnest. The policy towards which he inclined, as a young and ambitious man, was of a vigorous and somewhat daring sort. Much less attached to peace than was the party of Barnave, he was bent on restoring confidence in the government at home and respect for the nation abroad. When that was done—not before—the constitution might be recast. That to gain these ends he aimed at war from the first is by no means certain[3]; but he was resolved to strengthen France by reforming the army, to resist any interference in her affairs on the part of Europe, and to bridge over the gulf between the deputies and the ministry. Should his policy bring France into collision either with the Rhenish Electors or with Leopold he was prepared to accept the consequences. He was very definitely opposed to the somewhat subservient attitude towards the Emperor

---

[1] The petition came from the members of the departmental directory of Paris. It was signed by Talleyrand, Larochefoucauld, etc. *Hist. Parl.*, XII. 232.

[2] Narbonne's appointment was announced on the 7th. *Arch. Parl.*, XXXV. 627. See too Glagau, pp. 60 sqq.

[3] Sorel (II. 336) speaks as if he did. Narbonne himself declared, a year later, that he had acted on the policy of insuring peace by making every preparation for war. *Déclaration de M....de Narbonne dans le procès du Roi* (London, 1793), pp. 6, 7. Cp. below, p. 161.

that his colleague Delessart and the triumvirate had adopted. In his attempt to win the favour of the Assembly Narbonne met with considerable success. He is said to have been 'the only minister who could ever command a majority[1].' His firm foreign policy, and his friendship with many men of advanced views, made him acceptable up to a certain point to Brissot. The marked deference with which he treated the representatives of the nation contrasted favourably with the contempt for them which the followers of Barnave felt and took no special pains to conceal.

On the 14th Dec. Louis went across from the Tuileries to the Salle de Manège to deliver his formal response to the message of Nov. 29. It is probable that the speech which he made on that day was inspired neither by the Queen nor yet by Narbonne but by the still influential triumvirate. He announced that all his policy had been directed to one end, namely the avoiding of war. But, rather than compromise the dignity of France, he had threatened the Elector of Trèves with war if, within a month, he had not taken measures to disperse the emigrant gatherings. Other harbourers of emigrants were to receive a like warning. The Emperor, who had already shown his goodwill by his treatment of the French in the Low Countries, would be requested to bring pressure to bear on the Electors. It was expected that representations from that quarter would not fail of their effect. In conclusion His Majesty appealed to the Assembly ' to show foreigners that the French nation, its representatives,

---

[1] Vaublanc, *Memoirs*; quoted by Glagau, p. 78.

and its King, were but one.' The speech was received with stormy applause:—from one side of the hall only[1].

Then Narbonne rose to explain the practical measures by which these threats were to be supported. Speaking with warmth and vigour he expounded the plan which the King, in his devotion to the constitution and in spite of his known love of peace, had seen fit to adopt. One hundred and fifty thousand men were to gather on the frontiers within a month. They were to be formed into three great armies, under Lafayette, Luckner, and Rochambeau. Pending the mobilisation of these forces the minister was to visit the North-Eastern frontier in person; there to inspect the strong places and superintend the military preparations. As usual Narbonne received a favourable hearing.

Next day the Assembly voted a very cordial letter of thanks to the King for his gracious compliance with its suggestions; on the 17th His Majesty replied in an equally cordial strain[2]. It might have been thought that the various authorities in France were in complete harmony with one another. But it was not so. As M. Sorel says, 'whilst Narbonne was preparing a strictly limited war with the Elector of Trèves and the Emperor, whilst Barnave was preparing a benevolent mediation on the part of Leopold, and the court an armed intervention of all the powers, the Assembly and the people of Paris let loose a true and passionate war, a national war in which the secular hatred of Austria

---

[1] *Arch. Parl.*, xxxvi. 109 sqq.
[2] *Arch. Parl.*, xxxvi. 122 and 173.

was inflamed by all the enthusiasm of revolutionary propaganda[1].'

At this moment that secular hatred and revolutionary enthusiasm were still further excited by the publication of two successive despatches from Vienna. To understand these documents it is necessary to return to the policy of the imperial court.

[1] Sorel, II. 340.

CHAPTER VII.

Austria in direct conflict with the Assembly. Completion of the Austro-Prussian Alliance. Dec. 1791—Feb. 1792.

No settlement of the still-vexed question of the Alsatian princes had yet been arrived at. The imperial Diet had declared the action of France illegal, and therefore null and void. For this decree Leopold was in part responsible; yet he allowed it to remain unratified from August to December, to the great discomfort of those Rhenish princes whose interests it so nearly affected. The violent language of the new Assembly touching the protection extended to the emigrants was more than discomforting. It caused much alarm among the prince-bishops and other ruling personages. The Elector of Mainz had for months been begging the court of Vienna to act. He had entirely disapproved of the suspension of the concert in October, and had told Kaunitz, with some indignation, that it was an emperor's plain duty to protect the outlying circles of the empire against the aggression of foreign democrats[1]. On the other hand Delessart, in the interests of the Feuillant policy of a benevolent mediation, had written on Nov. 14, requesting the Kaiser to put pressure on the Princes, and so effect quietly the much-desired dispersal of the emigrants. For a month Kaunitz did not take the trouble to reply. But gradually the representations of the Queen, the Electors, and the emigrants began to produce some effect. When to them was added the intemperate talk of the Brissotin orators against Austria there was much indignation, and even a little alarm, in the council of ministers at Vienna. Obviously it was high time that a few plain words should be addressed to these Parisian demagogues. Kaunitz thought that the plain speech of Padua had saved the French monarchy in July. One who knew him well wrote at this time:— "he is accustomed to suppose that his pen carries conviction and terror to whatever quarter its dictates are directed[2]."

As a preliminary measure Leopold was caused to take up again the grievances of the Alsatian princes and despatch a reply to the French communications of 1790. The old accusation of a breach of the Peace of Westphalia was repeated. A confident hope was expressed that all the illegal innovations since August 1789 would soon be abolished[3]. Together with this letter there was sent to Paris the Emperor's formal

---

[1] Vivenot, I. 108 sqq.: letters of March and April, I. 235; of August, I. 260. Mainz to Kaunitz, Oct. 2.

[2] Sir R. M. Keith to Lord Grenville, Jan. 28, 1791. Keith, *Memoirs*, II. 497.

[3] Vivenot, I. 287.

ratification of the 'conclusum' of the Diet in which the decrees of the Constituent Assembly were stigmatised as acts of arbitrary usurpation. Nor did Leopold confine himself to the question of Alsace. He expressed incidentally his indignation at the attempts of the French to spread the seeds of discontent and revolution abroad in the Empire. These complaints were read to the Assembly on Dec. 24[1], and excited much ill-feeling in Paris. One intelligent observer even states that they were generally regarded as a declaration of war[2].

But a yet more formidable document was already on its way from Vienna. The threat of war sent in December to the Elector of Trèves had increased the alarm of the archiepiscopal court. The Elector resolved to make his position secure on both sides. On the 18th he wrote to the Emperor claiming protection; and on the 21st he assured Delessart, with some fervour, that he had already put a stop to all military preparations on his lands and scattered the French malcontents[3]. At the Austrian court measures were already being taken to secure him against an attack from France. On the 21st Kaunitz handed to Noailles, the French ambassador, an "office," as the document was technically called, in reply to Delessart's friendly note of Nov. 14[4]. The chancellor's words were plain, even rough:—his master and the Elector of Trèves had both dispersed the emigrants; but the Elector had

---

[1] *Arch. Parl.*, xxxvi. 348.
[2] Pellenc to La Marck, Jan. 2, 1792. Bacourt, iii. 280.
[3] Schlitter, p. xc, and *Arch. Parl.*, xxxvi. 478.
[4] *Arch. Parl.*, xxxvi. 698, and Vivenot, i. 566.

demanded help of the Empire; orders were accordingly being given to Marshal Bender, the imperial general in the Low Countries, to defend him in case of need. Not that the Emperor doubted the friendliness of the French government, but because the provinces and municipalities of France were so full of violence and misrule that raids into German territory were by no means unlikely. On the following day arrangements were made for despatching the necessary instructions to Marshal Bender[1]. The Austrian government had not the least intention of declaring war. In promising to defend the Elector it was merely carrying out an elementary duty of the head of the Empire. But the parade of the measure and of the motives which prompted it made by Kaunitz to Noailles was superfluous. It was intended as a strong hint to the factious democrats who were insulting their king and threatening to disturb the peace of Europe. Kaunitz enormously overrated the strength of the distinctly royalist party in France, and made the further mistake of identifying the royalists with the still smaller party that was well inclined towards Austria. He therefore seems to have supposed that the mass of French politicians would approve his action. He was to learn that the picture of France which he had sketched for himself was out of drawing.

Delessart read the Austrian "office" to the Assembly on the last day of the year. Ever since the

[1] Leopold to the President of the Council of War, Dec. 22. Should the French attack Trèves, or should it become certain that they would do so, Bender was 'to repel force with force without further forbearance.' Schlitter, p. xc.

royal sitting of the 14th the various parties that were ready or anxious for war had rivalled one another in the violence of their proposals. Narbonne had demanded in the King's name an extraordinary vote of twenty millions, and had spoken of 'the necessary preparations at the opening of a campaign.' Dumas had suggested an increase in the number of marshals. Isnard had turned a petition of the section of Lombards into a motion demanding the impeachment of all the emigrant leaders. Vergniaud had laid before the Assembly a draft of a warlike address to the nation couched in the most violent terms. It spoke of the gathering of troops on the frontiers; of rumoured plots against liberty; of the 'senseless hand' which had turned aside the blows aimed by the Assembly at sedition and fanaticism; of the evil men who lived only to slander the representatives of the people and ruin the national credit by speculation on the exchange; of the horrid results that a counter-revolution and the re-establishment of the noblesse would entail. Crublier d'Optère, of the military committee, had mentioned the possibility of a speedy march across the frontier to crush the rebels encamped on German soil, and had advocated various measures for increasing the military strength of the country[1].

The speech that perhaps throws most light on the policy of what might be called the revolutionary, as opposed to the royalist, war party at this time was

---

[1] Narbonne, Dec. 18; Dumas, Dec. 24; Isnard, Dec. 25; Vergniaud and Crublier d'Optère, Dec. 27. *Arch. Parl.*, xxxvi. 233, 336, 381, 440, 451. On the 24th Leopold's note on the Alsatian question was referred to the diplomatic committee.

delivered by its leader, Brissot, on the 29th[1]. He began by proving, and that very completely, that no one of the great powers was at all likely to attack France forthwith. The argument is clear and sound; many of the reflections are remarkably acute. Of these one example must suffice: 'Catherine seems to want to make of France an apple of discord wherewith to excite disputes in Europe, in the midst of which she may reconquer the empire of the East.' That was precisely what Catherine did want. Brissot went on to say that, though there was no real danger, yet it was necessary to speak and act sternly in order to 'bring to an end the comedy which the crowned heads were playing'; and, quite apart from all such considerations, war would be a national blessing. One very suspicious circumstance had not escaped his notice. 'It is rumoured that the executive power, which to-day actually provokes war, after having for so long made show of an opposite system, may be suspected of having secret schemes.' Even this alarming, and as we now know most well-founded, suspicion in no way curbed Brissot's violence or interfered with his desire for active measures. He sneered at the court, the ministers, and the powers; he urged that Leopold and his fellows must be taught that the French constitution was no affair of theirs; that no mercy should be shown to the Elector of Trèves; and concluded by proposing that the French ambassadors should be recalled at once from those courts which had refused to recognise the constitution, namely Stockholm, St Petersburg,

---

[1] *Arch. Parl.*, xxxvi. 596 sqq.

Madrid, and Rome. Then Hérault de Séchelles rose and in a few prophetic words expressed a thought which, one is bound to suppose, had already sprung up in the minds of many members of the revolutionary war party[1]. It is true, said Hérault, that Leopold only can hurt us, and true that even he is not likely to attack as yet; but we need war, for 'in time of war measures can be taken that would appear too stern in time of peace. War will justify all your steps; for, in brief, it is at home that war must be made on rebels before it is carried abroad. All the measures that you may adopt for the safety of the State will be just, as was the consular authority created...in times of distress.... It is time to take a veil and throw it over the statue of Liberty.'

By a strange irony the Assembly, after listening to these speeches, proceeded to accept a declaration, drawn up by Condorcet, in which the French nation was made to renounce all ideas of conquest and to declare that war was being forced on it against its will. A second vote sanctioned the grant of twenty millions for military purposes that the King and Narbonne had demanded[2]. Thus before the last day of the year the advocates of war had succeeded in exciting both Assembly and nation. And Kaunitz' "office" seemed, even to moderate men, to confirm all that had been said of the insolence and counter-revolutionary spirit of the Emperor. The Feuillants were alarmed beyond

---

[1] The particular sentence quoted is not in the speech as printed in the *Arch. Parl.*, but is in the *Moniteur*. I do not know which is the more correct version. The thought is common to both.

[2] *Arch. Parl.*, xxxvi. 596 and 620.

measure at the enormous amount of ill-feeling that it aroused[1].

The Assembly as usual referred the letter to the diplomatic committee and postponed the formal debate on the question of peace and war until the committee should have reported.

It seemed that, in spite of the Feuillants, those who wished for war would very shortly carry their point. The followers of Brissot were ready to declare war in spite of their distrust of the court. But certain of the extreme republicans, supported by a section of the Parisian mob, feared the King so much that they were reluctant to plunge into war while he remained in authority, surrounded by royalist ministers. The members of this group bore names that were soon to become "tolerably known in the Revolution":— Robespierre, Billaud-Varenne, Collot d'Herbois, Danton, Marat, Dubois Crancé and others. Robespierre had retired to his native town of Arras at the close of the constituent Assembly. He was not heard again in Paris until November 25[2]. On that day he appeared at the Jacobins to criticise the policy of leaving the decision of peace and war in the King's hands. For his part he advocated a direct summons from the Assembly bidding Leopold to scatter the emigrants on pain of incurring the enmity of the French nation. Throughout December the idea that Louis and Narbonne intended to exploit the coming war in the interests of monarchy was expressed in many forms by Jacobin orators and Jacobin editors of the more

---

[1] Arneth, p. 280. Below, p. 152.
[2] *Hist. Parl.*, xii. 402.

extreme sort¹. *L'Orateur du Peuple* and *Les Révolutions de Paris* even began to treat Brissot as a royalist because of his eagerness for war and his understanding with the minister².

Twice, in the early days of January, Robespierre delivered set speeches on the great topic at the Jacobins³. He argued thus:—the prospect of war is welcome to the court, to the ministers, and to those who direct the ministers; as these men are secretly in league with the allied powers anything that pleases them cannot be for the good of the nation; therefore so long as such men are in power a war is more likely to bring misfortune than profit. It will be admitted that these preliminary contentions were not altogether wide of the mark. Robespierre next handled an argument which certain Girondin speakers were fond of using: that France had a mission to free her neighbours. His criticism was short and effective. 'No one loves armed missionaries.' As a matter of fact the first duty of the French nation was to set its own house in order. Was not the seat of evil rather nearer than Coblence? Would not a successful war turn to the profit of aristocrat generals and the reactionary government that they served? War might be necessary; but let it be declared first of all against conspiracy and despotism at home; when these had been crushed it would be time enough to attack Leopold. In an article published the day after the

---

¹ Robespierre spoke several times in Dec. It is not necessary to give accounts of all his speeches.

² Extracts in *Hist. Parl.*, XIII. 7 sqq.

³ Morse Stephens, *Orators*, II. 304 sqq.

delivery of Robespierre's second speech Prudhomme echoed these opinions and made a furious attack on Narbonne and the generals[1]. Danton and Marat, in speech and writing, did what they could to combat the views of the war party. How much these men were influenced by a real hatred of war, how much by fear of the King, and how much by jealousy of the Gironde, only a long and careful analysis could show. It is certain that their attitude did little or nothing to delay the contest. For by this time the force which was driving all parties towards war was the conviction that the existing state of things was unendurable and could best be terminated by some appeal to violence. This conviction the extreme Jacobins shared with their colleagues in club and assembly and their foes in cabinet and court. Their action inflamed rather than calmed public opinion. Had the appeal to violence taken the form which their language implied, namely an immediate overthrow of the King, it would certainly, in the state of Europe at the time, have accelerated rather than delayed the actual outbreak of hostilities. Their policy is rather interesting to a student of the Revolution as a whole than important in an account of the causes of the war.

The party with which Narbonne was connected had meanwhile worked out a definite system of policy; a system which it pursued with considerable skill and enterprise, though with very moderate success. Both Narbonne and the Feuillants wished to strengthen the King's authority, and finally to remodel the constitution

---

[1] In *Les Rév. de Paris* for Jan. 12. *Hist. Parl.*, XIII. 38.

in the interests of a limited but real monarchy. But whilst the Feuillants desired the aid, or even the protection, of the Emperor, Narbonne favoured the more spirited and patriotic means of repelling any attempt at interference and saving France by a reform of the army and perhaps by war. With Europe in general he had no quarrel. He even attempted to secure the alliance, or at least the neutrality, of England and Prussia. In company, as it would seem, with Me. de Staël he had devised a striking scheme for the furtherance of this policy. He suggested that Duke Ferdinand of Brunswick, reputed the ablest general of the day, might be prevailed upon to give his sword to France, like Marshal Saxe before him, and restore both army and monarchy. Ferdinand was known not only for his generalship but for his 'enlightenment' and hatred of Austria; it was therefore thought that his acquiescence was not out of the question. The scheme seems wild enough to a nineteenth century mind, accustomed to a sharp opposition of French and German, and familiar with the rôle that Brunswick played seven months after it was brought forward. But a man trained in the military and diplomatic traditions of the eighteenth century, although he might see difficulties of execution in plenty, would be hardly likely to regard the device as impossible of success or absurd[1].

[1] Contemporaries sometimes asserted that there was a plan for deposing Louis in favour of Brunswick. M. Sorel has proved that this story is entirely without foundation. For the whole matter see his study of Narbonne in *Le Temps*, Oct. 1878, and *La Revue Historique*, 1876; also the corresponding sections in his history and in that of Glagau. The King's assent had been secured. The Queen

The Brunswick scheme did not commend itself to Delessart, the minister of foreign affairs; but after a time he was induced to withdraw his opposition. Early in January François Custine, a young man of twenty-two, son of that General Custine who was to become notorious a year later, was despatched to sound the Duke. Ferdinand heard him politely but made no response to his offers. The young agent's skill and enthusiasm were alike remarkable; but he was dealing with an excessively cautious and definitely anti-democratic individual, who was already regarded as the probable commander of the combined Prussian and Austrian troops in a war against France. Such being the case it is not surprising that the whole affair came to nothing.

Narbonne's plan for detaching Prussia from Austria also miscarried. An elaborate scheme for bribing Bischoffwerder, and so gaining the ear of the King, had been devised by Biron. Its failure was due, at least partly, to the fact that the Feuillants were at this very time carrying on a separate negotiation at Berlin. They too wished to bring influence to bear on Frederick William; but their aim was to induce him to work in conjunction with the Emperor at the pacification of Europe. At the end of December they had sent the Count de Ségur to the Prussian court. Ségur was a diplomatist of good name, but unfortunately he was personally distasteful to the cabinet with which he had to deal. Scandalous stories were told of him:—that

spoke of the scheme as 'une idée folle'; and added, "Je ne doute pas que le duc refuse, et c'est même nous servir." To Fersen, Dec. 25. Fersen, I. 312.

he was plotting to overturn all the governments of Europe; that he had been furnished with a well-lined purse to be used in clearing the obstacles from his path[1]. Every such rumour was gladly received and diligently circulated by Roll, the agent of the Princes. The Prussian ministers were civil to Ségur but far from cordial; whilst the King made not the least effort to conceal his intense dislike of him. After his first month at Berlin Ségur was in despair. The King, he wrote, could not bear his presence; no member of the court party had any dealings with him; his mission had been ruined by the slanders of which he had been the victim; it had better be terminated with all speed[2]. The agent of the party of Narbonne, one Jarry, who had left Paris on Jan. 7, soon perceived that where Ségur had so signally failed he was not likely to succeed. He stayed but a few days in Berlin.

On the side of England Narbonne was more successful; though here too his disagreement with Delessart produced unfortunate results. He was well served—and to a great extent led—by the man who was to become the chief of European diplomatists, M. de Talleyrand, the ex-bishop of Autun. Talleyrand, like Mirabeau before him, had visions of an Anglo-French alliance[3]. At his own request he was sent

---

[1] Sorel, *Le Temps*, 1876. M. Sorel gives reasons for supposing that rumour had got hold of Biron's plan and fastened it on Ségur. Morton Eden wrote of Ségur on Jan. 14 (to Grenville), "His reception here has been perfectly cold, and he, I know, feels very sensibly mortified and disappointed."

[2] To Delessart, 8 Feb. 1792. Pallain, *La Mission de Talleyrand à Londres en 1792*, p. 63.

[3] Tall. to Biron, Jan. 5, 1792, "J'ai extrêmement insisté sur ce

unofficially to England, in the middle of January, to sound the cabinet of St James's. He assured Lord Grenville that the French government was disposed to "enter into the strictest connection with Great Britain[1]," but his unofficial character was a bar to regular negotiations. Had this not been the case his more ambitious schemes would have been very effectually frustrated by the action of Delessart, who hardly ever wrote to him and gave him no positive instructions[2]. However, he received private assurances, on more than one occasion, that England would certainly remain neutral in the event of war; and when he returned to Paris in March he remained convinced that the Anglo-French alliance was still not impossible[3].

At Paris the interval between the arrival of Kaunitz' December office and the opening of the debate to which it gave rise was well utilised by the minister of war. His understanding with Brissot and the Gironde enabled him to secure the weight of their support in the Assembly. On January 4 Isnard delivered a vicious speech, which was nevertheless most useful to Narbonne.

---

qu'il fallait envoyer en Angleterre"; to Delessart, Jan. 31, "Mon opinion est toujours que votre meilleur terrain est l'Angleterre." Mirabeau to Biron, July, 1786. Pallain, pp. 32, 56, and 38, note.

[1] Grenville to Gower, March 9, 1792.

[2] To Delessart, Feb. 14. Complaints of neglect, ending, "Je vous jure que c'est mal." Pallain, p. 84.

[3] Tall. to Delessart, 2 March. Pallain, p. 133. Grenville to Gower, March 9:—"...I had no difficulty in saying to him individually...that it was very far from being the disposition of the Government to endeavour to foment or prolong the disturbances there [i.e. in France] with a view to any profit to be derived from them to

He first declared that a war, 'indispensable for the consummation of the Revolution,' was about to break out. Next he attacked the royalist party with the utmost bitterness, pointing to the massacres of Avignon as a type of the fate to which the crime of royalism inevitably led. Then, turning to the Ministry, he demanded that they should provide France with allies. 'To succeed it is only necessary to try.' Surely Prussia, the land of the 'philosopher King' Frederick, could be induced to join a free nation; surely England would listen to 'a national language[1].' On the 11th Narbonne reported in person the results of his brief tour of inspection along the N.-E. frontier. He gave a glowing, and not too accurate, account of the state of the military preparations. But in spite of his desire to please he was forced to refer to the painful and patent fact that the frontier armies, with a nominal strength of 150,000, actually contained under 100,000 fighting men. However, he gratified his supporters by lauding the Assembly, the constitution, and the declaration of Condorcet[2]. Against Narbonne and the Gironde combined the unpopular Delessart could make little way. He attempted to hold back the Assembly from war by reading repeated pacific and humble messages from the Elector of Trèves, who was nervously anxious to prove his perfect good faith[3]; but the attempt met with no success.

The report of the diplomatic committee was laid

[1] *Arch. Parl.*, xxxvii. 85.
[2] *Arch. Parl.*, xxxvii. 233.
[3] *Arch. Parl.*, xxxvii. 106, 161, 447. Notes read on Jan. 6, 8, and 16.

before the house by Gensonné on the 14th of January[1]. Throughout the report Austria was treated as the faithless ally. All her misdemeanours since the first treaty of 1756 were enumerated in detail. The greatest of these misdemeanours were the protection given to the French rebels and the formation of a concert to modify the French constitution, and so reduce France to the level of an Austrian dependency. The orders given to Marshal Bender and the alliance formed with Prussia, without consulting France, were also treated as grievances. Gensonné advocated war for the usual reasons:—it would quicken the nation, restore credit, and check all unpatriotic movements. The conclusion of the whole matter was that France should strike suddenly and swiftly, as Frederick had struck at Silesia, unless a full and satisfactory explanation of her various unfriendly acts were given by Austria before February 10; and that meanwhile military preparations should be continued with all speed. Gensonné was followed by Guadet, who with a short, impassioned, but certainly well premeditated speech persuaded the Assembly to decree out of hand that it was a treasonable action to take part, either directly or indirectly, in a congress for the discussion of French affairs, in a measure of compromise between the nation and the emigrants, or in any agreement for granting to the Alsatian princes a compensation other than that promised to them by the Constituent Assembly. The decree was aimed directly at the plans

[1] The debates of the 14 are in *Arch. Parl.*, xxxvii. 410 sqq. Gensonné's report and Guadet's speech also in Stephens, *Orators*, I. 390 and I. 419.

of the Feuillants and the court. The last clause was intended to put a stop to all schemes for securing to the German princes compensation in land, the only form of compensation which they were prepared to accept[1]. The decree was carried to the King at once, with the request that it might be communicated to all the powers. Louis replied to the deputation gently and falsely:—'you know my attachment to the constitution; assure the National Assembly that I shall never neglect anything that may conduce to its security.'

The discussion of the report began on the 17th. There can be no doubt that already the majority in the Assembly was in favour of war. Pellenc wrote explicitly on this head to La Marck:—' Brissot, the majority of the Jacobins, almost all the diplomatic committee, and, in the present state of affairs, the majority of the Assembly' were reported warlike[2]. The phrase 'the present state of affairs' indicates the uncertain and composite character of that majority. Once more Koch tried to promote moderation and delay by insisting on the Emperor's readiness to disperse the emigrants. Once more Brissot advocated a declaration that the treaty of '56 was broken and an immediate appeal to force. Dumas accused the war party of encroaching on the constitutional rights of the King—as indeed it

---

[1] There had been some talk of a grant of Polish lands, which could easily be stolen for the purpose. Guadet probably feared a cession of French territory.

[2] Jan. 14. Pellenc was acute enough to add:—"Si la guerre commence, quel qu'en soit l'issu, il va s'agir de la destiné du genre humain." Glagau, p. 112 and p. 285.

was—and even dared to defend the Austrian alliance; but his arguments were drowned by a clamorous speech from Vergniaud. Another speaker, who wished France to make every preparation for war, but yet to let Europe know that peace was her aim, was shouted down after the same fashion by Isnard[1].

But the extreme party did not succeed in inducing the Assembly to neglect all forms by making its decree an actual declaration of war. The decree as passed was warlike enough but yet hardly so violent as Brissot would have wished. On the last day of the debate (Jan. 25) Daverhoult—a constitutional royalist—proposed that the Emperor should be requested to explain the nature of the concert and his relation to it, and to transform the treaty of 1756 into a national treaty, by which the new French constitution would be implicitly recognised; further, that the Emperor should be given a full month in which to decide on his reply. After Condorcet, in a long and most able speech, had urged the desirability of an English alliance, Hérault de Séchelles tried to frustrate the plan of Daverhoult by insisting that Leopold's answer should be required before Feb. 15[2]. But, although certain of his suggestions were received, he failed to carry the Assembly with him on this point. In its final form the decree stated

---

[1] The debates, Jan. 17—25, are in *Arch. Parl.*, xxxvii. 462—658. It would be wearisome to analyse all the speeches of the war party. The substance of their argument has already been given.

[2] Condorcet treated the question historically and tried to prove that England was the natural ally of France. He thought that no obstacles would be raised by Pitt, whose zeal for reform he commended, provided France were to abstain from the annexation of Belgium.

that Leopold had infringed the treaty of 1756 by his alliance with Prussia, his office of Dec. 21, and other like measures. So much was borrowed from the Brissotins; the next clause was the work of the more deliberate party. Leopold was to be asked whether he intended to live 'in peace and good intelligence' with the French nation and whether he was prepared to renounce all treaties derogatory to its sovereign rights. Should his reply be unsatisfactory, or should he fail to reply before March 1, his action would be regarded by the Assembly as a declaration of war. (It is always to be borne in mind that the Assembly had—under the constitution of 1791—no right to declare war.) In a supplementary clause the King was invited to continue all the military preparations already taken in hand.

Whilst the great war debates were in progress at Paris the war policy of the Queen produced its intended effect at Vienna. Marie Antoinette's most passionate cry for help must have reached Mercy in Belgium about the 20th of Dec.[1] He despatched within a few days a long letter to Vienna into which he inserted large sections from that of the Queen. On Jan. 4 Leopold announced with evident anxiety to Count Reuss that Mercy's courier had arrived with such information as rendered the taking of serious action against France absolutely necessary. He was desirous that Bischoffwerder should be sent from Berlin to discuss the matter and arrange with him some plan for a combined

---

[1] Above, p. 124. The various letters etc. quoted here are in Vivenot, I. 304—40. For a study of this correspondence see Lenz, *Preussische Jahrbücher*, 1894.

demonstration on the part of the German powers. Kaunitz also took the alarm and wrote to tell Ludwig Cobenzl that, as the French King had asked for help, it was necessary to resume the active concert. He then proceeded to draw up an elaborate memoir to be laid before the council of ministers[1]. The memoir took the form of an answer to the question:—Can Austria and the powers of Europe in general continue any longer a policy of simple observation? By way of answer an account of the spread of revolutionary doctrines in France was given:—how the apostles of these doctrines 'were promising the earth to the poor as Christianity promises heaven.' There followed an analysis of Mercy's despatch of Dec. 24, with many verbal extracts from the Queen's letter. Then came a report on the spread of the democratic disease in Belgium. In conclusion, it was urged that, as there was now no doubt whatever that the policy of the French court was one of elaborate dissimulation, the moment for action had arrived.

On the 17th of January the council of ministers, having considered the arguments of Kaunitz, decided to demand from France the suspension of military preparations on the frontiers; compensation for the absorption of Alsace; the restoration of Avignon and the Venaissin to the Pope; protection for the King and his family; and the retention of a monarchical form of government. As a preliminary measure the mobilisation of some 40,000 men was agreed on. Some

---

[1] The memoir as published is not signed; but there is little doubt that it is from Kaunitz' hand.

compensation for so disinterested an action would naturally be expected; and this matter too was discussed by the council. A few days later the whole series of resolutions was communicated to the Prussian court[1].

Austria was at length decided to act. But she was not prepared to act alone; she was not committed to any scheme of counter-revolution or even to an immediate war. She hoped to gain much by a mere display of force. The Austrian statesmen dreaded expense and did not like war. "There exists here," wrote Sir R. M. Keith, "as great a want of money as of resolution—and the evil day is put off as long as possible." That was on the fourteenth. On the eighteenth he was assured, "by a person of undoubted credit," that the mobilisation orders of the previous day were "nothing more than an empty parade[2]." It is certain that the Emperor did not want war, although he was beginning to regard it as almost inevitable. Nor did Kaunitz want war, but he was prepared to declare it should the democrats insolently disobey his orders. Both hoped that much might be gained by keeping in touch with the French 'moderates.' Mercy, by whose advice they were to a considerable extent guided, was in favour of war but not of an open attack on the French principles. He held that war should be begun on some ordinary diplomatic pretext, without express reference to the French constitution; that further pretexts should then be found for con-

---

[1] Kaunitz to Reuss, Jan. 25. Herrmann, *Forschungen*, v. 281.
[2] Keith to Grenville, Jan. 14, Jan. 18.

tinuing the fighting until the violent democratic passions of the French were exhausted; and that when at last moderate counsels began to prevail they should secretly be encouraged by Austria. So France would be constrained to effect her own counter-revolution, which would not be the less lasting because thus brought about[1].

Such were the calculations which induced the Austrian statesmen to remain on good terms with the Feuillants in spite of the Queen's known aversion to the leaders of that party. In the early days of January her agent Goguelat had travelled from Paris to Belgium once more. He explained to Mercy that the document he brought was really not the work of his mistress but of Barnave[2]. It was of the customary Feuillant type, hopeful, full of general statements, and somewhat didactic. In an introductory survey of the state of France its author maintained that in stripping the crown and the two first estates of their vicious privileges the French nation had done wisely. But, save in the case of the clergy, of whose 'definite destruction' Barnave apparently approved, the work of stripping had gone too far. It is surprising to find anyone who could write in this strain flattering himself that he had the ear of the King. The writer went on to say that the republican party, composed in part of

---

[1] Mercy to Kaunitz, Jan. 7, 1792. Herrmann, *Forschungen*, v. 288, and Glagau, p. 279.

[2] The memoir in Arneth, p. 240. Goguelat's explanation is in a letter from Mercy to Kaunitz, Jan. 14, '92. Feuillet de Conches, v. 92. Goguelat also carried a letter to Fersen, dated Jan. 4, so we may presume that he left Paris on that day. Fersen, II. 2.

scoundrels but mainly of honest theorists, was not really strong. 'By means of a firm and sustained policy' it would be possible to destroy it. Leopold was advised to repudiate all connection with the emigrants and rely on the support of the sane, constitutional majority of the nation. In a postscript, added after Dec. 31, the Emperor was informed of the disastrous effect that his office had produced:—men were now convinced that he was actually in league with the emigrants. To avoid war he must disown publicly all ideas of aggression and send no troops into the Electorate of Trèves until the Archbishop had complied fully with the French demands.

Leopold's reply to this communication was anything but unfriendly; but one can discern in it traces of two separate influences, that of the Feuillants and that of the Queen[1]. He protested his horror of all schemes for restoring the *ancien régime,* but spoke indignantly of the violence of the extreme minority, that was bent on driving him into war. The new concert, he concluded, was based on three principles:—no aid was to be given to the emigrants; there was to be no interference with the internal affairs of France, save to protect the King and his family; and no attempt would be made to overthrow the constitution. This reply appeared to the Queen neither more nor less than 'detestable[2].' She could not understand her brother's cautious procedure. For about this time her horror of the Revolution was increasing daily and with

---

[1] Dated Jan. 31. Arneth, p. 282.
[2] To Fersen; see his diary for Feb. 21. Fersen, II. 9.

it her eagerness for the powers to act. Leopold's method of paying retaining fees of promises to the Feuillants was in consequence not to her liking. Before the Emperor's reply was known to her she had prevailed upon the Russian ambassador, Simolin, to explain her real opinions at Brussels, Vienna, and St Petersburg. Simolin left Paris on Feb. 1. His task was to sweep away all excuses for hesitation and to induce Leopold to adopt the policy which the King had explained to Breteuil in December. 'Tell the Emperor,' the Queen had said, 'that there is no fear for us; the nation needs the King...and as for me I fear nothing. I would rather endure anything than live in my present state of degradation; anything would seem preferable to the horror of our present position[1].'

It is possible that, had it not been for the influence of the Feuillants, the Queen might have prevailed upon Louis to utilise the Assembly's warlike decree of Jan. 25 to bring on the long wished for crisis. He could have done so with ease. As Gouverneur Morris wrote to Washington, "the whole nation, though with different views," was "desirous of war[2]." There were however two levers by which the Feuillants were able to

---

[1] The Queen's note of introduction for Simolin and his long reports to Catherine of Russia are in Feuillet de Conches, v. 214, 255, 308. There is a second account of his conversation with the Queen in a letter from Fersen to Taube. Fersen, II. 167.

[2] Feb. 4, 1792. In the same letter he states that:—"The King's true interest (and he thinks so) seems to consist in preserving the peace." He does not state the source of this piece of information. Morris, I. 509.

move the King into the position which they desired:—his real love of peace and his royal pride. He naturally resented the interference of the Assembly and was easily induced to make no use of its advice. A royal message of Jan. 25 reminded the legislators that the constitution forbade them to discuss questions of peace and war save at the King's solemn request. Their petition, however—the King went on to say—was not to be neglected; indeed his views coincided with their own. 'More than a fortnight ago' he had written to the Emperor in the strain which they now adopted; he rejoiced to be able to give this further proof of his fidelity to the constitution and his love of peace[1].

This lamentable message was doubly false; it did not express the true sentiments of the King nor were its statements of fact accurate. On 5th Jan. Kaunitz had written curtly to Delessart to announce the dispersal of the emigrants assembled on the territory of the Elector of Trèves; to complain of the threatening attitude of the French army and the scandalous license of the Assembly, the clubs, and the press; and to repeat that the Emperor intended to resist any slightest violation of German territory. Delessart's reply, dated Jan. 21—exactly a week earlier than the message just referred to—was a most moderate, not to say inadequate, substitute for the fiery ultimatum of the Assembly[2]. The minister first pointed out, humbly enough, that a certain phrase which occurred in Kaunitz' December office was calculated to awaken

---

[1] *Arch. Parl.*, xxxvii. 717.

[2] Kaunitz' note of Jan. 5 and Delessart's of Jan. 21 in Vivenot, I. 567 and 384.

suspicion in France. The phrase in question was a reference to the 'sovereigns united in concert for the maintenance of public tranquility and for the safety and honour of crowns.' Then, somewhat more boldly, he went on to state that any attempt to alter the constitution by force would inevitably unite all Frenchmen in opposition. To go to war to avenge a few intemperate words or deeds, which were after all but the inevitable outcome of any revolution, was unworthy of the Austrian dignity. And, from the point of view of interest, Austria would gain nothing by provoking a general war, even if her arms were everywhere victorious and France, robbed by England of colonies, navy, and mercantile marine, should be reduced to the level of a second-rate power. So wrote Delessart. When a French minister spoke thus it is not surprising that Kaunitz should have continued, almost to the last, to believe that he could give orders to France.

A week after the arrival of this letter in Vienna the signature of the treaty between Austria and Prussia, the preliminaries of which had been agreed on in July 1791, still further strengthened the hands of the Imperial Chancellor. In Jan. 1792 the Prussian court was fully prepared to listen to proposals for an active concert, provided that some satisfactory settlement of the question of indemnities accompanied them. The King, the favourite, and certain of the military magnates had long been in favour of vigorous action. In the autumn of '91 French affairs had almost absorbed the interest of the King[1]. By December the rumour

---

[1] Above, p. 98.

that fifty thousand men would march on the Rhine in the spring was going the round of military circles in Berlin[1]. And even those statesmen who did not favour the King's policy began to fear that the violence of the National Assembly would "render the interference of the powers of the Empire absolutely necessary[2]." On the 14th of January, Frederick William wrote to assure Louis that the project of an armed congress of the powers met with his entire approval; but on the same day he informed Louis' agent, the Baron de Breteuil, that, anxious though he was to send troops to the aid of his brother the French King, he would be lacking in his duty towards his own people were he not to insist on some 'fair recompense[3].'

About the end of January the decisions arrived at by the Austrian council of ministers on the 17th were reported in Berlin by Reuss. The Prussian King promptly summoned the Duke of Brunswick to Potsdam to discuss with him a plan of campaign. Curious observers saw an official cross the court of the castle, with a map of France under his arm, and enter the room where the King was conferring with his general. The same evening the staff officers, now confident that war was at hand, drank to the confusion of the National Assembly and the speedy fall of Paris[4]. But although

---

[1] Massenbach's Diary (Massenbach was a royal aide-de-camp) quoted in Chuquet, *La première invasion Prussienne*, p. 30.

[2] Morton Eden to Grenville, Dec. 13. Similar news in a letter of Jan. 28.

[3] Fersen, II. 128 and 130. Cp. Frederick William to Schulenburg, Dec. 3. Ranke, p. 107.

[4] Massenbach; Chuquet, p. 20.

the King was probably in sympathy with such displays of enthusiasm, the circumspect Duke of Brunswick, who came straight from his conferences with Custine, and the majority of the Prussian ministers, who cared for other concerns than those of France, were not. Yet alarm at the reckless behaviour of the French prevented the ministers who disliked the new connection with Austria from interfering with the signature of a definite treaty. It had been agreed that this signature should not take place until the peace between Russia and the Porte should have been completed. The suspension of the active concert had further delayed matters. But on Jan. 9 the long-drawn Russo-Turkish negotiations at last came to an end and at the same time Austria took up again the active concert.

On February 7 Reuss, representing Austria, and Finkenstein, Schulenburg, and Alvensleben on the part of Prussia attached their seals to the treaty[1]. In form it was a simple defensive alliance; but it was obviously intended to serve as a basis for a European coalition against France, since the seventh article contemplated the ultimate adhesion of Russia, the Maritime Powers, and Saxony, whilst the eighth guaranteed the various German constitutions, evidently with a view to the infringement of imperial rights by France in the matter of Alsace. In the first separate article the contracting powers agreed to promote a concert for the settlement of French affairs. In the second they promised one another assistance in case of internal troubles. The

---

[1] Neumann (*Traités de l'Autriche*, I. 470) gives the text and three separate articles. Ranke, p. 276, and Vivenot, I. 370, give two other secret and separate articles.

third touched a more delicate question. The Austrian Cabinet had been anxious to guarantee the existing Polish constitution—that of May 1791—and had accordingly drawn up an article by which 'the free constitution' of Poland was formally recognised. To this however the Prussians took exception; they succeeded in carrying their point, so that in the final draft of the treaty the article merely stipulated for '*a* free constitution[1].' The two secret articles dealt with differences between the contracting parties, the existence of which limited the efficiency of the treaty so far as French affairs were concerned. The first related to the fate of the two Frankish Principalities of Anspach and Baireuth, which had just been taken over by Prussia, after the resignation of the reigning prince[2]. The territorial aggrandizement of Prussia was always unpopular at Vienna; so it might very safely have been concluded that the promise to settle the fate of these provinces amicably would be a cause of discord rather than of harmony. In the second secret article two exceptions were made to the guarantee of assistance in case of attack. Neither party was bound to defend certain remote possessions of its ally:—Belgium in the case of Austria, and the Westphalian provinces in that of Prussia. Such a stipulation rendered the treaty defective even as an instrument of defence against France. It was in no way an efficient weapon of attack

[1] See the account of the negotiations sent to the King of Prussia on Feb. 3 in Herrmann, *Forschungen*, IV. 429.

[2] Sybel, I. 458. It was a family arrangement. The King of Prussia was the nearest agnate of the childless Markgrave of Anspach and Baireuth.

for it contained not even a provisional settlement of the question of indemnities. It was not officially intended to be a weapon of attack; at least the ministers who signed it hoped that it would not be put to that use. They were undoubtedly anxious to avoid a French war. The King's party was not. But both parties fancied that France would hardly dare to refuse those demands which Kaunitz was about to make for the last time, now that he could speak in the name of the two great German military powers. The King probably looked forward to an armed congress, from which he would return in triumph, having helped to reestablish the French monarchy and having secured some indemnity in land. He would not have regretted an opportunity of meeting the democratic hordes in the open field. The ministers hoped to see those democrats effectually routed, but by less expensive means[1].

[1] Morton Eden to Grenville, Feb. 14. "I have repeatedly mentioned...the assurances which the Prussian ministers have given me of their earnest wishes to avoid a war for various reasons.......His Prussian Majesty himself would not, from pique perhaps as I have already stated, be averse to hostile measures...." Feb. 16. "This ministry still insists on the prudence and moderation of the intention of the two courts, and on their firm expectation that their grievances will be redressed by the French nation, without the necessity of coming to a rupture...."

CHAPTER VIII.

The Critical Events of Feb. and March, 1792.

The month of February in Paris was a time of eager waiting. All parties knew that the Emperor's reply to the official communications of the latter part of January, and his attitude on hearing of the decree of the twenty-fifth, would practically decide the question of peace and war. Each utilised the delay to strengthen its own position as far as possible. In the strife for popularity and power between Robespierre and Brissot there begins to be shadowed forth the struggle of Mountain and Gironde. The disorder and misrule in the provinces, now become almost chronic, and the violent language of club orators and journalists had begotten fierce suspicions in the mind of the people which boded ill for the coming months. Throughout January and February the revolutionary press was filled with savage attacks on Narbonne, on his patroness Me. de Staël, on the Queen and the Princess de Lamballe. There were, as always, alarms of a new plan of escape and rumours that the court was instigating speculators to raise the price of bread[1]. Brissot, whose popularity was on the wane, strove to retain his position and to secure an effective tool wherewith to overturn the throne by humouring the passions of the Paris mob, that 'colossal brute' which at this time 'the Girondins introduced into the political arena[2].' Brissot did more than any other prominent politician to encourage the systematic manufacture of pikes, which began in January, and to popularise another significant innovation—the wearing of the red cap of liberty. Meanwhile at the Jacobins—where a famous but fruitless reconciliation scene between Robespierre and Brissot took place on Jan. 20—the orators of the extreme revolutionary party advocated many measures which subsequently became famous as characteristics of the reign of terror[3]. This rapid development of the symptoms of the revolutionary disease in its most virulent form explains fully the alarm of the Feuillant journals and the tragic appeals of the Queen.

As to the ministry, it was absolutely unharmonious. Narbonne and Delessart were in almost permanent disagreement. In fact Narbonne was rapidly becoming isolated. He was ready to go to war, but he did not share Brissot's love of war for its own sake[4]; nor was his ultimate aim that of the Brissotins. In consequence

[1] Extracts in *Hist. Parl.*, XIII. 69 sqq.
[2] Taine, II. 146. A dark picture of France in the early months of 1792 is to be found in Chs. III. and IV. of this volume.
[3] e.g. Robespierre's speech of Feb. 10. *Hist. Parl.*, XIII. 266.
[4] The following passage throws light upon the state of his mind at this time:—" cette guerre que nous avons tant et de si bonnes raisons à craindre est peut-être encore la seule ombre d'espérance qui nous reste." To Biron, Feb. [date not given]. Pallain, p. 89.

his alliance with that party had never been satisfactory. Royalists disliked his liberalism, Feuillants his warlike policy and his rather ostentatious regard for the wishes of the Assembly. His popularity in the country could not easily withstand the sustained and savage assaults of the Jacobin press and his friendship with the now discredited Lafayette. Realising his isolation he decided to stake all on a bold bid for the support of the King. On Feb. 24 he handed in a memoir, in which Louis was invited, as he had so often been, to side honestly with that patriotic constitutional party of which Narbonne regarded himself as the true representative. The republican party, it was urged, was weak; the aristocrats were false friends. The King's inaction encouraged both these extreme parties, as did also his too notorious attachment to men of aristocratic disposition. The anger of Narbonne was particularly fierce against a policy which he attributed, and not without reason, to the King and some of his advisers:—that 'good would result from excess of evil.' Not only was it dishonourable, he wrote, but also highly impolitic; since it tended to alienate that most important class, the selfish bourgeoisie, who sought for nothing but quiet[1]. The whole was an attempt to turn the King against his Feuillant advisers and ministers, who were against all active measures and eager to see the Assembly discredit itself by half ruining the country. It was also aimed at Bertrand de Molleville, the one remaining royalist of the older type in the ministry. But it was a complete failure.

[1] The memoir is in Rœderer's Works, III. 252. Compare Glagau, p. 186 sqq.

For the King and Queen had already adopted once for all the policy that Narbonne denounced. 'The excess of evil' by means of which they hoped to find salvation was the evil of a foreign invasion. In December a fresh plan of escape from Paris had been elaborated by Gustavus of Sweden. This plan—of which the republican press somehow got wind—was laid before the royal family by Fersen in the middle of February[1]. At great risk the faithful servant of the Queen had returned to her palace prison. But he could not persuade the King to fly. 'The fact is,' wrote Fersen, 'that he has scruples about it, having so often promised to stay; for he is an honest man. He has, however, consented, when the armies shall have arrived, to go with some smugglers into the forests and have himself taken prisoner by a detachment of light troops[2].' With this compromise the poor King's honesty was content. After a last long conversation with the Queen Fersen made his way back to Brussels.

The important events in the Assembly during the month of February are few and disconnected. On the 1st Koch, in a long and learned report, justified the action of the Constituent Assembly in the matter of Alsace. The same day a vote of want of confidence in Bertrand de Molleville, the minister of marine, was thrown out. Seeing how well known his royalist views were, the fact is a striking testimony to the moderate, non-republican, opinions of the majority. The decree of accusation against the emigrant princes and their

---

[1] The plan—too long to be inserted here—is in Fersen, I. 279.
[2] Diary for Feb. 14. Fersen, II. 2.

advisers was finally adopted on the 6th; and on the 9th the Assembly declared that, as the nation deserved some compensation for the expense that its defensive measures entailed, the goods of the emigrants should be confiscated. In the course of the month Delessart made further attempts to hold the war parties in check, by protesting that the Elector of Trèves had very completely dispersed the armed French rebels on his territory, and by asserting that the rumours of warlike preparations on the part of the King of Sardinia were false[1].

The Austrian reply to the humble communication (of Jan. 21) by means of which Delessart had tried to stave off the war reached Paris on Feb. 27. The next day Goltz, the Prussian minister, informed Delessart that his court agreed entirely with the principles upon which it was based; and reminded him that France had been repeatedly warned that any violation of German soil would be treated as a declaration of war[2]. The court of Vienna hated two things—war and "the Jacobins." It was in no fit state for war. Men and money alike were short. But it continued to believe that it might crush "the Jacobins" without fighting. Leopold and Kaunitz still enormously exaggerated the influence of the Feuillants, and imagined that all Frenchmen who disliked mob rule and the methods of the extreme democrats shared the Feuillants' contempt for the

---

[1] Attacks on Bertrand had already been made on Dec. 29 and Jan. 13. The decrees etc. here referred to are in *Arch. Parl.*, xxxviii. 66 (Feb. 1), 196 (Feb. 6), 314 (Feb. 9) and 728 (Feb. 21).

[2] *Arch. Parl.*, xxxix. 253. See too Lenz, *Preussische Jahrbücher*, 1894, p. 311.

Assembly and fear of war. They interpreted the news that came to them from Mercy and the Queen somewhat after this fashion. All Frenchmen might be classed under two mutually exclusive categories, "moderates," who wanted monarchy and peace, "Jacobins," who aimed at anarchy and war. After some hesitation the Emperor and his chancellor agreed to despatch the arrogant, bullying, letter that Delessart received on the 27th. It is said, and by one whose information was usually of the best, that the most violent passages in that letter were inserted by the Emperor "with his own pen...with the mistaken hope of intimidating France[1]." The main argument was the work of Kaunitz, and the document of course bore his name.

The whole tone of the letter, when it was not bullying, was querulous. His Imperial Majesty, it began, had already explained twice his action with regard to Marshal Bender and the European concert, but he would repeat his explanations. As to the emigrants it was sufficient to state that they had been discouraged without any advice from France. A concert *had* been set on foot in July '91 and had never been entirely abandoned. Now, since France—on Delessart's own showing—was still in a state of disease, it was only natural that the powers should continue this precaution against infection. As to the cause of the disease:— that was exclusively internal; fear of an emigrant attack had nothing whatever to do with it. All the

---

[1] Sir R. M. Keith to Grenville, Sept. 10, 1792. See Appendix II. The letter itself (dated Feb. 17) is in Vivenot, I. 372, and *Arch. Parl.*, xxxix. 248.

misfortunes of France must be attributed to 'the influence and violence of the republican party.' That party ruled the Assembly, plotted against the King, fostered religious hatreds, favoured anarchy because it suited its own ends. It was that party which had caused an army of 150,000 men to threaten the handful of Austrian troops in the provinces adjoining the French frontier. It had encouraged revolt in the Low Countries. Finally, by its insolent decree of Jan. 25, it had insulted an ancient ally and spoken 'as if the rules and proprieties consecrated by the public law of nations were subject to the whim of a French legislature.' Yet fortunately this offensive republican band was nothing more than a factious minority which the sane body of the nation would in time overcome. Until that triumph of sanity should arrive, Austria and Prussia proposed to act as joint guardians of the peace of Europe.

Together with this long official note Kaunitz forwarded a copy of the circular of Nov. 12, 1791, by which directions for a suspension of the concert had been given, and a separate letter to Delessart. In this letter he again expressed surprise at the demand for further explanations, and spoke in strong terms of the 'pernicious sect' of the Jacobins, whose fatal ascendency was a danger for France and a menace to all Europe.

Delessart was not a little disconcerted and alarmed by the imperial chancellor's method of procedure. Kaunitz had so worded his reply that it had to be read in connection with his previous note of Jan. 5 and with the French minister's communication of the 21st. Now Delessart, wishing to soothe the Assembly, had kept back the former. As to the latter, its very date convicted him of authorising a public falsehood, and its style was not calculated to commend it to men of rather intemperate patriotism[1]. But there was no way of escape; so on the first of March the whole series of documents was read to the Assembly:—the whole series with the exception of one phrase in the minister's own despatch of the 21st to the authorship of which he dare not confess[2]. The reading was often interrupted by fierce murmurs and cries of dissent. Delessart, anxious to remove the bad impression that he had just produced, proceeded to announce his intention of demanding from Austria a frank and explicit repudiation of the concert. Some days later he assured Blumendorf that he approved of Kaunitz' policy. Meanwhile the promised categorical demand had been made at Vienna[3].

At this point two important breaks occur in the story of the movement of France and Austria towards war:—the death of the Emperor and the fall, first of Narbonne, and then of the whole Feuillant ministry. Leopold was only taken ill on Feb. 28; on March 1 he was dead. Though lacking in determination, he had

[1] Above, p. 154.
[2] Compare the copy in Vivenot, I. 384, with that in the *Arch. Parl.*, xxxix. 246. The passage referred to ran as follows (Delessart is speaking of Austria):—"Je supposerai tout ce qu'il y a de plus favorable pour ses armes [qu'elles seront partout victorieuses; que nous serons attaqués de tous côtés et que nous ne pouvons résister nulle part; que les Anglais...s'empareront de nos colonies et anéantiront pour jamais notre marine et notre commerce]. Eh bien! qu'en résultera-t-il?" The words in square brackets were omitted on March 1. This is pointed out by Glagau, p. 196.
[3] Blumendorf to Kaunitz, 17 March. Glagau, p. 198. Noailles to Kaunitz, March 11. Vivenot, I. 415.

succeeded, by means of political suppleness, a readiness to compromise difficult questions, and a real sympathy with the reforming if not with the democratic tendencies of his age, in winning back, within two years, the majority of those provinces whose confidence his brother had forfeited. His sympathy with the French court had been real. But he had intended that his sister should imitate him in swimming with and not against the stream. Nor had he ever been altogether prepared either to subordinate his own interests to hers or to promote the complete restoration of France. A man of many words and many promises, thrown on evil times, he has acquired in certain quarters a reputation for gross duplicity. Yet he made a really serious effort to understand and follow the wishes of the court of Paris; and much, though not all, of his hesitation and apparent indifference may fairly be ascribed to the difficulty of his position and the counsels of his chief adviser. Like the Feuillant party, with whose policy he was so much in sympathy, he had hoped to the last to avoid war; and, although he made preparations for it, it is evident that, a fortnight before the end, he had no intention of attacking and hardly even expected to be attacked[1]. His general foreign policy can not be called successful. How utterly unsuccessful it had been with regard to France was yet to be proved. He had, it is true, steered with wonderful skill at times; yet the Russian alliance, to which his brother had trusted, was almost destroyed, and in its stead there had grown up the unsatisfactory partnership with the hereditary enemy Prussia.

[1] Leopold to Marie Christine, Feb. 18. Schlitter, p. 255.

Francis, his son and successor, was a young man of weak health who hitherto had lived entirely apart from political affairs. His education had been first in the hands of his uncle, then in those of his father. In consequence no one could tell what policy he was likely to adopt, for Joseph and Leopold had agreed on few matters. He had however received a thorough military training under Marshal Laudon, and it soon became evident that he was somewhat more warlike in disposition than his father[1]. At first he naturally followed the advice of his father's ministers. And among the ministers the old chancellor, who had already served three monarchs, still held the foremost place. He had lost some of his influence under Leopold. Many of the measures of that prince's short reign had been adopted against his advice. But he remained influential. Age had increased his vanity, irritability, and arrogance. For years he had never condescended to attend a ministerial council. His opinion was always sent in writing. His powers were failing and he no longer pursued any well-sustained policy[2].

At the moment of Francis' accession Kaunitz was in a state of active irritability. He intended to maintain

---

[1] He was twenty-four years of age. "Perhaps no heir of a crown, arrived at the age of manhood, was ever less known to the higher classes of his father's subjects, or to the corps diplomatique at his court..." Keith to Grenville, March 1, 1792.

[2] See Appendix II. The following extract from a letter of Keith's in Dec. 1791 is typical of many:—"We have observed of late that the Prince never gives credit to anything that hurts his pride or threatens to disturb his indolence; and his language has varied so frequently in regard to French affairs that no solid conclusions are to be drawn from a few of his vapouring phrases."

the Prussian alliance and to bully France into obedience[1]. He was half-disposed to fight, should his strong representations fail. The messages already sent to Paris were to be followed by a joint declaration of the allied powers. This might lead to war. A defensive war, he thought, would suit the allies best, for it would 'put right on their side and authorise them to make conquests, if they could, and to keep them legitimately in compensation for the expenses of the campaign.' 'In short,' he wrote on March 3, 'it seems to me that it is time to oblige France to comply [with the demands of the powers,] or to make war on us, or to justify us in making war on her[2].'

Late in February Bischoffwerder had come to Vienna in response to Leopold's invitation[3]. But the Emperor was already on his death-bed, so that the Prussian favourite for some days was unable to carry on any business. Bischoffwerder was perhaps among all the Prussian and Austrian statesmen the one most eager for an attack on France. He now exerted himself to the utmost to set the lumbering Austrian cabinet in motion. "I am not a little surprised to find," wrote Keith, "that he carries his exhortations to immediate and vigorous measures against France to a much higher pitch than could well have been imagined[4]." Francis

---

[1] Noailles said that Kaunitz, seeing that his masterpiece the treaty of 1756 was to be destroyed, "préféra de la rompre avec éclat." Noailles' account of his embassy at Vienna, written in June '92. Feuillet de Conches, v. 453—70.

[2] Kaunitz, "Considérations sur les affaires françaises," March 3. Vivenot, I. 403.

[3] Above, p. 148.

[4] To Grenville, March 7.

seemed disposed to listen to him. He had already written in the most friendly strain to Bischoffwerder's master; and in his first conference with the favourite he showed himself equally cordial[1]. There were royalists at Vienna who began to hope great things of Francis. Fersen was there; and he promptly announced the favourable symptoms to the Queen. Simolin was there too. His conferences with Leopold had been not altogether satisfactory, those with Kaunitz hitherto entirely unfruitful. Now he wrote hopefully to Catherine and elicited a warm eulogy of the new King of Hungary from that astute sovereign[2].

Before returning to the course of events in France it will be well to give a summary account of the state of Europe at this crisis. The attitude of the Prussian court is reflected in the instructions given to Bischoffwerder[3]. The object of his mission, he was informed, was the arrangement of a plan of action against France. Prussia meant to act in accord with the Emperor, and was not prepared to take any independent action whatever. She was anxious to see the command of the allied armies entrusted to the Duke of Brunswick. The question of indemnity was of first-rate importance. If the powers should succeed in terrifying the French factions into submission by a mere display of force they might call upon France for a money compensation. If

---

[1] The letter in Vivenot, i. 403. For the conference, Ranke, p. 131.

[2] Fersen to the Queen, March 9. Fersen, ii. 202. Simolin's reports in Feuillet de Conches, v. 255 and 308 and Catherine to Francis, April 12. Beer, *Leopold II.*, *Franz II. und Catharina*, p. 172.

[3] Dated, Feb. 18. Ranke, Appendix, p. 278.

war became necessary the compensation might be taken in land. Austria might occupy Alsace and Lorraine provided that, by means of some exchange, the duchies of Jülich and Berg were secured to Prussia. The sixth article of the instructions dealt with the affairs of Poland. Bischoffwerder was to bear in mind that Prussia did not regard herself as bound by her treaty of 1790 to uphold the Polish constitution of 1791. The eighth article had reference to the question of Anspach and Baireuth. The general impression that the whole document produces is that Frederick William and his court were above all things eager to increase the territory of Prussia. At the same time it is evident that simple hatred of democracy and the democrats and sympathy for the wretched state of the French King had made them ready, even anxious, for war. It seems that Frederick William was delighted with the first letter of the new King of Hungary, and was fully prepared to support him in the forthcoming imperial election, in the hope that, as Emperor, Francis would be able to set all Germany in motion against the French[1].

The influence of the emigrants had helped not a little to arouse the warlike impulses of the Prussian King. But Austria detested them, and the French court disowned them. They were still confident, still noisy. Yet, either as politicians or as possible soldiers, their importance was now less than ever. Their allies were few and either poor or distant. In consequence their

---

[1] Frederick William to Bischoffwerder, March 6. Vivenot, I. 406. Cp. Ranke, p. 165.

funds were low. A satisfactory organisation or a complete policy they had never had. Spain had formerly given them some pecuniary assistance; but Spain was lost to them and to the concert by the fall of Count Florida Blanca from power at the end of February. His successor, Aranda, was a liberal, who during a former tenure of office had tried to reform the Spanish universities and limit the power of the Jesuits. He "by no means disapproved of the changes which had taken place in the French constitution." Further he was convinced that it was to the interest of Spain to maintain the French connection. In consequence he was determined to do nothing that might be treated in Paris as an excuse for war[1].

Sweden was remote and poor; yet she had seemed willing to take up the cause of the emigrants, and had condemned the leisurely policy of Leopold. But before the season was sufficiently advanced to enable her to send the long promised fleet Gustavus III. was dead. He was assassinated by Ankarstroem on March 16, and a few days later he died. Whether, had he lived, he could have done anything for the cause of the emigration is doubtful. His brother, the Duke of Sudermania, who acted as regent for the young Gustavus IV., was certainly in no position to meddle with French affairs. Sweden, like Spain, was lost to the emigrants and the concert[2].

[1] Lord St Helens to Lord Grenville, Feb. 28, March 12, April 9, 30, May 27. The quotation is from the letter of May 27, Appendix IV. Cp. Sybel, II. 367, and Sorel in *La Rev. Hist.*, 1879.

[2] Fersen wrote to the Queen in June, "Notre régent est bien pour vous mais il ne peut rien ou peu de chose." Fersen, II. 286.

No statesman any longer supposed that England could be induced to join in the proposed demonstration against France. The ministers were resolutely determined to remain neutral. The leading men of the nation seem, as a body, to have been indifferent to foreign affairs. The trading classes were prosperous, contented, and consequently pacific[1]. Yet, though the English cabinet was not prepared to assist in any coercion of France, that secret pleasure at her discomfiture which can be traced in almost all the correspondence of the period continued to find expression from time to time. "The rapid increase of anarchy" wrote Lord Gower from Paris,..." renders a war of some sort necessary, and if a bankruptcy should insue it is to be hoped that France will not remain entire[2]."

A few enthusiasts and half-informed persons had at times supposed that Catherine of Russia intended to give some substantial help to the cause of monarchy. It had now become apparent that she had no such intention. Ever since the Peace of Sistova she had been urging 'the courts of Vienna and Berlin to entangle themselves in French affairs.' The words are her own; what follows is even more outspoken. 'I want to engage them in these affairs in order to have elbow-room[3]'—elbow-room, that is in Poland. Her plan was known to the statesmen of all three nations. Brissot

---

[1] For the importance attached by diplomatists to these considerations see a letter of March 1792 from Lord Auckland to Lord Henry Spencer. *Auckland Correspondence*, II. 397.

[2] Feb. 10, 1792. Gower, p. 155.

[3] Written in Dec. 1791. Sorel, II. 216-17.

had announced it in Paris on Dec. 29[1]. About a month later Kaunitz sketched it in words that resemble closely those of the Empress herself[2]. Somewhat earlier Goltz, the Prussian minister at St Petersburg, had got sight of an official note containing orders for General Repnin to march on Poland as soon as Turkish affairs should be settled. 'If,' said the Empress, 'Austria and Prussia oppose me, which is likely, I will offer them compensation or a partition[3].' Already, on Jan. 9, Catherine's ministers had signed at Jassy the final treaty with the Porte, and in March she had the free hand for which she had been working. Austria made one last effort to check her advance. Reuss proposed at Berlin (March 10) that the two German powers should unite to support the reformed Polish monarchy[4]. Such a proposal was entirely contrary to the traditional Prussian policy and was therefore but ill received. Three days later a note from St Petersburg reached Berlin. In it Catherine suggested joint action in Polish affairs, and hinted that Austria might also be permitted to assist in the ultimate partition which that soft phrase implied. Frederick William had already expressed the opinion that after all a partition would be 'the most effective means of limiting the power of

---

[1] Above, p. 135.

[2] To Reuss, Jan. 25, 1792. Kaunitz suspects that Russia is only wanting: "bis sein Friede mit der Pforte geschlossen sei—bis Oesterreich und Preussen mit den französischen Händeln beschäftigt wären, um alles in Polen geschehene...wieder über den Haufen zu werfen." Vivenot, I. 358.

[3] Sybel, I. 459—60.

[4] Sybel, I. 462 sqq. Complaints were also made at St. Petersburg in April.

a Polish King'; now he did not hesitate to enter into the bargain that Russia suggested. Thus on the very eve of a war undertaken in the name of monarchy Prussia gave the lie to all her public protestations[1]. Austria, excluded from the transaction, watched with apprehension and jealousy the progress of a policy that she had consistently opposed. Henceforward it was certain that the alliance between the two German powers could not work well and that any action that they might take in French affairs would be at best half-hearted.

Had the Legislative Assembly been able to exercise a more direct control of matters affecting peace and war Kaunitz' February office must have brought about the final rupture. Knowing, as we now do, that he was prepared at all costs to press the demands therein put forward we may safely say that it rendered a declaration of war on the part of France inevitable. But the death of Leopold and the confused relations of parliament, ministry, and court at Paris postponed the declaration for seven stormy weeks. Even within the Assembly there was still some hesitation. It is curious to find that on the day after Delessart's reading of the office, a renewal of the diplomatic committee gave the moderates a majority in that body[2]. Meanwhile in the ministry

---

[1] Sybel's attitude towards the Polish partition contrasts curiously with his criticisms of the Revolution. 'Political necessity' is the excuse he puts forward for Prussia; an excuse never allowed in the case of France. See the bitter criticism in Janet, *Philosophie de la Révolution*, p. 133.

[2] The new members were Lemontey, Daverhoult, Jaucourt, Viénot-Vaublanc, Briche and Ruhl. Mercy reported the election with satisfaction on March 7. Glagau, p. 201.

the breach between Narbonne and these same moderates became every day wider. In February the minister of war had summoned his trusted allies, the three generals, to Paris, to take counsel with him on affairs of state, affairs both military and civil; among others the attitude to be adopted towards the revolutionary party in Belgium[1]. Narbonne was not aware of the relations of his colleagues with the court and the Emperor; but he shared the suspicions of the Gironde and the Jacobins as to the existence of an 'Austrian committee' at the Tuileries. It was becoming evident to him that his attempt to win over the King to his own way of thinking, by means of the memoir presented on Feb. 24, had been a failure. His quarrels with Bertrand continued. Once more he and Lafayette drew nearer to Brissot and the Gironde[2]. The generals supported the minister's complaints as to the policy of the court and its advisers. Narbonne declared that he and Bertrand could not hold office together; the generals pointedly and publicly begged him to remain at his post. But Louis and the Feuillants, disgusted with the interference of Lafayette, glad to get rid of his ally Narbonne, and anxious to thwart the democratic war party, took up the cause of Bertrand. On the ninth of March Narbonne was dismissed. 'People were astonished,' we are told, 'that the King still dared to disgrace anyone[3].'

[1] Lafayette, *Memoirs*, III. 323.

[2] "M. de Narbonne après une querelle...avec M. Bertrand a demandé au roi de renvoyer ce dernier." Pellenc to Mercy, March 5. Glagau, p. 206. On March 8 a fresh attack was made on Bertrand in the Assembly.

[3] Dumont, *Souvenir sur Mirabeau*, p. 371. For the whole inci-

This abrupt collapse of all their plans drove Narbonne and the party of Lafayette further towards the Gironde. The Girondin orators returned to the assault. In the sitting of the 10th the King announced the appointment of De Grave to the ministry of war, and expressed his firm intention of retaining the services of Bertrand[1]. These messages produced an excited debate and an interminable speech from Brissot. He proposed, in the first place, that the King should be invited to fix a date before which the Emperor would be bound to reply to Delessart's last note—that which demanded the abandonment of the concert—and that any minister who might hinder the King from so doing should be held responsible. Secondly, he enumerated the various acts of weakness, duplicity, and treachery of which the minister of foreign affairs had been guilty, and urged that they furnished matter for impeachment[2]. At a later stage in the debate Vergniaud, in the course of a furious onslaught on the court, pointed from the tribune towards the Tuileries and cried:—'I see the windows of the palace where they are plotting the counter-revolution, where they are devising the means whereby to plunge us once again in the horrors of slavery.' Carried away by enthusiasm and suspicion, but yet

dent:—Glagau, p. 206 sqq. Sybel, I. 366 sqq. The Lameth brothers were now the moving force in the Feuillant party. Barnave had withdrawn to his estates in January.

[1] *Arch. Parl.*, xxxix. 528 sqq.

[2] The charges were:—keeping back important documents; bringing dishonour on the nation by his cowardly note of Jan. 21; communicating details of the internal troubles of France to a foreign and hostile minister. Delessart was imprisoned, and murdered in September.

not without just and substantial motives for its action, the Assembly voted the impeachment of Delessart.

The Gironde pressed its victory. On the 11th Pétion, Mayor of Paris, came at the head of a deputation to support the attack on the ministry. On the 12th the six deputy members of the diplomatic committee, originally chosen to fill vacancies caused by illness or the like, were empowered to sit and vote with the regular members. This questionable measure produced the intended effect; the Feuillant majority on the committee no longer existed. The same day Guadet carried the attack on the Feuillants a stage further by denouncing Duport-Dutertre, the minister of justice[1].

A last desperate effort was made by the Feuillants to come to terms with the party of Lafayette. But the disagreement as to the exact measure of constitutional reform to be aimed at, which had always existed, was now further complicated by differences of opinion with regard to the war policy, and by the personal disputes that had arisen in connection with the fall of Narbonne. The only result of the negotiations, in the then warlike state of public opinion, was to increase considerably the following of Lafayette at the expense of that of the Lameths[2]. And meanwhile the Gironde, finding power within its reach, moved heaven and earth to secure it. The party, or group, that goes by that name cannot be described as in any way committed to a definitely

---

[1] *Arch. Parl.*, xxxix. 567 (Oct. 11), 599 (Oct. 12). The deputy members were Schirmer, Hérault de Séchelles, Jean Debry, Pozzo-di-Borgo, Lasource, and Vergniaud.

[2] Glagau, p. 232 sqq. Glagau's account is based largely on Pellenc's MS. letters.

republican system. Its members, however, believed firmly in the existence of a royalist plot, and sought for power, largely it may be for its own sake, but largely also as a means of checking the intrigues of the 'Austrian committee.' For they were oppressed by the incubus of a possible counter-revolution—full of fear and suspicion. We are told that their secret adviser, the Abbé Sieyès, 'in his sinister dreams saw his own head rolling on the floor[1].' They believed that Kaunitz' note of Feb. 17 had been concocted in collusion with Delessart and the King—a belief, after all, not without a measure of foundation. Their journals howled bitterly against the Queen, the court, and the Emperor. On the other hand they feared the rising strength of the Robespierrist Jacobins. Brissot disgusted one of his more moderate friends by admitting that the attack on Delessart was to a large extent a mere party manœuvre; 'for,' said he cynically, 'we need to get a start of the Jacobins[2].'

The savage utterances of the Gironde, the growing ferocity and daring of the Paris mob, the breakdown in the administration of the kingdom, all combined to terrify the court beyond measure. The King, it is said, wept and prayed and brooded over the story of Charles of England, the chances of deposition, and the advisability of abdication[3]. The Queen managed to despatch

[1] Dumont, p. 181. Dumont's account of the Gironde at this time rests on better authority and is altogether more complete than that of Mallet du Pan (*Memoirs*, I. 260), which has been adopted without criticism by Taine, II. 137.

[2] Dumont, p. 378.

[3] Pellenc, March 16. Glagau, p. 240. Beaulieu, *Essais sur la Révolution*, III. 129.

yet another secret agent to Vienna with a desperate appeal for help. The agent, the faithful Goguelat, left Paris on March 13. He was to demand speedy succour —the congress was at last completely abandoned—but to assure the Emperor that 'a counter-revolution, if carried out by the princes, would be more fatal to the King than his actual situation and would make him more of a slave than ever[1].'

To avoid unpopularity and gain time Louis resolved to appoint a ministry, the 'patriotism' of which should be beyond question. He began to negotiate with the leaders of the Gironde. (An acute observer noticed that Brissot's *Patriote français* promptly adopted a more kindly tone in speaking of the Queen[2].) It was impossible for any of the better known members of the party to hold office, so their adherents and nominees were utilised. The department of foreign affairs was given to Dumouriez, that of finance to Clavière, the interior to Roland de la Platière, the navy and colonies to Lacoste. In April the ministry of justice was handed over to Duranthon.

The new ministers by no means entered into office with the set purpose of helping to overthrow the King. On the contrary they are said to have been, without exception, well disposed towards him[3]. But they did

---

[1] Goguelat's letters of commendation from the King and Queen in Feuillet de Conches, v. 322. The words quoted were addressed by Goguelat to Ph. Cobenzl on March 30. Vivenot, I. 430. The court was specially alarmed at this time by a rumour of a plot laid by Sieyès to dethrone the King, try the Queen, and set up their son as King with a regent. The story, which is accepted by Sybel (I. 369), is not very well supported but is in itself not impossible.

[2] Pellenc, in his letter of March 16.   [3] Dumont, p. 386.

not altogether trust him, and they were influenced by the leaders of their party in the Assembly who, bidding for popularity against the Jacobins, advocated the most extreme measures and plunged deeper and deeper into demagogy. On March 19, for example, the Assembly voted an amnesty for the murderers of the Glacière at Avignon. Somewhat later the 'Swiss of Chateauvieux,' who had been sent to the galleys for their share in the military rebellion of Nancy, received an unmerited pardon. The Jacobins made heroes of them and organised the 'Feast of Liberty' in their honour. At the Jacobin club Robespierre continued to denounce the war, the aristocrat generals, and the Gironde who had formed with them an unholy alliance. But the great majority of the Assembly was now in favour of war; so that Robespierre's opposition produced hardly more effect than the last efforts of the Lameths[1].

[1] The Lameths, wrote Pellenc, "quoique mis presque à terre, font des efforts en tout sens pour détourner la guerre." April 2. Glagau, p. 256.

CHAPTER IX.

Dumouriez and the War.

THE month that preceded the outbreak of the war (March—April) might almost be treated, from the present point of view, as part of the career of Dumouriez; so much do the political events of that time group themselves around his policy. De Grave, the war minister, was a man of no remarkable force or ability, whose influence on events is imperceptible[1]. Dumouriez was already over fifty years old. He had served as a soldier in the Seven Years' War. As a member of the secret diplomatic service of Louis XV. he had worked in Italy, Corsica, Spain, Portugal, Poland and Germany. He had been in the Bastille. From the first he saw in the Revolution a means of 'arriving,' and he plunged into it without caring particularly for its principles. At the end of 1791 he held an unimportant military command at Niort. Late in February, 1792, he came to Paris and found the times ripe. He was an old

[1] Dumont, p. 373, with whose estimate historians have generally been content.

servant of the Crown whose name was familiar to many royalists. His bitter hatred of Austria and his friendship with Gensonné served to recommend him to the Gironde. His really great knowledge of foreign affairs marked him as a likely successor to Delessart. On the 16th March he announced his appointment to the Assembly[1].

Dumouriez had been an admirer and personal friend of Favier. He was devoted to the political system that Favier had advocated[2]. When he came into office the policy which he intended to adopt was already worked out in all its details. He felt certain that the German powers intended to treat France as a second Poland. He would prove to them that she was still a force in Europe. The war game with Austria should begin with the traditional opening—an attack on the Low Countries. Those provinces were to be overrun and revolutionized. This move was particularly desirable at the moment because the state of the French finances necessitated the support of her armies by some conquered district. That he might be able to concentrate all the force of the nation in this one assault on the old enemy, it was Dumouriez' intention to isolate Austria, by inducing all other powers to observe a strict neutrality during the coming struggle. He was convinced that Prussia, 'the natural ally,' the home of men who had known Frederick, would never act in unison with the Hapsburg and might be detached from her new friend.

---

[1] For his early career see his *Memoirs*, Vols. I., II., and the critical appreciations of M. Sorel, in the *Rev. des Deux Mondes*, 1884, and his history, II. 403 sqq.

[2] Above, p. 6.

The assumption was justified by the past and was to be confirmed in the future. But for the time being it was mistaken. Dumouriez, the exponent of a traditional diplomacy, hardly realised that the most powerful force which was driving Prussia towards war was not love of Austria, nor even land-hunger. It was the Revolution itself that the war party at Potsdam detested.

The first act of the new minister was to despatch an agent to stir up the Belgians[1]. The agent was Maret, the future Duke of Bassano. François Custine had been acting as *chargé d'affaires* at Berlin since the discomfiture of Ségur. On the eighteenth Dumouriez wrote to him, appointed him minister plenipotentiary, and ordered him to ascertain the attitude of the Prussian court towards the new system. To aid, and it may be to watch, Custine certain subordinate agents were sent from Paris. One of these, by name Benoît, was charged with a very delicate mission. Dumouriez, the nominee of the Gironde, was secretly attached to the policy of Narbonne. He intended, should a suitable opportunity present itself, to restore the influence of the Crown. It was this intention that Benoît was instructed to explain at Berlin. He received a patient hearing, but his proposals were not sufficiently definite to elicit any formal response[2]. Custine met with no success. The

---

[1] Details from Sorel, as above.

[2] Sybel, I. 377. Benoît left Berlin, saying:—'The last word is not yet spoken, I will return when and whither you wish; perhaps it will be well for our negotiations that a Prussian army should be in France.' This was after all hope of the immediate neutrality of Prussia had been abandoned. The main interest of the story lies in its relation to the dealings of Dumouriez with Prussia after Valmy.

influence of Bischoffwerder, the emigrants, and the royal mistresses proved too strong for him. The court was terrified at the news of the assassination of Gustavus of Sweden, which it regarded as the outcome of some Jacobin intrigue. The further news of the amnesty granted to the criminals of Avignon confirmed Frederick William in his conviction, that the policy of the party for which Custine was pleading was one of murder and devastation. Even had this not been the case the Prussian negotiations with Vienna were now much too far advanced to allow of any retreat. On April 6 Custine was officially informed that the King had nothing to say to him and the attempt to break Prussia from Austria had failed.

Still more important in Dumouriez' eyes than the Prussian negotiation was a scheme for securing from England not merely a declaration of neutrality—which had already been promised—but in addition some assurance of friendship and perhaps even of prospective alliance. Could England's friendship be secured, all danger either from Spain or Holland would be at an end. And when the war with Austria was over, the two great constitutional monarchies of the West might together dictate to Europe and monopolise the ocean commerce of the world. So dreamed Dumouriez. The plan was not new. It was that advocated by Talleyrand, and to Talleyrand its execution was now intrusted. War had already been declared when the embassy left Paris; but some account of the policy from which such great things were hoped will not be out of place here[1].

---

[1] Talleyrand returned from his first mission (above p. 142) on March 10; he set out again on April 23. He carried a confidential

The great difficulty to be overcome arose from England's jealous guardianship of the Low Countries. Consequently the first task of the French diplomatists was to explain that their government had no intention of absorbing the Belgian provinces; that it was attacking them merely for reasons of military expediency[1]. It was hoped that England would assent ultimately to the establishment of a Belgian federal republic, and, in the meantime, would not look with too unfavourable an eye on the northern advance of the French. For the more remote future Dumouriez formed vast designs. A new Anglo-French treaty of commerce was to be firmly established; together the two powers were to effect the liberation of the Spanish colonies of the West; together they were to enjoy the opportunities for great commercial undertakings to which such a measure would lead; finally, they were to uphold constitutional liberty and guarantee the peace of Europe. What England thought of all this does not now concern us. It is sufficient to endorse M. Sorel's very just observation that 'these were no vulgar notions, no chimerical designs.'

The Northern powers were no longer to be feared. Sweden had retired, so to speak, from active life, and Dumouriez knew the undercurrents of European diplo-

letter from Louis to George III. which closed with the words—"j'ajouterai, que réunis, nous devons commander la paix à l'Europe." Pallain, p. 215. The letter would be the work of Dumouriez. Probably the King disapproved of it; for in February "a confidential person" had desired Morris to assure Washington that the French court did not sympathise with the earlier overtures to England. Morris, I. 512.

[1] Réflexions pour la Négociation d'Angleterre en cas de Guerre, March 30. Pallain, p. 172.

macy too well to be imposed upon by the apparent drift of Catherine's policy. To ensure the neutrality of Spain, the minister trusted rather to the inquietudes of Aranda and the indirect influence of England than to any official negotiations. The studied rudeness with which the court of Madrid received the new French agent Bourgoing can consequently have caused little alarm in Paris. Sardinia was to be bought off at the expense of the house of Hapsburg. In the instructions for Sémonville, which were drawn up on April 6, an exchange of Savoy and Nice against the Milanese was suggested. But Sardinia was the only state that refused a hearing to the agents of the new policy. The King became violent at the bare mention of Sémonville's visit, and gave orders for his detention at the French frontier on the pretext of an irregularity in his passports[1].

There remained the various minor princes of the Empire. Their support would be of inestimable value to France; for if by any means the election of Francis to the imperial throne could be prevented or postponed, Austria would be in no position to attack and might even be partially incapacitated for defence[2]. The Rhenish Electors also would fall an easy prey, so long as there was no Emperor to whom they could appeal for help. Even if it proved impossible to exclude the Hapsburgs from the post that had come to be regarded

---

[1] April 19. A second unsuccessful attempt to win Sardinia was made in July.

[2] Talleyrand wrote to Biron—March 21—that the postponement of the election was of the utmost importance. "Il faut," he added, "exciter toutes les ambitions en Allemagne." Pallain, p. 121.

as almost theirs of right, there remained the chance of securing the neutrality of the Empire in the coming war. Dumouriez therefore filled Germany with his agents. Those courts—such as Zweibrücken—which had suffered losses in Alsace were to be soothed with promises of fair compensation or persuaded to accept the indemnity already offered. Others, that had specific grievances against Austria, might be induced to seize an opportunity of thwarting her. Bavaria in particular, whose lands the statesmen of Vienna had long lusted after, might be expected to give a ready hearing to the plans of the French minister. The movements of the Empire were as notoriously dilatory as its petty princes were self-seeking, so that this part of Dumouriez' great scheme had every chance of success. And indeed this part alone proved unmistakeably successful.

Whilst his subordinates were negotiating and intriguing in all the capitals of Europe, in Paris Dumouriez was toiling to win the support of the various parties in the government, the Assembly, and the city. The court was to all appearance with him. That Louis was in favour of a war of aggression cannot be confidently affirmed. True he had consented in February to Fersen's scheme for an invasion. But that character which his brother had once compared to 'oiled billiard-balls that one tries in vain to hold together' was capable of extraordinary revulsions[1]. His love of peace and his religious horror of bloodshed overcame almost periodically all other sentiments. But the letters of

---

[1] The Count of Provence to Lamarck, Oct. 1789. Bacourt, I. 124.

Marie Antoinette may be taken as the best record of the aims and policy of the Tuileries. There is no doubt that her opinion usually prevailed over that of her husband; and what that opinion was the letters show clearly enough. Writing to Mercy on March 2, she gave a suggestive hint as to what appeared to her the reforms essential to any re-establishment of the royal authority:—'the multiplicity of powers, popular elections, and, in short, the force given to the people' must go[1]. That the throne might endure until the coalition was ready to act, and that an emigrant invasion might be anticipated, she favoured the aggressive policy of Dumouriez. 'Our position,' she wrote on March 30, 'is still frightful, but yet less dangerous if it is we who attack[2].' Four days earlier she had told Mercy that the council of ministers had just agreed to an attack on the Low Countries by way of Liège and another on the territories of the King of Sardinia in Savoy[3]. Her provocation was great; it is hard to call her a traitor; but if her enemies in Paris suspected and denounced her treachery they very certainly cannot be blamed.

Dumouriez hardly received from his colleagues the same encouragement that was given him by the court. Roland and Clavière, both men of moderate ability and little daring, were fearful of incurring the heavy responsibility connected with a declaration of war. De Grave was equally apprehensive—and with abundant reason—of the possible utter breakdown of the military organ-

[1] Arneth, p. 254.
[2] Fersen, II. 220.
[3] March 26, Arneth, p. 259. On March 30 she told Fersen that she had warned the court of Turin three weeks earlier.

ization[1]. But the party which had carried them to power was stronger than they, and they bowed to it. Nothing checked the hysterical excitement and the morbid imaginings of the Gironde; nothing turned aside the wild flood of their declamation. Brissot, involved more closely week by week in the struggle with Robespierre at the Jacobins[2], looked upon war as the cure of every ill. War would save France, his party, himself. One extraordinary story of the man's state of mind is preserved by Etienne Dumont:—as a means of winning a surprise vote of war from the Assembly, he actually proposed that some bands of soldiers, disguised as Uhlans, should be sent to raid the French frontier villages[3].

Robespierre, with the extreme Jacobins and those who sympathised with them, continued to lay stress on the weak points of the war policy. Their wide sweeping suspicions could not fail to fasten on the minister. When, on March 19, Dumouriez, wearing the red cap of liberty, declared before the club that he would either secure a solid peace or wage a decisive war, the applause of the members was stilled by Collot d'Herbois and Robespierre himself. They urged that it was well not to applaud until words had begotten acts, and that a minister was not, merely by reason of his station, more deserving of acclamation from free men than were tried patriots of the unofficial sort. To this Dumouriez

[1] Dumont, p. 418, mentions Condorcet, along with Roland, Clavière, and De Grave, among those who voted for war without approving of it.

[2] See March and April debates. *Hist. Parl.*, XIII. and XIV.

[3] Dumont, p. 311.

replied by throwing himself into the arms of his critic; but, throughout the Revolution, such scenes were more often the witnesses of an existing disagreement than pledges of future harmony[1]. To the last these orators of the extreme democratic party retained their position:— criticising, or condemning, the war, the court that desired it, the generals to whom its conduct was to be intrusted, and the directing minister.

Of the Feuillant leaders nothing further need be said. Their day was past. Lafayette and his adherents had profited nothing by a change of ministry which they had contributed to bring about. But they showed no outward signs of ill-feeling. They knew Dumouriez and were on the best of terms with him. He was delighted to receive the support and advice of such an important group[2]. The reality of the coalition between the 'Fayettists' and the Gironde is easily proved. The latter defended Narbonne, both in the Assembly and the press, against the attacks of the extreme Jacobins[3]. The Jacobins, in their denunciations of Brissot, repeatedly accused him of complicity with Lafayette, the bloody monster of the massacre of the Champ de Mars.

The great majority of all parties was undoubtedly for the time being with Dumouriez. Encouraged by this general approval, he began to rival Kaunitz in the matter of plain speaking and even to adopt the bullying tone of the Austrian chancellor. His first despatch to Vienna—dated March 19—was, however, somewhat

---

[1] *Hist. Parl.*, XIII. 402 sqq.

[2] Glagau, p. 247. (A letter of Pellenc, dated April 2.) See too Gower, March 23, p. 163.

[3] *Arch. Parl.*, XLI. 85, and Glagau, p. 250.

cautious. He was not as yet certain of the effect produced by the death of Leopold and wished to sound the Austrian court[1]. He referred, rather in the manner of Delessart, to the unwisdom and probably unprofitable nature of any attack on France; but he concluded with a firm request for immediate disarmament and the repudiation of that 'political monster' the concert. He was not aware that Kaunitz and the Austrian cabinet intended to stand by the declaration of Feb. 17. At Vienna it was still "the general hope, as well as wish, to see matters amicably adjusted with France[2]," but the adjustment was sought by means of a suppression of "the Jacobins."

On the 11th of March Noailles had communicated to Kaunitz Delessart's last message—that in which a formal repudiation of the concert had been first demanded[3]. Such a demand increased the irritation of the chancellor. A week later he had completed his reply. How much assistance he received from his colleagues or from the new King does not appear. The English Ambassador noticed that the language of this document, "though it be intended to prevent hostilities on the part of France, may in the actual state of parties in the National Assembly produce a contrary effect[4]."

[1] The letter is in *Arch. Parl.*, XLI. 605. The news of Leopold's death had made business men in Paris hope for peace. On the Bourse paper rose 15 p.c. Sybel, I. 368.

[2] So wrote Keith to Grenville, March 7.

[3] Vivenot, I. 415. Above, p. 167.

[4] Keith to Grenville, March 21. Keith shrewdly remarks, "I have not concealed from him [the Prussian ambassador] a notion which has taken root in my mind that the very repeated and violent attacks made by the Austrian ministry on the club of the Jacobins

In Paris it was regarded, on its arrival, as the most violent of all Kaunitz' official despatches[1]. No further explanation, it was stated, would be given by Austria; for none was needed. Nothing whatever had been done within the Austrian dominions to justify France in complaining of military preparations; in fact no military preparations properly so called had been made. The new King of Hungary fully accepted his father's policy. He had not the least intention of abandoning the concert. How could he be expected to do so, how could the concert cease, until France should have complied with the demands that it had been created to enforce? The delay in compliance was due to the 'sanguinary and furious' faction of the Jacobins. In conclusion Kaunitz insinuated that the French nation, should it find itself unable to grapple with this satanic faction, might welcome the friendly help of the powers. He was arguing on the Feuillant hypothesis. When his argument was read to the excited Assembly (March 29) the Feuillants were already fallen. The impression which the despatch produced may be imagined. It sounded like a Rehoboam's declaration from the young King of Hungary.

A second letter to Noailles had already left Paris. It is dated March 27, and shows a distinct advance in tone when compared with that of the 19th. Dumouriez demands a prompt and precise reply to the interrogations of the French government. Nothing else will

have been suggested by the French King and through Count Mercy to this court."

[1] Pellenc, March 31. Glagau, p. 262. The despatch itself, dated March 18, is in Vivenot, I. 425.

appease the just indignation of France. Unless the matter is satisfactorily decided before the middle of April she must resort to the sternest measures[1].

Noailles regarded the Austrian despatch of the 18th as final; it was indeed intended to be so. He consequently made no attempt to carry out the instructions contained in Dumouriez' letter of the 19th, which reached Vienna in the last days of March. Writing to the minister on the 1st of April he explained his conduct:—nothing more could be done; he begged for leave to retire; he himself had advised Kaunitz to make no reference in his official correspondence to the internal affairs of France; Dumouriez was well aware how little effect that advice had produced; France could not stoop to further negotiations with the man who had signed the despatch of the 18th and who was actually making that document public in Vienna[2]. But on the receipt of Dumouriez' second instructions Noailles humbled himself to make one last effort. He visited the vice-chancellor Cobenzl, who was by this time aware of the fall of the Feuillants, and explained the French demands. Cobenzl assured him that the King of Hungary had no wish to interfere in the internal affairs of France; but that he was determined to obtain justice for the Princes of Alsace and the Pope, and to secure some guarantee of strong government in France, since that was essential for the safety of Europe. Two days later—April 7—Cobenzl remarked further that the despatch of March 18th must be regarded as

[1] *Arch. Parl.*, XLI. 605.
[2] Noailles wrote in this strain both privately and officially. *Arch. Parl.*, XLI. 605.

Austria's sole and final answer to all the questions recently put to her[1].

Yet the Austrian cabinet was not altogether so harmonious and confident as it wished to appear. Under the influence of Bischoffwerder and his master the young King, and certain of his inner circle, were inclining not only towards war but towards a war of aggression. Bischoffwerder carried on his negotiations behind Kaunitz' back; for the old chancellor, imperious though he was, had no wish to bear the responsibility of an invasion of France. Perhaps his experience had taught him that offensive operations are not often carried on successfully by a coalition. Certainly he had no wish to restore France to any sort of prosperity. He was anxious only to keep her from doing injury to the interests of the other powers; and he believed that the threats of an armed concert would suffice to bring her to reason. Yet he knew that a general concert was out of the question; and he was beginning to fear lest some even of the German states should refuse to fall in with his ideas. Apparently the intrigues of Dumouriez at the German courts were becoming known; for on April 13 Kaunitz made a desperate attempt to induce the whole Empire to take action against France. He wrote to the various circles of the Empire in an exaggerated style, pointing out that the French barbarian hordes were eager to treat all neighbouring lands as their predecessors had treated the Palatinate in the days of Louis XIV[2].

---

[1] *Arch. Parl.*, XLII. 189. Noailles had received Dumouriez' ultimatum of March 27 on April 4. Dumouriez received the replies—April 5 and 7—on April 14 and 15.   [2] Vivenot, I. 453.

The excitement aroused in Paris by the reading of the March office increased in the early days of April. The extreme Jacobins and their adherents were preparing the demonstration in honour of the Swiss of Chateauvieux. That demonstration was used as an opportunity for displaying the immense force of the party. By a small majority the Assembly had decided to admit the liberated Swiss to the sitting of April 9th. With them poured in a mob of national guards and a mixed multitude of women and children. The orator of the Faubourg St. Antoine came brandishing a pike to announce that ten thousand such were already in the hands of the citizens of Paris[1]. From the provinces came the old monotonous story of disorder and alarm. From the army Luckner reported a lamentable deficiency of supplies and even of men[2]. It is not surprising that, when Dumouriez made public his despatches of March 19 and 27 and the refusal of Noailles to conduct further negotiations, the Assembly, irritated by the apparent disobedience of the ambassador, proceeded to impeach him out of hand. However, when the report of his last interview with Cobenzl was made known, the decree of impeachment was promptly rescinded. This was on the 19th of April[3].

The final and decisive step, so far as the King and his ministers were concerned, had already been taken. At the council of ministers held on April 16, Dumouriez had read a rather wordy report on the situation. Two

---

[1] The majority referred to was 281 to 265. The proceedings of the 9th are in *Arch. Parl.*, XLI. 389.

[2] In a letter read on April 10. *Arch. Parl.*, XLI. 424.

[3] The two decrees are in *Arch. Parl.*, XLI. 610, and XLII. 175.

things, he said, were always offensive to tyrants, a monarch who loves the law and a people that has ceased to be servile. Hatred of these two things accounted for the threatening attitude of Austria. He went on to speak of Austria's misuse of the treaty of 1756; of her attempt to stir up Gustavus of Sweden and the 'successor of the immortal Frederick' against France; of her persistent adherence to the concert scheme; and of her anxiety to set the French nation against its King[1]. After criticising severely the orders given to Marshal Bender and the note of Feb. 17, he drew his conclusions thus. The treaty of 1756 had obviously been broken. The attempt to form a concert was an act of hostility. The refusal to reply to the representations of France amounted to a declaration of war. Noailles must be at once recalled. Finally Dumouriez proposed that, in accordance with the constitution, the King should formally invite the Assembly to declare war on the King of Hungary[2]. The council was unanimously in favour of this proposal and Louis gave his assent. That night Dumouriez wrote to Biron, 'You understand, my friend, that it is our dear ally Austria alone that we declare our enemy; taking care to separate her from the other powers which form what is called the concert, that is to say an infernal league against us[3].'

On the 20th the King, surrounded by his ministers,

---

[1] Dumouriez rightly observed that Kaunitz, in addressing 'the French Government' and not 'the King of the French,' was insulting both King and nation and attempting to separate their interests.

[2] *Arch. Parl.*, XLII. 189 sqq.

[3] Pallain, p. 214.

entered the Assembly, 'to converse with it,' as he said, 'concerning one of the most important matters with which its attention could be occupied.' After Dumouriez had read his report to the council, the King announced that he and his advisers had given their assent thereto :—' All would rather have war than see the dignity of the French people outraged and the National Assembly menaced. It has been my duty hitherto to exhaust every means of maintaining peace; I come to-day, according to the letter of the constitution, to propose to the Assembly war against the King of Hungary and Bohemia.' The President, in the name of his colleagues, promised to give his Majesty's proposal the very serious consideration that it deserved. Louis left the hall 'amid some applause and cries of Vive le roi.'

In the evening sitting, when the discussion began, the united war parties carried all before them. A few speakers, such as Becquet and Dumas, pleaded that peace was necessary for the maintenance of the new constitution; that an attack on Brabant would probably lead to a general European war; that the concert was defensive and that its demands could be readily satisfied. Murmurs and interruptions came from every side and they could barely secure a hearing. But when Condorcet rose to read a declaration justifying the war, a declaration that began with the words ' every nation has the power to make laws for itself and the inalienable right to change them at will,' he was received with wild applause. The applause only became more furious when Vergniaud proposed that the French people should cry aloud to Europe—' we will live free or die; the whole constitution, without modification, or death.' Before the sitting closed war had been declared. The vote was almost unanimous. In the long preamble to the final resolution mention was made of the protection afforded by Austria to the French rebels, the formation and continuance of the concert, the promise of support to the Alsatian princes, the attempt to divide France against itself, and the refusal to disarm or resume negotiations. The Assembly declared that France was forced to take up arms in self-defence. She remained true to the principle that wars of conquest and wars against liberty were iniquitous. In the coming contest she was prepared to wage war with all possible humanity, and to welcome all who might seek to escape from tyranny by uniting themselves to a free people[1].

On April 29 Noailles received orders to leave Vienna. The day before the attack on Belgium had begun in a manner altogether disastrous for France. A French column marching against Tournai was seized with panic at the sight of a small body of Austrian cavalry, fled, and in its flight murdered Dillon, its general. On the first of May Schulenburg told Custine that Prussia intended to fight. So early was the collapse of one section of his great scheme made known to Dumouriez. Had he been less completely under the influence of diplomatic tradition he might before this have hit upon the painful truth:—that Prussia, so far from favouring France, had for some time been pushing the court of Vienna into an offensive war.

[1] *Arch. Parl.*, XLII. 189 sqq.

CHAPTER X.

THE WAR AND THE INVASION.

It would be possible to close the story of the causes of the war of 1792 with the declaration of April 20; but it will be well to carry the narrative somewhat further and sketch the events that affected the invasion of France by the allies. And that for two reasons. The invasion, and not the first futile attack of the French on the Low Countries, is the episode which makes the first year of the revolutionary wars memorable; for had Austria and Prussia contented themselves with carrying on a mere defensive war, or had they been ready to attack in May, the whole history of the Revolution might have been other than it is. Further, the scheme for an invasion was developed, and actually adopted, by the allied courts before news of the French declaration reached them. Therefore it is impossible to treat the invasion as a mere result of the declaration; for invasion and declaration alike were the results of the whole series of causes that brought about the war.

The Austro-Prussian alliance of February was ostensibly defensive; but it was understood at the time of its conclusion that the joint representations at Paris, which were its direct outcome, would very probably lead to war. The character of the war would depend on the attitude of the democrats on hearing of the preparations of the allies. Should the democrats prove obstinate the invasion, and even the dismemberment, of France might become necessary. At Berlin the King and the predominant party in the ministry had been advocating a war of aggression since the beginning of the year. The King was bent on war both because he hated the Revolution and because he saw in it an opportunity of extending his territory. The way in which the Dutch and Belgian revolutions had collapsed at the mere approach of Prussian or Austrian troops encouraged the assumption that no serious effort would be necessary to overthrow the Parisian mob and the demagogues who hounded it on[1]. There was a party in the ministry at Berlin that disliked the policy of aggression; but it was fear of Austria and of the possibly unprofitable character of the war, rather than regard to the fate of France, upon which this dislike was based[2]. The two ministers to whom the negotiations with Austria after the French declaration were entrusted, Haugwitz and Schulenburg, had no great confidence in the Austrian 'system;' but they prepared

---

[1] As Catherine of Russia wrote:—"L'exemple de la Belgique a démontré combien il faut compter sur la résistance d'une anarchie; c'est certainement de toutes les résistances celle qui en a le moins." Larivière, *Catherine II. et la Rév. Franç.* p. 369.

[2] Ranke, p. 159. Sybel, I. 467.

to carry out their master's orders and to turn the coming war to the profit of Prussia. Schulenburg, wrote Custine to Dumouriez,—speaking of his conversation with the minister on May 1,—'did not conceal that indifference as to our future existence, and as to the calamities that await us after a counter-revolution; that the desire of vengeance for the past, and that of securing the tranquillity of governments for the future, were the sole motives of their present resolutions.' Eight days later, at the moment of quitting his post, Custine wrote:—'The court of Berlin is to-day the one which most desires the rapidity and irresistibility of the expedition against France[1].'

The eagerness of the Prussian court for an aggressive war had one great obstacle to overcome at Vienna, the opposition of Prince Kaunitz. Since the accession of Francis, Bischoffwerder had carried out his instructions with the utmost zeal—urging "war, immediate and offensive war," in season and out of season[2]. Kaunitz had all along confidently expected that the Jacobins would submit to his threats; and he was prepared to come to terms with France as soon as they showed signs of so doing. For the French monarchy and its interests he was not concerned. It was even rumoured that after the accession of Francis, Kaunitz opined "that the engagements of Leopold as head of the German Empire, were not binding on his successor as King of Hungary, and that it was consistent with prudence and sound policy that his Apostolic Majesty should keep every door open to amicable accommodation

[1] Sorel, II. 446, 450.
[2] Keith to Grenville, Sept. 10. See Appendix II.

with France[1]." This being so, Bischoffwerder's task was a hard one, and though he abstained from addressing himself to Kaunitz he had still the utmost difficulty in traversing the chancellor's case.

As a result of the division of opinion and the dislike for war at Vienna, the various threats sent to Paris had not been accompanied by any very serious military preparations. There had been talk of mobilisation in January, but it was only on April 13 that the first definite orders were given for the march of additional troops towards the Rhine[2]. There were already some forty thousand men in the Low Countries, but from this number had to be subtracted all the garrison troops, so that no very considerable force was in readiness should the war become aggressive[3]. In March Bischoffwerder—following his instructions—had proposed that the command of the allied troops should be confided to the Duke of Brunswick. This suggestion was well received by Francis, who was rapidly adopting the Prussian view of the coming war. Early in April he wrote to Frederick William to discuss the plan of campaign and invited Brunswick to accept the post of commander-in-chief[4]. His conduct was highly appreciated at Berlin.

Meanwhile Kaunitz began to take more interest than formerly in the military preparations, but he gave no definite assent to the scheme of invasion. He was

---

[1] See Appendix II.
[2] Ranke, p. 167.
[3] Sybel, I. 384.
[4] Vivenot, I. 433, 434, 460. Francis' two letters are of April 3; Frederick William's reply, April 17.

busy reviving the European concert:—perhaps trying to create it would be a safer phrase. The 'two essential bases' of the concert were to be 'very considerable forces and the greatest moderation in demands.' Seeing that he was not very sanguine as to the stability of the Prussian alliance, one can hardly suppose that he expected much from the concert, which had never yet existed except on paper, in spite of the freedom with which references to it had been bandied between Paris and Vienna[1]. It was on April 21 that he presented to the representatives of the various foreign courts a document in which he proposed the resumption of the active concert. During the following week copies of an explanatory memoir were forwarded to the different capitals. Kaunitz sketched the history of his previous efforts and pointed to their success, in July 1791, in securing the temporary safety of the French monarchy. It was now clear, he added, that as the overthrow of the King was the object of the extreme party in France the suspension of the concert was no longer expedient. There could be no doubt that it was the duty of Europe to interest itself in the fate of Louis XVI.; although a complete counter-revolution was not to be thought of[2]. It is clear that Kaunitz had no intention of advocating extreme measures.

[1] Kaunitz to Reuss, April 13; to L. Cobenzl, April 12; and to Stadion, April 18. Vivenot, I. 451, 439, 464.

[2] Vivenot, II. 1 sqq. Sybel lays stress on the fact that France attacked Austria for adhering to a concert which did not exist on April 20. But Kaunitz had assumed its existence in most of his despatches and had made no secret of his intention to utilise it for the amendment of the French constitution.

Prussia had for some time been waiting anxiously for a definite expression of opinion from Vienna on the question of aggressive war. The notion of purely defensive measures was distasteful to Frederick William and his advisers. They felt probably that a defensive war would profit them little; for no Prussian lands marched with those of France, and they had no mind to defend Austrian territory without either helping Louis XVI. or benefitting Prussia directly. Accordingly Reuss reported to his court that until Prussia saw some prospect of the adoption of an aggressive system she would not begin to put her troops in motion. This called for some definite decision on the part of Austria. The final discussion of this most important point took place at a ministerial conference on Saturday, April 28. The news of the declaration of war had not yet reached Vienna. Kaunitz sent to the conference in writing a strong statement of his reasons for objecting to an offensive war. But his opinion was not adopted; we are told that it "was treated by several of the cabinet counsellors as the effect of age and timidity." The counsel of Bischoffwerder won the day, and it was decided that should the King of Prussia see fit to adopt the policy of presenting a manifesto to the French, as soon as the allied armies were in position, and of following up that manifesto—if it produced no effect—by an invasion, he might expect the entire concurrence of the King of Hungary[1].

On hearing of this decision the Prussian ambassador

---

[1] Report of the conference: Vivenot, II. 10; with additional details from Keith's despatches of May 2 and Sept. 10. See Appendix II.

at Vienna promptly despatched a messenger to his court. But before the official report of the conference had been sent to the Prince of Reuss, and on the very day after the conference took place, news of the French declaration of war reached Vienna. The news was of importance. It arrived, as Sir Robert Keith wrote on May 2, "in the precise nick of time to furnish an opportunity to this court of throwing the whole odium of aggression, and an offensive war, on the French nation." "From that moment," he wrote on another occasion, "the madness as well as injustice of French *aggression* were in every mouth, and not a whisper was heard of the violent resolutions so lately adopted in this cabinet."

The Prince of Hohenlohe-Kirchberg hurried to Berlin in the beginning of May to make arrangements for the coming campaign. He found the Prussian Court eager to meet his proposals, as was to be expected. On the 13th, at Sans Souci, Frederick William and his council discussed with him the plan of invasion[1]. It was finally decided that the command of the allied forces should be entrusted to the Duke of Brunswick. Forty-two thousand Prussians were to assemble at Coblence and move on Paris by way of Luxemburg, Longwy, and Verdun. On the Meuse the Austrian army from Belgium was to join them. A second Austrian corps, advancing from the Breisgau, was to operate on the left of the main army along the Saar and the Moselle; whilst a detachment of emigrant troops was to create a diversion by crossing the Rhine in the neighbourhood of Bâle.

[1] Ranke, p. 175. Sybel, I. 473.

The emigrants had expected greater things. Just before the outbreak of the war they seem to have fancied, to judge by a letter written by the Count of Vaudreuil to Artois on April 19, that the allies would probably assume the part of mere auxiliaries to their army. The news of the paltry rôle assigned to them in the plan of campaign caused the liveliest disgust at Coblence[1]. That rôle would probably have been still more paltry had not Prussia and Austria been anxious to conciliate Catherine of Russia, who patronised the princes. The latter could not imagine that the Prussian cabinet—excluding perhaps Bischoffwerder and the King—cared almost as little for their fate as for that of Louis, provided that the democrats were crushed and some compensation was secured.

Late in May the Prussian troops began to gather at Magdeburg; early in June they were moving towards the Rhine. But Austria hung back. Francis wished to be crowned Emperor; his advisers were anxious to settle the question of a territorial indemnity before plunging into the thick of the war; his armies were not so mobile as those of Prussia. Prussia was therefore given to understand that her ally could not join in the attack until the latter part of July. Nor was this the only discouraging circumstance. It soon became evident once more that nothing was to be expected from the concert scheme. Spain, under the influence of Aranda and somewhat in dread of incurring English displeasure, would not move. England pursued her former course, observing and criticising but not acting. Talleyrand

[1] Provence and Artois to Catherine, May 9 and 19. Feuillet de Conches, vi. 39, 50.

had arrived in London at the end of April, with no official post—for Chauvelin was the nominal ambassador—but charged, in conjunction with Duroveray, with the delicate negotiation that the minister had planned. Grenville received him with politeness, but with no warmth. The court and London society treated him as a sort of political leper. "I am very happy, however," wrote King George, "M. de Talleyrand and De Roveray may be directed by the French Secretary of State to Lord Grenville; that they have no credence to me and therefore may receive the contempt their characters entitle them to[1]." The proclamation of neutrality that was issued on May 25 by the English ministry proved that England would neither have any dealings with the concert nor listen to the advances of Dumouriez. The special appeal that Kaunitz had made to the Empire also miscarried. On this field alone was the diplomacy of Dumouriez altogether successful. To the great disgust of Austria and Prussia, the minor states of Germany, led by Hanover refused to take any part whatever in the coming struggle. The one exception was Hesse-Cassel, whose prince, proud of that little army which he was wont to let out on hire to other powers, promised to join the invasion with some five or six thousand men[2].

The utter failure of the French attack on Belgium gave the allies every reason to anticipate an easy triumph, in spite of the indifference of the other great

[1] To Grenville, April 28. *Dropmore Papers*, II. 267. See also Pallain, p. 250, and Dumont, *Souvenir sur Mirabeau*, Chs. XXI. and XXII.

[2] Vivenot, II. 57. Sybel, I. 476.

powers. During the month of May and the early part of June a few minor skirmishes resulted in successes for the French, but the plan for a speedy conquest of the Low Countries failed most lamentably[1]. Lafayette, who was in charge of one of the armies, was constantly looking back at Paris[2]. There the first bad news increased the violence of the Gironde. It seemed to confirm the prophecy of Robespierre that nothing would be well until the enemies at home had been crushed. The attacks on the Queen and the 'Austrian committee' were taken up with fresh vigour and fresh bitterness.

The court watched the play of parties in Paris and the growing force of the ultra-Jacobin mob with the utmost alarm. On the last day of April, Marie Antoinette sent to Mercy a series of suggestions for the forthcoming Austrian manifesto:—there was to be no mention of the King; no hint of interference in internal affairs; the war was to be given the appearance of a political war of the ordinary type[3]. Three weeks later —May 21—the Genevese publicist, Mallet du Pan, left Paris to convey the last wishes of the court in connection with the conduct of the coming invasion. His message deserves some consideration. The princes, he was commissioned to state, were not to be assigned any prominent part; for a civil war was above all things to be avoided. What the court desired was a "guerre

---

[1] Chuquet, *La première invasion prussienne*, p. 64.

[2] He had now, it would seem, given up all hope of a successful war and was concentrating his attention on the restoration of the royal power. To this end he had again come into connection with the Lameths and had made advances to Mercy. Glagau, *Hist. Zeit.* 1899.

[3] Arneth, p. 263.

étrangère faite de puissance en puissance," and not one of Kings against peoples. It was hoped that the powers would issue a manifesto, so worded as to separate—by a judicious mingling of threats and promises—the Jacobins and other factious persons from the nation at large. The Jacobins were of two sorts; the followers of Sieyès—Brissot, Condorcet, Vergniaud, and others—who were working for a republic or a change of dynasty; and the more violent lower-class party under Robespierre and Danton. Both these factions were to be punished without mercy. The constitutionalists of various shades, on the other hand, were to be well-treated and so won. The manifesto was to contain an assurance that no project for the dismemberment of France existed. No particular political system was to be advocated in it; it was to refer merely to 'the reestablishment of monarchy and the legitimate royal authority.' Finally the powers were to declare the National Assembly, the various municipalities, and Frenchmen in general responsible for the persons of the royal family; and they were to insist that the liberated King was the only person with whom peace negotiations would be carried on. After the King's release " un plan général de restauration sous les auspices des puissances" was to be elaborated. Such was the last scheme of the court. Its moderation and the anxiety to avoid bloodshed that it reveals do infinite credit to the King; yet its very existence proves the substantial justice of those attacks on the 'Austrian committee' at the Tuileries in which the Gironde indulged[1].

[1] Mallet, *Memoirs*, I. 280, 429. The actual memoir that we have was drawn up by Mallet himself; but the substance of it had been arranged between him and the King.

Mallet reached Frankfort in the middle of June. There he awaited the arrival of the Kings of Prussia and Hungary, who were to meet on the occasion of the imperial election and coronation.

Week by week hatred of the court and the failure of the northern campaign were driving the Assembly further and further along the path of violence. On May 27, the transportation of all non-juring priests was decreed; on the 29th, the King's constitutional guard was dissolved; on the 8th of June, Servan, who had succeeded De Grave at the ministry of war, suggested that 20,000 of the national volunteers, the "fédérés," should be placed in a great camp under the walls of Paris—ostensibly to defend the capital, practically to watch the King. Louis determined to veto the first and last of these decrees, but to permit the dissolution of his guard. Whereupon Roland presented to him a long didactic remonstrance, the work, it is said, of the minister's famous wife. Dumouriez, who was no longer in sympathy with his Girondin colleagues, took this opportunity, supported the King, and aided him in getting rid of Roland, Clavière, and Servan (June 13). A new ministry was hastily put together, composed of Feuillants and friends of Lafayette—for the hero of two continents declared himself against the fallen ministry and demanded the suppression of the Jacobins club, in a letter that reached Paris on June 17. The reply of the Jacobins was the rising of June 20. The rising was the outcome partly of the veto, the changes of ministry, and the consequent intrigues of the Gironde; but primarily of a plan that had for some time occupied the mob-leaders of the Faubourg St Antoine, who intended to celebrate the anniversary of the tennis-court oath by a great popular demonstration that should serve as a warning to the King. Louis' admirable firmness and presence of mind in face of the mob on that occasion produced a momentary revival of loyal sentiment.

Had Lafayette possessed the confidence of the court something might yet have been done to support the throne and render the invasion of the allies superfluous. The general left his post and came to Paris, on June 28, to denounce before the Assembly the 'sect which was usurping the sovereignty of the nation.' The Assembly, when not carried away by excitement or terror, was moderate as it had always been. On July 7, in the famous scene of the "baiser Lamourette," it solemnly denounced all schemes for modifying the constitution 'either by the establishment of two chambers or by that of a republic.' Yet on the 11th, as the direct result of a furious attack on the King delivered by Vergniaud on the 3rd, it sanctioned the decree that, noised abroad, shook all France:—'the fatherland is in danger.' The King's authority was daily growing weaker. The Gironde, holding that the time for a republic was not yet come, or fearing the rising force of the extreme party, was thinking of a regency and looking forward to civil war[1]. From all parts of France representatives of the most decidedly revolutionary class, deputed to attend the fête of the federation on July 14, were streaming into Paris. There they were being urged by the orators at the clubs and in the sections to demand the suspension of the King and the summons of a

---

[1] Pellenc on Sieyès, July 13 and 15. Glagau, p. 357.

national convention[1]. At this moment a scheme of escape from the capital was laid before the King, the last of the many schemes of the sort. It was the work of the old moderate reforming party of 1789, in conjunction with Lafayette. Louis agreed to make trial of it. But the Queen distrusted the 'constitutionals,' she hated Lafayette, and she had just been advised by Fersen to await in Paris the chances of an invasion. Her opposition wrecked the proposal[2]. Yet she fully realised her danger. On the 4th of July she wrote to Mercy beseeching him to hasten the issue of the manifesto that was to declare Paris and the Assembly responsible for the safety of the royal family. Five days later Mercy replied:—certainly the manifesto should be issued; but nothing definite could be done until after the imperial coronation, which was fixed for the 14th; let her gain time and, if possible, win some of the mob-leaders, Santerre for instance; early in August the allies would enter France. 'A month, then, and you will be saved[3].'

In proportion as France absorbed the attention of the West the manœuvres of Catherine against Poland prospered. Throughout the early spring her armies had been moving westward and her agents in Poland building up a party of opposition to the new system,

---

[1] The fédérés demand these things in the Assembly on July 3.

[2] On June 30, Fersen wrote:—above all do not leave Paris, "c'est là le point capital." The Queen wrote on July 11, "Les constitutionnels, réunis à Lafayette et Luckner, veulent emmener le roi à Compiègne...Le roi est disposé à se prêter à ce projet; la reine le combat." Fersen, II. 315, 326. See too Morris, *Diaries*, I. 556; Sybel, I. 417; Glagau, in *Hist. Zeit.* 1899.

[3] Arneth, pp. 265, 266.

whose complaints might serve as a pretext for interference. Catherine pretended to believe that the revolution in Poland, of which the chief object had been the strengthening of the royal power against the aristocracy, was essentially the same in character as that of France. 'As to the "jacobinière" of Paris,' she wrote on May 9, 'I will fight it in Poland[1].' Ten days later 100,000 Russian troops crossed the Polish frontier. Thereupon Stanislaus of Poland wrote to Berlin for help. He did not know that his ally Prussia hoped to share the spoils with Catherine and was eager to secure a treaty with the spoiler[2]. Frederick William in reply to his request explained that, as the state of things anticipated in the Alliance of 1790 had entirely changed, Prussia did not consider herself bound to defend the new constitution, of which she had never approved. Since the declaration of war by France the cabinet of St Petersburg seemed to have abandoned the notion of gratifying Prussia by a partition; so Prussia had fallen back on Austria, and was preparing to constrain Catherine to fulfil her promise by a combination of force and persuasion.

The Polish question became inextricably confused

[1] Forneron, *Les Emigrés*, p. 292. On May 31, Catherine sent the princes a million francs. It was, she said, all that could be spared—" au milieu des dépenses assés considérables qu'exige de moi l'arrangement de mes propres affaires." According to Feuillet de Conches (vi. 52), she had run her pen through the two words " en Pologne " which terminated the sentence as originally written.

[2] Custine divined this. He wrote to Dumouriez on May 9, " L'accord avec la Russie n'est plus douteux. Tout ceci présage et déterminera peut-être plus tôt qu'on ne pense un nouveau partage de la Pologne." Sorel, ii. 450.

with that of the compensation for the expenses of the French campaign. Once more German diplomatists fell to rearranging the map of Europe; and whilst engaged in this task both Austrians and Prussians were doing their utmost to obtain separate alliances with Russia[1]. On May 21, Schulenburg had suggested to Reuss a scheme for settling both the French and Polish questions. Austria and Prussia were each to send 10,000 men into Poland to protect their interests against Catherine. A simple and satisfactory division of the anticipated Polish and French spoils might be effected if Austria were to take all the latter and Prussia all the former[2]. This proposal led to a long and complicated negotiation, which was carried on by Francis and Spielmann without the knowledge of Kaunitz, to whom any such scheme would have been altogether distasteful. Such things had happened before, in the reign of Leopold; but that his youthful successor should have broken in this fashion with the chancellor's policy shows that the once mighty minister was losing control of the helm. In fact ever since the rejection of his opinion on the question of an aggressive war his influence had been on the wane. Spielmann and Cobenzl agreed to the Prussian proposal so far as Poland was concerned; for their own part however they preferred the old Austrian scheme for the exchange of the Low Countries against Bavaria to any increase of territory along the Rhine[3]. To this Schulenburg consented, thus breaking with the traditional Prussian

---

[1] They succeeded, Austria in July, and Prussia in August.
[2] Vivenot, II. 55. Sybel, I. 478.
[3] Vivenot, II. 120. Ph. Cobenzl to L. Cobenzl, July 2.

policy of protecting Bavaria at all costs. It was not until June 21. that the Emperor acquainted Kaunitz with this negotiation. Kaunitz declined to have anything to do with it, on the ground that it was opposed to all his political principles[1]. From this time forward his influence was gone; before the invasion began he had resigned.

Not until the 5th of July, on which date Francis was elected Emperor, did Austria begin to deal with France in earnest. On that day the official reply to the French declaration of war was circulated to the various Austrian embassies. Point by point the charges brought against the Imperial court by its enemies were discussed and answered. It was accused of assisting the emigrants and thus showing hostility to France. It replied by pointing to its dispersal of the emigrants in October 1791, and its request to the Elector of Trèves to do the like. 'The simplest ideas of monarchical government' were enough to justify the existence of the concert, and the attitude of opposition to the 'fatal principles' of the French democrats that its advocates had adopted. In the matter of Alsace, Austria did not stand alone in objecting to the conduct of France; further she had made every effort to bring about a satisfactory compromise. France was the true aggressor; for she had ordered 150,000 men to proceed to the frontiers, at a time when no corresponding armament had been undertaken by the court of Vienna. Consequently the demand for a disarmament made 'when she alone was armed for war' was the flimsiest of pretexts for

[1] Beer, *Hist. Zeitschrift*, 1872.

aggression. Next the French ministers were accused of garbling the Austrian despatches for publication; and finally it was pointed out—and with some justice—that if the concert *was* violating the sovereignty of the French nation, the French in their turn were every day provoking and abusing the sovereigns, and seeking to overthrow the governments, of all Europe[1].

The Prussian declaration, which had appeared before the end of June, resembled in the main that of Austria. Its heads of accusation against the French were the violation of treaties in the matter of Alsace, the revolutionary propaganda, the attacks on 'the sacred person and lawful authority of sovereigns,' the unjust war against the King of Hungary, and the 'disastrous principles of insubordination' that a ferocious sect was advocating in Paris[2].

On July 14, Francis II., the last of the Holy Roman Emperors, was crowned at Frankfort. Thence he proceeded to Mainz, where a stately interview with the Prussian King took place. Already the Prussian forces were close to Coblence. Ferdinand of Brunswick was with them. Brunswick had never loved Austria, and now, although in command of the allied armies, he was boiling over with indignation at the general Austrian policy and the utter inadequacy of the Austrian military preparations. For when the 42,000 Prussians and the 5,500 Hessians reached the Rhine, towards the end of July, they found that Austria had not fulfilled her share of the contract. No more than 14,000 men,

---

[1] Vivenot, I. 470.
[2] Ségur, *Tableau politique de l'Europe*, II. 347.

under Hohenlohe Kirchberg, were ready in the Austrian Rhenish provinces to cooperate with Brunswick; while only 15,000 more were to follow Clerfayt from the Netherlands[1]. Thus even including a few thousand emigrants, the great army of invasion would amount to little over 80,000 men instead of the 110,000 of which the Austrians had spoken in May. And before them lay the French armies, numerous and enthusiastic if not very efficient, holding famous fortresses, well supplied with artillery, and on the whole well provisioned; for France had availed herself to the full of the three months' grace allowed her by the allies[2].

At Frankfort and Mainz in July Mallet du Pan met the representatives of the German powers, Cobenzl and Spielmann, Schulenburg and Haugwitz. The ministers assured Mallet that the King's advice with regard to the manifesto should be followed, that they had no intention of dismembering France, and that they would hold the emigrants in check[3]. In pursuance of this last engagement it was agreed, on July 20, that not more than 17,000 emigrant troops should be permitted to take part in the war. Of these 8,000 under Provence and Artois might accompany the main army of Brunswick; 5,000 were to remain with the Imperial army in the Breisgau and apparently to have no share in the invasion; 4,000 more were assigned to the detachment

---

[1] Chuquet, *La première invasion prussienne*, p. 145. Sybel, I. 452.

[2] For the immense improvements effected in the French armies between April and August or September, see Chuquet, Ch. II. According to Chuquet the troops were better provisioned than in the same country in 1870.

[3] Mallet, *Memoirs*, I. 306. Sybel, I. 488.

under Clerfayt[1]. But the subject which engrossed almost all the attention of the negotiators at Frankfort and Mainz, the subject which is uppermost in all the diplomatic correspondence of these weeks, was that of the compensation; and upon this head no agreement had been arrived at when the invasion began[2]. The partition of France had been abandoned as impracticable; she would be called upon merely to pay an indemnity for the expenses incurred during the campaign. Austria proposed that the Elector Palatine should be transplanted from Bavaria and settled in the Belgian provinces with the title of King of Burgundy[3]. Prussia's compensation was to consist in the long-desired districts of Danzig and Thorn. But here a new difficulty arose. Bavaria would not yield as much revenue as the Netherlands, and the 'exact equality of acquisitions' was one of the articles of the Austro-Prussian treaty. Austria accordingly suggested that her ally should resign the lately acquired principalities of Anspach and Baireuth. This startling demand, even though linked with the suggestion that some land on the lower Rhine, or some more scraps of Poland might be thrown into the Prussian scale to equalise the balance, was most distasteful to Schulenburg and

---

[1] These figures are maxima: the three emigrant detachments might not be greater than this—in fact they were considerably less.

[2] Various documents, July—Sept. 1792. Vivenot, II. 120—80.

[3] The Austrians described this exchange as "das summum bonum der oesterreichischen Monarchie." Conference Protocol, July 17. Vivenot, II. 132. Charles Theodore of the Palatinate had succeeded to the Bavarian throne on the extinction of the younger line of Wittelsbach in 1777.

Haugwitz. At this point the negotiation broke down; it was never resumed.

In the intervals of these negotiations the scheme for a manifesto brought from Paris by Mallet came under the consideration of the allies. Unfortunately Mallet's advice was not taken. The document actually issued on July 25, and made known in Paris on the 28th, the famous Brunswick manifesto, was not that monument of combined persuasion and intimidation which the court had proposed. It was essentially an emigrant production, approved by Frederick William, tolerated by Francis, and issued in the name of the Duke, who had himself succeeded in softening some of its harshest passages[1]. It did not terrify the French, as was intended, but it did convince the revolutionary leaders that it would be impossible to make head against the invasion were the King not deprived of all power. A few days after its publication Brunswick began to move reluctantly towards the French frontier. His heart had never been in the enterprise entrusted to him and he saw no hope of bringing it to a successful issue with the forces at his command. So slow was his march that twenty days were spent between Coblenz and the little village of Redange, near which the Prussians first entered French territory on August 19[2].

---

[1] For the history of the manifesto see Mallet, I. 317; Fersen, II. 337; Ranke, p. 197; Sorel, I. 82 and II. 509. It is often stated that its publication produced great excitement in Paris; yet Gower (*Despatches*, p. 206, Aug. 3) says that it produced "very little sensation," and a correspondent of Mallet's wrote "on en rit" Mallet, I. 322.

[2] Chuquet, p. 160. Sybel, I. 543.

Nine days earlier the blow so long meditated in Paris had been struck, the throne had been overturned, and its late occupant made prisoner.

If anything whatever was to come of the crusade against the Jacobin schismatics, it was necessary that its leader should be in a position to take active measures and that speedily. But even before the cannonade of Valmy it was already almost certain that nothing decisive would occur in the autumn of 1792; for the Austrian and Prussian ministries, upon whose action as much as upon that of Brunswick the prosperity of the crusade depended, had not taken and were not taking the steps necessary to insure success. The jealousies and conflicting ambitions of the two courts were proving stronger than their desire to assist the French King, stronger even than their fear of the subversive principles of the Revolution. The army of invasion was too small for the work in hand because reserves had to be kept to deal with Poland. Its movements were uncertain because there was no harmony among the politicians who directed its action. An acute observer of European politics wrote in 1801 that this first campaign of the revolutionary wars served rather 'to bring the aims of the cabinets into the light of day than to effect the triumph of the powers[1].'

---

[1] Count Woronzow, *Woronzow Archives*, VIII. 289.

APPENDIX.

So much of the diplomatic correspondence of the revolutionary period has already been printed that the few extracts collected here are necessarily fragmentary and of only secondary importance. Some of them are given to justify statements in the text, others to throw a little fresh light on various questions connected with the origin of the war. Several of the most interesting come from despatches of Sir R. M. Keith not printed in his *Memoirs* [edited in 1849 by Mrs. Gillespie Smith]; others from the similar despatches of Lord Auckland. Rather disproportionate attention is given to Spanish affairs because the relations of England, Spain, and France at this time have been studied less carefully than the policy of Austria or Prussia. A few of the extracts from Ewart's letters from Berlin have already been printed—but in German—in Herrmann's *Geschichte des russischen Staates*, Ergänzungs-Band, 1866. The remainder, so far as I am aware, are now printed for the first time. All are extracts, not complete letters.

I. ENGLAND AND FRANCE.

1787. Oct. 18. *Duke of Dorset to Marquis of Carmarthen.* During the administration of M. de Vergennes, no measures were taken to cultivate the least connection with the court of Austria: that minister having always professed a jealousy of the system of politics adopted by Prince Kaunitz with a view to the destruction of the Turkish Empire...This conduct of M. de Vergennes gave great disgust to those who looked upon Austria as the safest ally for France, and who were therefore always at work (though without effect) to undermine him in the King's opinion.

Since the death of that judicious minister and experienced politician things seem to have taken a different course, and the Emperor's friendship appears now to be the object in view and systematically pursued: this plan is the more likely to be persevered in on account of the secret correspondence that has been uniformly held between the Archbishop of Thoulouse [Loménie de Brienne] and Prince Kaunitz ever since the marriage of the present King with the Emperor's sister....

Your Lordship may depend upon it that no great progress has as yet been made in this business, for the French are by no means cordially disposed towards the Austrians, yet still the plan is likely to be pursued though it be only with the view of revenge at some future opportunity on the King of Prussia....

Nov. 1. Wm. Eden to Carmarthen. He [Montmorin] told me that in the course of our discussions this country had been much nearer going to war than from a view of the circumstances I might suppose. He said that exclusive of all objects of external interest there had been some opinions of weight that a war was the best mode of finishing the internal troubles which had prevailed at the time of the King of Prussia's march.

1790. *Sept.* 1. *Duke of Leeds to Lord Gower.* ...You will omit no opportunity of letting it be understood that nothing but necessity can occasion any views to be entertained in this country hostile either to the general interests of France, or to the settlement of their newly established constitution; but that on the other hand any step of assistance to the court of Spain will naturally lead to our adopting such measures as may be most likely to render such assistance ineffectual.

1791. *Sept.* 20. *Lord Grenville to George Aust* [Under-Secretary for Foreign Affairs]. I inclose you an answer which His Majesty has been pleased to write to the letter from Monsieur which I received for His Majesty through the Chevalier de la Bintinnaye...You may read to that gentleman the copy of it, and I have also His Majesty's permission to communicate to M. de la Bintinnaye through you (as my absence from town prevents my seeing him myself) that His Majesty's resolution extends not only to the taking no part either in supporting or opposing the measures which other Powers may adopt, but also to the not influencing in any manner their determination in that respect. And as the letter from Monsieur refers to the answer given by His Majesty to the Emperor, you will further acquaint M. de la Bintinnaye that the first overtures which were made here on the part of the Emperor consisted only in the transmission of the circular letter and project of declaration, with which that gentleman is probably already acquainted, but which you are otherwise at liberty to show him; and you will read to him the answer returned by His Majesty to that letter. You will acquaint M. de la Bintinnaye that nothing specific has since passed on the subject; that M. de Mercy, during his residence here, avoided all particular conversation upon it; that M. de Stadion's language and communications relative to it have been entirely of a general nature; and that in return I have expressed the same general sentiments as are contained in the King's answer; that in the course of my conversation with M. de Stadion I adverted to the apparent danger of fresh disturbances in the Netherlands and to the difficulty of the King's explaining himself on the subject of the Emperor's interference in the affairs of France while any part of the business of the Hague Convention remained unsettled: and that, with that view, I mentioned the advantage which would have arisen from bringing that business to a point...; but that on the occasion of Sir R. Keith's return to Vienna he has been authorised to explain to the Emperor, in the same terms which have been used to other powers, the King's determination to take no part in the business of France, unless any new circumstances should arise which might have an influence on the interests of his subjects; that this is in a few words the result of all that has passed upon the subject, and that His Majesty's friendship towards Monsieur makes him desirous that he should be accurately informed, in order to prevent any mistaken conjectures which might be formed by the Princes or those connected with them, from any misrepresentation or misapprehension of the King's sentiments or conduct.

II. Policy of the Court of Vienna.

1790. *July* 16. *Lord Auckland to the Duke of Leeds.* [Reporting a letter written by De Haeften, the Dutch ambassador at Vienna, to his government.] M. de Haeften appears to consider the Austrian cabinet as under three separate directions :—first, that of Prince Kaunitz to whose impracticable haughtiness, aggravated by the infirmities of age, he attributes many particulars of language and recent conduct which are ill suited to the circumstances of embarrassment prevailing in every part of the Austrian dominions :—next, that of Count Cobenzl, who endeavours separately to draw to himself the influence that Prince Kaunitz has so long had in foreign affairs...The remaining direction is that of His Imperial Majesty personally, who frequently permits Prince Kaunitz and the Vice-Chancellor to take opposite lines in a business, and at the same time without contradicting or restraining either of them adopts and pursues some third mode totally distinct and separate from them both. It is impossible that a system so replete with inconsistencies can long be maintained, but it is interesting so long as it exists.

July 31. *Auckland to Leeds.* I have this moment received a letter from Sir R. Keith, stating that by his unremitting efforts and those of Mr Ewart, the basis of an accommodation is laid by the acceptance of the *status quo plenier*, on the part of his Hungarian Majesty, and that he can foresee no probable difficulty to prevent the immediate concurrence of the King of Prussia.

1791. *June* 24. *Colonel Gardiner [at Brussels] to Lord Grenville.* Upon the news of the French King's departure, a council of war was held here to decide upon the properest disposition of the troops, and it was determined to send as many as could be possibly spared...to the frontiers, putting the whole on the war establishment, but there was no mention of sending any out of the country, nor could, indeed, a considerable detachment be spared at this particular juncture, or would Their Highnesses venture such a measure without positive directions from the Emperor.

July 1. *Gardiner to Grenville.* A circumstance has been communicated to me, and as it comes immediately from the person employed by the French King with a verbal message to the Emperor [Count Durfort presumably] and who was present at...Mantua, it may possibly be depended upon. After the affair had been very fully discussed the Emperor expressed himself much against the measure of quitting Paris as dangerous, and unnecessary...; this answer being less encouraging than their French Majesties expected, was not well received, and they acted in conformity with their own opinions, upon the principle that the business was gone too far, and was too well prepared, to admit either of alteration or delay.

Oct. 1. *Sir R. M. Keith to Grenville.* I have it from good authority that the Emperor said to Baron Jacobi in his audience at Prague...that the French King's unconditional acceptance of the new constitution had put an end to the idea of the interposition of foreign princes, whilst that monarch and the nation seemed to agree so thoroughly. It is generally believed that the French Queen deprecates all military interference on the part of the Emperor.

Oct. 8. I saw Baron Jacobi last night and...I learnt from him in positive terms...that the Emperor is firmly resolved to abstain from every species of military interference in the affairs of France.

Nov. 13. ...A resolution has been adopted here that a circular letter shall be written to all the Imperial ministers at foreign courts (when occasion may require it) that although the free acceptance of the constitution by the French King has suspended the effect of the concert...yet, that any renewal of circumstances similar to those in which His Most Christian Majesty stood, when that concert was formed, would not fail to call forth the same exertions which were then agreed upon.

I am assured that in order to evince the freedom of the French King's late acceptance, some intimation will be given, in the above-mentioned circular letter, of the earnest wishes expressed by *both* their Most Christian Majesties, in their *private correspondence* with the Emperor, that no armed intervention should be employed from without, as that would only serve to render their situation more difficult and dangerous.

Dec. 14. *Keith to Grenville.* It has been remarked (by those persons who frequently pass some hours in familiar conversation with Prince Kaunitz) that within these ten days his language respecting the situation of the French King is somewhat altered, and that he again calls in question the personal freedom of that Monarch. Some people pretend that (since the election of the present Mayor of Paris) the French Queen has acquainted His Imperial Majesty that the King's situation and her own grow daily more precarious, and that they may stand in need of his powerful intervention.

Dec. 17. The suspicion grows that the French Queen has written again to the Emperor to represent the danger of her actual situation. Be that as it may I learn from good authority that this court entertains great apprehensions lest fresh tumults at Paris should renew the horrid outrages of the first days of the French Revolution and thereby necessitate the armed intervention of foreign powers. It is under consideration in this cabinet to publish another declaration intimating to the National Assembly of France the effectual measures which the powers in concert are determined to take in support of the liberty and security of the French Royal Family, if they should be again endangered.

Dec. 28. Prince Kaunitz hitherto affects making light of the menacing language in respect to the Elector of Trèves which has been held by the French King to the National Assembly, treating a possible irruption of the French into Germany as a degree of foolhardiness which passes all belief. But we have observed of late that the Prince never gives credit to anything that hurts his pride or threatens to disturb his indolence, and his language has varied so frequently in regard to French affairs that no solid conclusions are to be drawn from a few of his vapouring phrases.

1792. *Jan.* 14. This court, though much embarrassed and no less alarmed by the actual posture of affairs, continues to have recourse to palliatives and has hitherto adopted no steady nor vigorous plan of conduct. There exists here as great a want of money as of resolution, and the evil day is put off as long as possible, consequently no orders have been sent to make serious preparations for the assembling an army of observation on the upper Rhine.

Feb. 22. The Emperor looks upon the boasted efforts of Russia and Sweden, in the supposition of a war with France, as far too distant to be of any real utility. He begins to foresee that the whole burthen of such a contest may ultimately fall on his own shoulders. Yet he still hopes to intimidate the French by his warlike preparations; and for that reason he has rendered those preparations very public. But should they fail in producing the desired effect, His Imperial Majesty would find himself in a very difficult situation, as his treasury is so much drained that (according to the avowal of his ministers) if the sword must be drawn, he will be obliged to lay the heavy war-tax on his subjects at the opening of the first campaign.

March 21. He [Baron Jacobi, Prussian ambassador at Vienna] appears to me to adhere strongly to his original opinion that this court is at bottom averse to war,...but he does not call in question the justness of the remark I have made, that the language of the late declaration from hence, though it be intended to prevent hostilities on the part of France, may in the actual state of parties in the National Assembly produce a contrary effect. I have not concealed from him a notion which has taken root in my mind that the very repeated and violent attacks made by the Austrian ministry on the Club of the Jacobins have been suggested by the French King and through Count Mercy to this court.

May 2. The French declaration of war has come in the precise nick of time to furnish an opportunity to this court of throwing the whole odium of aggression, and an offensive war, on the French nation. This cabinet would indeed show themselves very inexperienced politicians if in their future manifesto, and in their subsequent addresses to the principal powers of Europe, they did not turn to the best advantage the means of justifying their most vigorous measures, which the precipitation of the French has at this moment put into their hands.

Nevertheless your Lordship may be assured that, in consequence of the strong remonstrances made by His Prussian Majesty last week (enforced as I am told by a private letter in his own handwriting to the King of Hungary) the definitive resolution was adopted in the Austrian council on Saturday last [April 28] to go all lengths against France which the King of Prussia thought advisable, and to give full power to the Duke of Brunswick, as Commander-in-Chief, to set on foot an offensive war as soon as the different corps of his army should reach the places of their destination.

Barón Jacobi sent an estafette to Berlin to give immediate notice to his court of this determination. But as the French declaration was received here previous to the departure of the messenger who was to be despatched to Prince Reuss at Berlin, it is not unlikely that this court may have employed in their instructions to that minister the language best calculated to paint the conduct of the French in the blackest colours.

July 21. The real motive which prevents the Emperor from opening the Bank of Vienna, or any loan on foreign exchange, proceeds from a sanguine (your Lordship will judge whether it may not deserve the epithet of overweening) belief that the war against France must be brought to a happy and glorious termination in a single campaign.

August 29. The situation of France creates here not only extreme anxiety but some doubts of the speedy success of the allied army. On this occasion the jealousy natural to the Austrians, on seeing their troops commanded by a Prussian officer, begins to vent itself, and Prince Kaunitz, who was always an enemy to the present war, cannot help making a merit with the public of the aversion to that measure which he formerly manifested. With all this, my Lord, I am persuaded that the first important blow struck with vigour by the Duke of Brunswick will put an end to all these gloomy predictions.

Sept. 10. [Keith is describing the causes of the war and of the retirement of Kaunitz.] The Emperor Leopold, who was often rash, though without resolution, precipitate in promising (but with a mental reservation of eluding performance) had, in a moment of extreme deference for his Prussian ally, and with the mistaken hope of intimidating France, added, *with his own pen*, to the rough draft of the declaration which Prince Kaunitz had prepared to send to Paris, about the middle of February, those very harsh expressions, level'd at the Jacobin faction, which carried *their* resentment to the utmost pitch.

It was almost the last act of Leopold's reign in relation to French affairs, as General Bischoffwerder who brought the decisive opinions of His Prussian Majesty, arrived here when the Emperor lay at the point of death in the last days of February.

War, *immediate and offensive war*, against France was the essential and almost the sole purpose of General Bischoffwerder's commission.

He endeavoured, from the first, to carry this point, without a direct reference to Prince Kaunitz, and this mode of proceeding became more and more advisable, as upon the accession of the young King the Prince's opinion soon began to transpire, that the engagements of Leopold, as Head of the German Empire, were not binding on his successor as King of Hungary, and that it was consistent with prudence and sound policy that His Apostolick Majesty should keep every door open to amicable accommodation with France.

Mr Bischoffwerder strained every nerve of his (very slender) abilities, to engage the Monarch Himself, as well as Counts Colloredo and Cobenzl, to adopt the sentiments of His Prussian Majesty; but he addressed himself most particularly to Baron Spielmann, whose favour with King Francis was visibly increasing....

On the 27th of April...the great question of peace or war was formally debated, in the Conseil de Conference.

On this day Prince Kaunitz (who during a long term of years had never deigned to attend any meeting in the Imperial Palace) gave, *in writing*, to his first official clerk, Baron Spielmann, a man who owed to him his whole fortune, the heads of his opinion, touching that important matter, with positive orders to make known, in strong terms, the Prince's aversion to offensive war, founded on the actual state of the Austrian monarchy, and the situation of Europe in general....

No definitive resolution being adopted in the first meeting, the same subject was resumed on the 28th, when Prince Kaunitz's advice came again to be quoted, and was treated by several of the cabinet counsellors as the effect of age and timidity.

Here it was that Baron Spielmann, who in virtue of his proxy from Prince Kaunitz, was permitted to speak, departed so widely from the injunctions he had received as to become the warmest and most eloquent advocate for immediate and offensive war against France. By this step he betrayed the interests of Prince Kaunitz, in so glaring a manner, that Prince Rosenberg, who singly, and constantly, had supported the known opinions of the aged minister, could hardly conceal his surprise, in seeing how successful General Bischoffwerder had proved in implanting Prussian notions in Baron Spielmann's breast.

His Apostolick Majesty had, very recently, received a pressing letter in the handwriting of His Prussian Majesty, which was thought to have given a new turn to his sentiments, in so far, that the Prince, together with three of his five cabinet counsellors embraced, at once, the final resolution of proceeding to immediate hostility against France.

The minutes of that council were sent to Prince Kaunitz together with an express order to draw up a declaration to that effect.

The Prince did not hesitate to obey (though if he had resigned his employment at that moment, he would have secured the veneration and gratitude of the whole nation) but, on the contrary, he took pleasure in giving full scope to the natural acrimony of his pen, and he committed to paper that intemperate Philippick, which had more the air of a manifesto against the Jacobine Club, than of a well digested justification of the offensive measures which were to be pursued against the French nation.

Happily for the honour of the Austrian councils, the blind temerity of the Parisian demagogues outstripped all expectations, and the French declaration of war reached this capital on the very day which followed the above decision on the part of Austria.

From that moment, the madness, as well as injustice of French *aggression*, were in every mouth, and not a whisper was heard of the violent resolutions so lately adopted in this cabinet. [Keith goes on to explain at length the subsequent stages in the fall of Kaunitz.]

III. Policy of the Court of Berlin.

1791. *July* 17. *Ewart to Lord Grenville.* This court now knows for certain that it was His Imperial Majesty who acted the principal part in arranging the escape of the royal family of France, and that he had taken his measures for supporting them by force of arms had it succeeded. In the last interview with Colonel Bischoffwerder, at Milan, he said much on this subject, and solicited the concurrence and co-operation of the King of Prussia; but I know that His Majesty has written himself to Colonel Bischoffwerder, to decline all further discussion on this subject; as he had no direct concern in it, et que c'étoit à l'Empereur de monter la brêche. His Majesty likewise gave a similar answer to the French emissary here, on his delivering to him a few days ago another letter from Count d'Artois, renewing his solicitations for His Majesty's assistance.

Aug. 2. Since writing my last [July 23] I have seen the King of Prussia's answer to the Emperor...the assurances of approbation and even of concurrence are much stronger than was at first intended, owing to the effect produced on His Prussian Majesty by the recent representations, proposals, and entreaties of His Imperial Majesty through Colonel Bischoffwerder. I am now convinced that should the Emperor take the lead, and act the principal part in furnishing men and money, the King of Prussia will co-operate; and I have every reason to believe that M. de Bischoffwerder has already gone great lengths at Vienna. [Printed by Herrmann.]

Aug. 4. ...On my asking Count Schulenburg what he thought His Prussian Majesty would do if the Emperor, satisfied with the neutrality of England, offered to employ measures of force; whether the King of Prussia would furnish such a corps of troops as that before mentioned, he said that his own private opinion was that he would co-operate with His Imperial Majesty. The Prussian Minister added that he had advised His Majesty to follow the line of conduct adopted by England but that he perceived his attachment to the common cause of Sovereigns prevailed.

Sept. 2. ...He [Schulenburg] told me the above declaration [that of Pilnitz] had been extorted from the two Sovereigns by the Count d'Artois, who first presented ten proposals, which he said he had seen, which had all been declined:—that having forced himself upon the Emperor at the moment of his departure, to propose the signature of an offensive convention, His Imperial Majesty had sent for the King of Prussia; and that after a long conference, at which were present the Count d'Artois, M. de Calonne, M. de Lascy, Baron Spielmann, Prince Hohenlohe, and General Bischoffwerder, the above declaration was signed and delivered to the Count d'Artois.

Count Schulenburg treated the paper as of no sort of consequence, and as proving the Emperor had no intention of using any measures of force in French affairs; but he expressed great regret at the King's having committed his dignity and political consequence. He further told me, that Baron Spielmann and M. de Lascy were both opposed to any interposition, and that Prince Hohenlohe was the only person at the conference who attempted to support the contrary opinion. He added, on this subject, that Count d'Artois and his adherents were extremely disappointed, and that he had wished to come to Berlin, but had been discouraged....

Sept. 9. ...With regard to French affairs, it seems to be only the King Himself and Prince Hohenlohe, who wish that any interference in them should take place....

Sept. 23. A messenger arrived here, two days ago, from Coblenz, with the publication made by the French exiled Princes...Baron Rolle immediately communicated it to the King of Prussia, whose sentiments respecting its contents I have not learnt, but everybody here treats it as a most extravagant performance which can only tend to make the cause of its authors still worse than it is.

Dec. 13. *Morton Eden to Grenville.* Apprehensions are entertained here that the very extravagant conduct of the French National Assembly, and particularly their decree of the 29th past, will, if persevered in, render the interference of the powers of the Empire absolutely necessary.

Jan. 28. On Thursday last...I had...a private conversation with Count Schulenburg. He indeed began it, by expressing his apprehension that this country would at length be forced into an open interference in the affairs of France, in consequence of the wild conduct of the National Assembly, and particularly the decree of the 14th instant. [Printed by Herrmann.]

Jan. 31. ...I know that hopes are entertained by this ministry that a rupture will still be avoided, unless the French actually invade the territory of the Empire. His Prussian Majesty is indeed personally irritated, as I have already mentioned to your Lordship, against some of the democratic party, and would most willingly, if it could be done conformably to the dictates of prudence, attempt coercive measures.

Feb. 16. In the act signed at Vienna its present limits [those of Poland] are indeed fully guaranteed—this I fear will prove but a feeble barrier, and if Russian troops overrun the country, and the Empress proposes a new partition, plausible arguments will easily be found for the political necessity of its being accepted. Resistance even would be difficult, if this court and that of Vienna be once fully embarked in the project of an armed negotiation with France:—for as in that business it does not appear probable that the Empress can take any effective part, she will be left the sole arbiter of the fate of Poland....[Printed by Herrmann.]

March 24. His Prussian Majesty as I have often observed would not be averse to hostile measures, but I still think that his conduct in this important affair will depend on the impulsion given by the court of Vienna through the medium of Mons. Bischoffwerder. Count Schulenburg is certainly averse to war but he notwithstanding his ability is of too little weight and is too much attached to his place to risk a steady resistance to the will of the favourite.

April 17. It is the general opinion here that war is inevitable. The best officers say that with a trifling force they will undertake to repel the attack; but that an invasion of France will be attended with great difficulty, particularly if it should become necessary to take up winter quarters in that country.

April 24. I have always represented His Prussian Majesty as desirous of vigorous measures. The incongruity of the conditions [*i.e.* of Prussia urging Austria to act] is a further proof of the impatience with which he saw the indecision of the court of Vienna; and is another urgent call on His Hungarian Majesty for a full and explicit explanation of his intentions, an object which the ardour of General Bischoffwerder, whose journey was principally intended for that purpose was unable to attain, and which it is possible that the arrival of affairs at such a crisis as to render a decided conduct unavoidable will alone be able to bring about...Luckily for humanity, the sentiments of the court of Vienna are more moderate, and it is every day more evident that the French, unless they become the aggressors have nothing to fear on the side of Germany. No public orders have as yet been given, but such preparations continue as will in case of necessity greatly facilitate the readiness of the troops to march.

April 24. Since I wrote off my despatch of this day, I

am credibly assured that orders for putting 56,000 men on the war establishment have been issued.

April 28. Your Lordship will probably be surprised to learn that His Prussian Majesty has signified his intention of taking himself the command of his troops....This resolution...has probably arisen from the reproaches that have been so frequently thrown out of His Majesty's indolence and love of pleasure....

May 1. The event [the declaration of war] was expected and of course caused but little surprise....Certain it is that the enterprise is very unpopular and even reprobated.

May 5. The operations of the campaign are talked of by those in place as likely to be very trifling and of short duration; but the undertaking continues to be very unpopular, and it is even said that it would be wiser to draw a cordon as in the time of the plague to prevent the spirit of innovation from entering the country, than to send so many men out to imbibe its pernicious principles.

IV. POLICY OF THE COURT OF MADRID.

1789. *Jan.* 16. *Wm. Eden to the Marquis of Carmarthen.* The great and leading object of this government is to avoid being involved in war. It is the prevailing idea, and perhaps wisely so, in everything that is said or done in the foreign department.. The disagreements of other powers if they do not tend to affect the tranquillity of Spain, are regarded with little anxiety and perhaps even with complacency.

March 30. [There exists in France] a considerable party who under the pressure of the present embarrassments...would think it right to precipitate the nation into a foreign war, though at the expense of a public bankruptcy. Count Florida Blanca himself inclines to the opinion that such an experiment, however desperate, might become the best palliative for France; but however much he may regret the increasing distress of so near an ally to Spain, he cannot, he says, wish to see her relieved from them, by plunging Europe into new wars, which might become general.

July 5. *Merry* [*Consul-general*] *to Carmarthen*. Count Floridablanca...expressed a kind of disregard to whatever France might do; and spoke of that country as if he held it in a very cheap light. He even said that because her present position allowed her to do nothing, she wished to make a show of influence.

July 27. His Excellency [Florida Blanca]...showed great uneasiness at the reports which prevailed, and after observing that the case was highly interesting to all the sovereigns of Europe, he hinted at some assistance which Spain might give to quell the disturbances, but his expressions relative to this last point were very diffuse, and made use of in a hurry, and when he had dropped them he concluded by saying with much warmth and agitation, that he did not know what could be done, since there was no head in France to govern the machine....I do not find that he made to anybody but to me the suggestion of His Catholic Majesty's succouring the French King....

Aug. 10. I am assured that above two months ago the court of Spain made an insinuation to that of France by means of a letter from Count Florida Blanca to Count de

Montmorin, which was desired to be communicated to the French Council, stating that the alliance between the different branches of the House of Bourbon, solemnly confirmed by the Family Compact, did not allow that any alteration should take place in the form of government of the kingdoms belonging to that family; and that the King of Spain, as being head of the house, felt himself particularly interested to see the monarchy in France preserved on the same footing on which it has hitherto subsisted...M. Montmorin, in his answer, is said to have given assurances, that all the measures conducive to this end would be pursued, and that those they were then using were for maintaining the disunion between the three orders of the National Assembly.

1790. *Feb.* 4. The precautions used by this government to prevent, if possible, any spirit of Liberty breaking forth here, are carrying to such lengths as are more likely to defeat their own purpose, than to operate the desired effect. All correspondence is opened, and spies are employed in every quarter to watch what is said.

April 12. I can see only one circumstance which may incline the King of Spain and his ministry to war—it is the idea that it might be the means to re-establish the royal authority in France, as that kingdom would naturally take a part.

May 20. Notwithstanding the natural vanity of Spain has been so much increased of late, as well by the situation of France, as by the manner in which she has been flattered by the Imperial Courts, and by communications from other quarters, it is astonishing that she should have carried it to such a length, and that she should not be sensible of her inability to support it.

May 20. *Fitzherbert [at Paris, on his way to Madrid] to the Duke of Leeds.* In general I am inclined to think that M. de Montmorin is perfectly sincere in the desire that he professes to see our difference with Spain terminated amicably...; but I can plainly see that many of the other members of the aristocratical faction are anxious to avail themselves of the opportunity in order to bring on a war... However their opponents begin to be aware of this drift and it seems to have been principally with a view to guarding against such designs that the latter have chosen the present time for carrying into execution their plan of transferring the power of making war and peace from the Crown to the National Assembly.

Aug. 19. *Fitzherbert [Madrid] to Leeds.* Count Florida Blanca's present language is, that Great Britain having made a formal demand of the succour stipulated by her treaty with the States General, he had thought it right for form's sake to make a similar application to the National Assembly, but that he had never looked for real assistance from that quarter, nor in truth did he desire to receive any at the immediate risk of introducing by that means into this kingdom those democratic principles now so universally prevalent among all classes of men in France, including the army and navy. These expressions may perhaps be dictated in part by disappointment, but the truth is, that nothing can exceed Count Florida Blanca's anxiety to prevent any intercourse between France and Spain at the present crisis, insomuch even, that he some time ago seriously talked of treating the former kingdom upon the footing of a country infected with the plague, and of cutting off all communication with it as such by the establishment of a regular cordon from sea to sea.

Sept. 16. [The King of Spain regards] the National

Assembly...with the utmost horror and detestation...[he] is extremely averse to the adopting of the species of treaty proposed by that body, conceiving that such a step, as it would imply a recognition on his part of their authority, would be highly injurious to his personal dignity and might possibly in the end produce the most fatal consequences to the tranquillity and well-being of his kingdom.

Sept. 16. [Separate despatch.] From everything that has passed between Count Florida Blanca and myself during the course of the present negotiation, I have the strongest reason to be persuaded not only that this court is really and unfeignedly anxious for an accommodation with Great Britain, but that this anxiety is principally occasioned by the King of Spain's personal repugnance to the national compact proposed to him by France....

Nov. 28. It appears to me...that this court, though they remain firm in their original determination not to enter into any such compact as that proposed to them by the National Assembly, will not consent (unless absolutely forced to do it, by the proceedings of that body, or some other inevitable necessity) to break in upon the Family Compact so long as there remains any prospect of the re-establishment of the royal authority on its former footing.

1791. *Feb.* 7. I have at length traced out and had an opportunity of conversing with the person through whose channel the French exiled princes have hitherto carried on their communications with this court. He tells me that the Count of Artois' two last letters...are still unanswered, though he delivered them more than six weeks ago, and that he has moreover lately heard Count Florida Blanca express himself in very disparaging terms respecting that

Prince and his followers, saying their levity and indiscretion rendered them utterly unfit for the conducting of any business, much less for that of so important an enterprise as the restoration of the French monarchy. From these circumstances my informer (who is a very judicious person and fills a station of some eminence about this court) is decidedly of opinion that Count Florida Blanca is weary of that connection and is resolved to break it off—a conjecture which seems in fact to be on many accounts highly probable.—However it seems to be at the same time pretty certain that he was not led to this resolution by any desire to keep measures with the French Revolutionists, as his animosity against that party is no less violent and undisguised than before....

May 16. *Lord St Helens* [*Fitzherbert*] *to Lord Grenville.* ...All the high roads communicating with France are occupied by detachments of soldiery who suffer no persons to pass into this kingdom but such as are furnished with the most unexceptionable testimonials....

June 15. [Florida Blanca said] that he knew enough of the Emperor's character to be confident that they [the Princes] had nothing to expect from that quarter. M. de Florida Blanca has received what he considers as an authentic report of what passed at the interview at Mantua between that monarch and the Count d'Artois, and he told me that he had learnt from it (to use his own words) that His Imperial Majesty had talked a great deal upon that occasion but said absolutely nothing.

June 23. I have reason to believe that some supplies have in fact been sent from hence to the Count d'Artois by the way of Italy but the smallness of the sums so remitted (their amount being according to my informant no more than £10,000) seems to indicate plainly that they must have been intended merely for his personal support. On the other hand this court have just conferred a very essential favour of the same kind on the present French government by the grant of a particular license for the exportation to France of 2,000,000 dollars in specie:—an indulgence that had been earnestly solicited by the latter as a means of alleviating the distress...from the scarcity of gold and silver coins.

June 30. The supply of specie...appears to have been granted with great readiness....It is certain that he [Count Florida Blanca] has rendered them upon this occasion a most important and seasonable piece of service and that by his conduct in the present instance he has even sacrificed in some sort the interests of the opposite party. In fact... many circumstances indicate, that he has for the present determined to keep well with the National Assembly, in the hopes, as it should seem, of inducing them, by motives of gratitude, to refrain from and discourage any attempts to disturb the interior tranquillity of this kingdom.

July 4. The news of the evasion and recapture of the French Royal Family was received here by the last post....

Aug. 15. [I have gathered that Florida Blanca's answer to the Padua circular] highly extolled the Emperor's zeal for the relief of the French monarch, and approved in general of the plan traced out for that purpose. Its chief purport was to recommend earnestly the waiting for events, and particularly for the completion of the French constitutional Charter, which this court affects to hope may so far ameliorate His Christian Majesty's condition as to supersede the necessity of any foreign interference on his behalf. It has been confided to me, that the answer to the application from the King of Sweden, whose immediate object seems to have been the obtaining a considerable advance of money, was conceived in terms equally ambiguous, and indeed the fact is (as I often took the liberty to observe) that independent of Count Florida Blanca's natural predilection for a temporizing system this court cannot now in prudence pursue any other.

Oct. 3. It seems that the last French messenger was charged with a letter from His Most Christian Majesty to the King of Spain, written in his own hand, and as in his personal capacity, containing a long apology for his having laid aside the ensigns of his several orders of knighthood, and particularly those of the Golden Fleece. M. de Florida Blanca's language respecting this letter has hitherto been that it merits no kind of attention, having been evidently extorted from the French monarch by the threats of his oppressors, but the general tenour and style of the letter seem to contradict this assertion....

Oct. 13. ...The fact certainly is that some fresh remittances have been made from hence to that quarter [to the Princes] by the way of Genoa.

Oct. 17. It is now strongly rumoured here that the Courts of Vienna and Berlin are disposed to admit the validity of His Most Christian Majesty's acceptance of the new constitution, and Count Florida Blanca is of course the more alarmed by this report, as it is obvious that his late declaration on that head, should it be the only one of its kind, must from that circumstance appear doubly odious in the eyes of the French Nation, and that it may therefore render the breach between the two Governments absolutely irreparable.

Nov. 3. Count Florida Blanca's language and conduct respecting French affairs are more wavering and uncertain than ever—on the one hand he has just granted to the French Government a licence for the exportation of a considerable quantity of grain for the supply of the S. Provinces of that kingdom...and he has moreover formally acknowledged M. Dartubise as Chargé d'Affaires of the French crown...; on the other hand his ostentatious language respecting the invalidity of His Catholic Majesty's [should be Most Christian Majesty's] acceptance of the constitutional act is precisely the same as before, and I know from the best authority that he also continues to encourage the French exiled princes to persevere in their present measures.

Dec. 8. ...Even in the present moment, notwithstanding the embarrassment of the National Assembly, and the little degree of attention that they have hitherto given to the hostile language and preparations of this Court, the French cordon on the frontier...is by much the stronger of the two.

Dec. 29. ...The design which has been formed by the French exiled Princes to invade that kingdom with their own force only has been approved by this court, and in order to facilitate its execution His Catholic Majesty has just advanced to them a million of French livres, in addition to their usual monthly subsidy, the amount of which last is seven thousand pistoles, or about £45,000.

⨯ 1792. *Feb.* 9. The Austrian and Prussian cabinets have desisted for some time past from communicating with the Spanish minister on the subject of their views and intentions with regard to French affairs, being aware that they are not likely to derive any solid or effectual support from this quarter; but the King of Sweden continues to pay his court here with the utmost assiduity.

Feb. 28. ...I am assured Count Florida Blanca is at this time by no means anxious for an invasion of France, partly because he suspects that the secret object of the preparations now carrying on by the Emperor and the King of Prussia may be to effectuate a dismemberment of that kingdom, and partly because he has really good grounds for the opinion...respecting the probability of a counter-revolution....

[On Feb. 28 Florida Blanca was dismissed, and D'Aranda succeeded him.]

March 12. [I expect D'Aranda] will be less favourable than his predecessor to the interests of the monarchical party....

April 9. In fact his own personal desire to keep up a good understanding with the present French Government appears plain from the whole tenour of his conduct towards them.

April 30. I am confident that he is still determined to persist in his plan of remaining neutral, or at least waiting for the event, so as to be at liberty to join the stronger party, a system which is much favoured by the death of the late King of Sweden. Since Count Florida Blanca's engagements with that Prince on the subject of French affairs were more positive and specific than those that he had contracted with any other of the confederated powers.

May 27. He endeavours to keep upon good terms with all parties, but his inclinations are evidently in favour of France, partly, as I conceive, because he considers it as the interest of Spain to keep up its connection with that country in all circumstances, and partly because (as he has often intimated to me before he came into office) he by no means disapproves of the changes that have taken place in the French constitution.

V. The Powers and the Belgian Revolution.

1789. July 10. *Fitzherbert [at the Hague] to the Duke of Leeds.* Mr Van de Spiegel has informed me in confidence, that he had an interview, not long since, with an emissary from certain members of the Estates of Brabant, who, it seems, in consequence of the late suppression of their privileges, have united themselves in a secret confederacy, the immediate object of which is no less than to shake off entirely their allegiance to the Emperor, and erect the two above-mentioned Provinces, together with Austrian Flanders, into an independent Republic, under the protection and guarantee of Great Britain, Prussia and Holland.

I must confess, I was not a little surprised to find that...the Grand Pensionary could condescend to listen, for a single instant, to a project which to my apprehension appears wild and chimerical in the extreme; however he certainly does consider it as by no means unworthy of attention....The Grand Pensionary shew'd me likewise a letter from M. de Rheede which mentioned that this scheme had also been communicated to the Court of Berlin, where it had met with a very favourable reception....

Sept. 5. Ewart [Berlin] to Leeds. The Flemish emissary, Van der Noot, has been here some time....[The Prussian King] permitted M. Hertzberg to insinuate verbally that if the States of Brabant, after having published a manifesto, establishing their lawful rights and independence, should address themselves to him, in their quality of ancient members of the German body, and also to Great Britain and Holland, as parties and guarantees of the Barrier Treaty; in that event His Majesty would be disposed to concert with his allies such measures as might appear advisable for defending the Netherlands against the entry of French or other troops that might be sent against them; and that His Majesty would immediately communicate to the allies the proposals of Van der Noot, together with the verbal answer returned in order to settle some eventual concert concerning the line of conduct to be pursued, should the States of Brabant, duly qualified, reclaim the good offices of the allies.

Sept. 14. *Leeds to Ewart.* On the whole...it is His Majesty's earnest wish to prevail on the court of Berlin to desist altogether from any enterprise, either in the Netherlands or in Galicia, and, at all events, it is impossible to pledge this country beforehand to the consequence of measures, which go beyond the limits of a Defensive Alliance, and which might incur, without any sufficient justification, the risque of a general war.

Dec. 1. *Leeds to Fitzherbert.* ...It appears to the King's servants that the two principal objects which the allies ought as far as possible to prevent are, first, the Emperor's establishing such a degree of power in those provinces, as must not only destroy every part of their ancient constitution, but at the same time render him a dangerous neighbour to this country and Holland. Secondly, the independence of those provinces (in case of the insurgents succeeding) being established in such a mode as might connect them with France, and thereby be productive of such additional power to that kingdom, as might be equally fatal to the most important interests of the allies....Yet...we do not conceive the allies are called upon for any immediate interference by force, or by acknowledgement of the independence of the provinces because it is probable that, whatever turn events in that country may take, we shall be able to secure the main objects of our policy as above stated with greater advantage, by not having pledged ourselves beforehand.

In the meantime we think it will be highly expedient for the allies to keep up (though privately) a direct intercourse with the insurgents, so as to establish the most favourable impression on their minds of the importance of our friendship.

1790. *Feb.* 2. *Colonel Gardiner* [*Brussels*] *to Leeds.* [The Belgian leaders are dealing with] a M. Simonville, an *avocat du Parlement*, who is here, certainly deputed to the Estates, but not, I believe, by public commission; the original business he came upon was simply to convey, that when the independence of the provinces was acknowledged by any other nation, France would add her concurrence, but he means to continue here some time, and is therefore supposed to wait for events in order to endeavour at the formation of some treaty.

Feb. 12. M. Simonville cannot restrain his disappointment, and his discontent [at the news that the Triple Alliance was preparing to interfere in Belgium]; he sometimes affects to join with those who deny the existence of the treaty, and on other occasions he says that a war would be most desirable and advantageous to France, and that on the smallest movement of a Prussian army, 50,000 troops would instantly march into this country; he even goes so far as to mention the commanders, who are, M. de Rochambeau, M. le Marquis de Bouilli, and M. de la Fayette. I suppose he would not hazard what he advances without good authority....

Feb. 19. *Fitzherbert to Leeds.* M. de Rheede...has not failed to intimate to the Grand Pensionary that His Prussian Majesty has it in contemplation to recognise the independency of the Belgic States forthwith, and without waiting for the concurrence of Great Britain and the Republic.

March 9. *Leeds to Fitzherbert.* My sentiments are fully known upon the question of expediency respecting the independence of those provinces, and should Holland ever acknowledge that independence, until every possible method of preventing it taking place had been attempted, I have only to wish, that when both the Netherlands and myself are independent, the Government of the two maritime powers may feel no greater mischief than the loss of the services of one insignificant individual.

March 16. *Leeds to Lord Auckland* [*now at the Hague*]. My great object is to prevent the mishaps which must result to this country from their being either really or nominally independent, which I am persuaded can alone be prevented by their returning to the Austrian government, so far limited however as that the ancient Constitution and privileges of the provinces shall be secured to them against any encroachment of their Sovereign, by the guarantee of Great Britain and her allies.

Aug. 2. *Gardiner to Leeds.* M. du Morrier [Dumouriez, whose arrival in Brussels Gardiner had announced in a letter of July 26] is returned to France, after having compleated his memorial for M. de la Fayette; his description, both of the military department, and that of the finances, is as unfavourable as possible, and his objections to many other parts of this government strongly expressed ...though he was not otherwise inimical to the Belgic alliance....

VI. Miscellaneous Extracts.

1790. *Sept. 7. Auckland to Leeds.* The Pensionary... inclines to believe that a war with France ought above all things to be avoided; not because her circumstances make her formidable; he believes her helplessness in every military and naval point of view to be extreme, beyond all example among nations; but because a necessity to arm against Great Britain might give to the leaders of the Assemblée Nationale, a pretext to make a more compleat Bankruptcy than they have yet been able to arrive at, and which they would embrace with eagerness.

1790. *Sept. 21. Auckland to Leeds.* [Extract from a letter of the Grand Pensionary of Holland relating to the schemes of Artois for a counter-revolution.] Je trouve le projet à tous égards injuste, impolitique et dangereux... Je crois que les puissances de l'Europe devoient plutôt se prêter les mains, pour étouffer le détestable germe d'anarchie et de licence, qui ne laissera pas tôt ou tard d'éclore parmi elles. Que la France soit ruinée par elle-même, et à la suite de ses beaux principes de philosophie! Ce sera un terrible exemple pour en inspirer de l'avenir de l'aversion aux autres nations.

1791. *Aug. 14. Colonel Gardiner to Auckland.* I presume you have been informed that Mr Craufurd (whom you knew at Paris) is in England upon a particular mission: the fact is, that having been upon most intimate terms with M. de Fersen, he was persuaded by him to accompany him to Aix-la-Chapelle, where he had repeated interviews with the King of Sweden, who at last induced him to undertake this voyage to England, charged with letters, in the King of Sweden's own hand, to His Majesty and Mr Pitt, at the same time that M. de Fersen was sent off to Vienna, with similar despatches to the Emperor. Craufurd has been received uncommonly well, and particularly by His Majesty, who naturally must be partial to any project for the support of royalty; M. de Fersen, when he wrote, was only just arrived at Vienna, and had not then had his audience.

So far proceeded as well as possible;...unluckily...the Chevalier de Coigni passed through Brussels with letters for the Count d'Artois and the Emperor, from the King and Queen of France, entreating the former to return, and the latter, to suspend every hostile intention in their favour, as they were determined to accept the crown on the terms proposed to them by the Assemblée Nationale. This has every appearance of some private arrangement between their French Majesties and that Assembly....

The question now is, My Dear Lord, what part will the Emperor act. If he considers the safety of his sister only, he will most likely proceed in the most cautious manner; but if he takes up the cause as the general interest of all sovereigns, and as material to the tranquillity of Europe at present, and of its balance of power in future, he will not be withheld by any remonstrance of the Queen of France from joining with those other powers who may be so inclined, to overturn the present most dangerous system....

Aug. 30. Gardiner to Grenville. Yesterday evening an assembly took place at the Duc d'Uzès on rather uncommon principles, he, with the Duc de Villequier and M. de la Queuille sitting as a sort of court, for the distribution of future honours and rewards, to those who are to assist at the Contre-Revolution; the French were accordingly summoned, and desired to bring memorials of their pretentions and services, that the recompense might be proportionate to the deserts, and a vast number actually obeyed this strange invitation....

By such traits it will appear what sort of people the French emigrants are, and how well they are calculated to undertake the arduous task which they are desirous of entering upon.

Sept. 6. Gardiner to Grenville. What has greatly added to the animosity [of the restored Austrian government] against the States [of Brabant] is an intrigue, lately found out, between them and certain emissaries sent from the French National Assembly, to persuade them to throw themselves upon their protection ; the States sat in private debate on this proposal, and finished by rejecting it ; upon the principle of the views of the two countries being so diametrically opposite. Yet, as this refusal was produced more by personal interest than attachment to the Emperor, the States are looked upon as equally culpable. Unfortunately the emissaries were fled, before their mission was discovered, or they certainly would have been hanged without any process, and the knowledge of this affair...would certainly justify any vigor of proceeding against them [the States], though it is thought better to suppress the matter, and not allow it to become public.

1792. *June* 1. *Auckland to Grenville.* Whatever may be the final success of the combined armies, perhaps in true policy it would have been better for mankind and for the permanent interests of good government, if the French Revolution had been left to its own course and crisis, and to the fatal consequences which would naturally have resulted from the new constitution.

INDEX.

Alsace (Alsatian Princes), 19, 38, 98, 115, 130, 131, 145, 217
Alvensleben, 71, 157
Ami du Roi, 105
Ankarstroem, 173
Anspach (and Baireuth), 158, 220
Aranda, 173, 208
Artois, Count of, 7, 22, 23, 34, 75, 89 sqq., 110, 219; at Mantua, 48 sq.
Auckland, Lord, 13, 16, 37 n., 60 n., 98 n.
Augeard, 24, 29 sqq., 63
Austria, 5, 7, 8, 71 sq., 149 sqq., 155 sqq., 217
Avignon, 18, 38, 112, 121, 182

Barnave, 86, 126, 151
Bavaria, 189, 216, 220
Becquet, 197
Bender, 64, 133
Benoît, 185
Bertrand de Molleville, 95, 162, 163, 177 sq.
Billaud Varenne, 137
Biron, 141, 198
Bischoffwerder, 23, 63, 67, 70, 84, 141, 148, 170, 186, 196, 203
Blumendorf, 167
Bourbon, Duke of, 22
Bourgoing, 188
Breteuil, 123, 124, 156
Brissot, 105 sqq., 108, 113, 114, 127, 135, 146, 160 sq., 175, 178, 191, 211
Brunswick, Duke of, 140 sq., 156, 171, 204, 218 sqq.; his manifesto, 221
Burges, 16
Burke, 32, 91

Cahier de Gerville, 118
Calonne, 22, 75
Catherine II., 8, 14, 34, 73, 83, 84, 100, 174 sq., 188, 208, 214 sq.
Champ de Mars, massacre, 86
Charles IV. of Spain, 13, 25
Chateauvieux, regiment of, 182, 197
Chauvelin, 209
Clavière, 181, 190, 212
Clerfayt, 219
Cobenzl, 149, 195, 216, 219
Collot d'Herbois, 137, 191
Cologne, Elector of, 20
Condé, Prince of, 22, 110
Condorcet, 113, 136, 147, 199, 211
Constituent Assembly, 86, 132, 145
Constitution of 1791, 78, 93
Crublier d'Optère, 134
Custine, 141, 157, 185 sq., 203

Danton, 137, 139, 211
Dantzig (and Thorn), 60, 77, 83, 220

C.

INDEX.

Daverhoult, 118, 147
De Grave, 178, 183, 190, 212
Delessart, 117, 118, 119, 127, 130, 132, 133, 143, 144, 154, 161, 164, 166, 179
D'Escars, 101 sq.
Diet (Imperial), 21, 30, 117, 130, 132
Diplomatic Committee, 137, 144, 176
Drottingholm, Peace of, 101
Dubois-Crancé, 137
Dumas, 133, 146, 199
Dumouriez, 42, 113, 181, 191, 192 sqq., 197 sqq., 212; career and policy, 183 sqq.
Du Port, 86
Duportail, 126
Duport-Dutertre, 179
Duranthon, 181
Durfort, 49
Duroveray, 209

Elgin, Lord, 67 sqq.
Emigrants, 21, 109 sqq., 172 sqq., 208
England, 10, 59 sqq., 98, 174, 186 sq., 208
Esterhazy, 75
Ewart, 61, 98

Family Compact, 13, 40
Favier, 6, 184
Fersen, 44, 50, 80, 82, 94, 100, 121 sqq., 163, 171, 214
Feuillants, 86, 88 sqq., 108 sqq., 118, 125, 136, 139, 146, 151, 153, 164, 179, 192, 212
Finkenstein, 157
Florida Blanca, 13, 32 sq., 40, 99, 173
Fontbrune, 12, 29 n.
Francis II., 169, 196, 204, 208, 216, 217 sq., 221
Frederick William II., 9, 17, 23, 59, 61, 97, 122, 155, 156, 159, 172, 175, 186, 202, 207, 215, 221

Galatz, Treaty of, 72, 85

Genêt, 74
Gensonné, 105, 145, 184
George III., 31 sq., 37 n., 209
Gironde, 105, 139, 160 sq., 178 sqq., 190, 210, 212 sq.; critics of, 106 sqq.
Giurgevo, Armistice of, 62
Goguelat, 151, 181
Goltz (ambassador at Paris), 9, 23, 164
Goltz (ambassador at St Petersburg), 175
Gower, Lord, 174, 221 n.
Grenville, Lord, 73, 143
Guadet, 145, 179
Gustavus III., 3, 14, 34 sq., 74, 75, 100, 121, 163; death, 173

Hanover, 209
Haugwitz, 202, 219, 221
Hérault de Séchelles, 136, 147
Hesse-Cassel, 209
Hertzberg, 9, 11, 13, 60, 61, 68, 83
Hohenlohe-Ingelfingen, 23, 63
Hohenlohe-Kirchberg, 207, 219
Holland, 10, 13, 26, 37

Interference, policy of, 26
Isnard, 105, 119, 143, 147

Jacobins, 23, 104, 137, 138, 164, 211
Jarry, 142
Jassy, Treaty of, 157, 175
Joseph II., 9, 12, 37, 41 n., 65
Jülich (and Berg), 63, 172

Kaunitz, 17, 42 sq., 47, 51, 56, 59, 63, 66, 68, 81, 83, 94, 96, 130, 132 sq., 149, 150, 154, 164 sqq., 169, 175, 193, 196, 203 sqq., 216 sq.
Keith, 72, 150, 170, 207
Keller, Count, 65
Koch, 19 n., 117, 119, 146, 163

Lafayette, 40, 42, 87, 125, 128, 162, 177, 179, 192, 210, 212 sqq.
La Marck, 92, 112, 146

INDEX. 259

Lamballe, Princess, 160
Lameth (the brothers), 86, 116
Lebrun-Tondu, 112
Leeds, Duke of, 60 n.
Legislative Assembly, 92, 95, 103 sqq., 113, 147 sqq., 176
Leopold II., 12, 20, 21, 29 sqq., 46–57, 59, 61 sqq., 64, 65, 69, 79, 81, 89, 94 sqq., 111, 122, 130, 148, 152 sqq., 164 sqq., 167 sq.
Liège, revolution of, 66
Lombards, section of, 134
Lorraine, 20, 98
Louis XVI., 17, 24 sq., 45 sq., 54, 55, 91, 114, 116, 120 sqq., 146, 163, 180, 189, 211 sqq., 214
Louis, Abbé, 90
Luckner, 128, 197

Mainz, Elector of, 117, 130
Mallet du Pan, 210, 212, 219, 221
Malouet, 87
Mantua Conference, 48 sq.
Marat, 137, 139
Maret, 185
Marie Antoinette, 6, 24, 29, 44 sqq., 50 sq., 75, 80, 82, 90 sq., 114, 120 sqq., 124, 148, 151, 152 sq., 160, 163, 180, 190, 210, 214
Marie Christine, 43, 110, 113
Mercy (Argenteau), 43, 44, 50, 52, 64 sq., 90, 91, 122, 124, 148, 150, 214
Merlin (of Thionville), 118
Mirabeau, 45, 47, 86
Mirabeau Tonneau, 31, 110, 117
Montmorin, 27, 115, 118
Morris, 27, 153
Mounier, 24
Moustier, 98

Naples, 13, 73
Narbonne, 125 sqq., 128, 133, 139, 143, 144, 160 sqq., 167, 177, 192
Netherlands, 11, 26, 37, 41, 43, 64 sqq., 111, 216
Noailles, 132, 193, 195, 197, 200
Non-juring clergy, 116, 120, 212

Nootka Sound affair, 39 sq., 61

Oczakow, 60, 67, 73
Orateur du Peuple, 138

Padua circular, 55 sqq., 73, 88
Palatine, Elector, 20, 63
Patriote Français, 105, 181
Pellenc, 92, 146
Père Duchesne, 105
Pétion, 179
Pilnitz, conference of, 71, 75; declaration of, 76 sqq., 84
Pitt, 4, 39, 68, 98
Poland, 14, 72, 82 sqq., 100, 158, 214 sqq.
Polignac, 53
Propaganda, society of the, 36
Provence, Count of, 22, 75, 115, 219
Prudhomme, 139
Prussia, 12, 17, 31, 58, 63, 66, 71 sq., 97, 155 sqq., 171, 206, 218

Reede, 61
Reichenbach Convention, 61 sqq., 66
Reuss, Prince of, 61 sqq., 148, 156, 157, 175, 207
Révolutions de Paris, 138
Robespierre, 137, 138, 160 sq., 182, 191, 211
Rochambeau, 128
Roland, 181, 190, 212
Roll, 23, 63
Rome, 13
Ruhl, 118, 119
Russia, 14, 66, 100 sq.

Sardinia, 13, 33 sq., 73, 100, 164, 188
Savoy, 37
Saxe-Teschen, Albert of, 110
Saxony, 84
Schulenburg, 71, 157, 200, 202, 216, 219 sq.
Ségur, 141 sq.
Sémonville, 41 sqq., 188
Servan, 212

Sieyès, 104, 180, 211
Simolin, 153, 171
Sistova Congress, 62, 67, 70, 72, 83
Sorel, M. Albert, 79, 128, 187
Spain, 32 sq., 73, 99, 188, 208
Spiegel, Van der, 65
Spielmann, 52 n., 61, 94, 216, 219
Spires, Bishop of, 20, 30
Staël, 34, 96 n.
Staël, Me., 125, 140, 160
Stanislaus of Poland, 215
Stedingk, 74, 101
Strasburg, Bishop of, 117
Sudermania, Duke of, 173
Sweden, 14, 100, 187
Switzerland, 100

Talleyrand, 28, 175, 142 sq., 186 sq., 208 sq.
Taube, 35, 100
Trèves, Elector of, 20, 110, 117, 127, 132, 144, 152, 154, 217

Trevor, 34 n.
Triple Alliance, 10, 14, 41, 65, 68 sq.
Tuscany, 100

Varennes, flights to, 44 sqq., 87 sq., 103
Vaudreuil, 23, 52 sq., 208
Venaissin, 19, 112
Vergniaud, 105, 115, 134, 147, 178, 199, 211, 213
Victor Amadeus, 22, 34
Vienna circular, 56 sq.
Vonckists, 112

Walckiers, 112
War, and internal politics, 3; in 18th century, 3, 4; declaration of, April 1792, 197 sqq.
Wimpfen, 117
Woronzow, 222

Zweibrücken, 20, 189

www.ingramcontent.com/pod-product-compliance
Lightning Source LLC
Chambersburg PA
CBHW032131230426
43672CB00011B/2303